A Need for Care?

Elderly Applicants for Local Authority Homes

JUNE NEILL
IAN SINCLAIR
PETER GORBACH
JENNY WILLIAMS

*National Institute for Social Work
Research Unit*

Avebury

Aldershot · Brookfield USA · Hong Kong · Singapore · Sydney

Published by

Avebury

Gower Publishing Company Limited,
Gower House, Croft Road, Aldershot,
Hants. GU11 3HR, England

Gower Publishing Company,
Old Post Road, Brookfield, Vermont 05036
USA

ISBN 0 566 05716 6

Printed and bound in Great Britain by
Athenaeum Press Limited, Newcastle upon Tyne

Contents

Tables

Acknowledgements

This study was financed by the Department of Health and Social Security (DHSS) Local Authority Social Services Research Liaison Group (LASS RLG). We have greatly valued the help and encouragement from Dr Marguerite Smith and from our consecutive Research Liaison Officers - Jack Barnes, Hazel Canter and Sue Moylan.

Our work in the study authority was made possible by the trust and co-operation we received from managers, social workers and clerical staff in the health and social services departments. All members of the Interdisciplinary Panel (listed overleaf) willingly gave their help and advice and their ideas are encompassed in this report. We would especially like to thank the Director of Social Services, Nigel Grindrod, for allowing us access to his department; Ken Morley for his unfailing support; Brenda Sheppard for her friendship and co-operation and David Kirkman and Dr Doreen Hobson who helped, encouraged and guided the research team at all times. Peter Carpenter and his clerical staff provided a desk and a welcome in an already overcrowded office. Debbie Burchell and Mary Jones provided efficient temporary help with coding and tracing information on the outcome of applications.

The social workers in area offices, hospitals, the rehabilitation section and the Heads and residential care staff in all of the Part III Homes were generous with their time and interest. We would especially like to thank Joan Haward and Sheila Woolacott for responding with such good humour to our particularly heavy demands on their time.

Much of this report is based on interviews conducted by Ela Burstyn-O'Farrell, Pat Longbottom and Mary Ternouth who combined skill and commitment with compassion for the people they met. Ward sisters provided facilities for private conversation and the elderly people, their relatives and friends trusted us with their opinions and feelings knowing that this would not benefit them personally. We are grateful to Dr Anthea Tinker who, in a personal capacity, read our drafts at a late stage and provided very constructive criticism and advice.

We have received help from our colleagues at the National Institute, particularly from Enid Levin who gave helpful comments on the report, the statistical assistants (listed earlier) and Guistina Ryan and her staff in the NISW Library.

Elma Sinclair spent many patient hours editing our drafts and we much valued her enthusiasm, perceptive comment and her sharp eye for jargon, contradiction and ambiguity. We are also grateful to Dr Rea for editing the final draft of the book and compiling the index.

Finally, we owe much to the secretaries in the Unit and especially thank Debbie Smith and Rachel Davidson for the skill and intelligence with which they coped with the drafts and the patience and good humour with which they coped with us.

1 Background to the research

Introduction

It shall be the duty of every local authority, subject to and in accordance with the provisions of this part of this Act, to provide residential accommodation for persons who by reason of age, infirmity or any other circumstances are in need of care and attention which is not otherwise available to them.   (National Assistance Act, 1948)

I suppose it's best as long as the Home's nice.   I'm getting too much for her. I'd really like to go to sleep and not wake up. I've had a good life. I'm not bothered about going.   (Client, old lady in hospital)

I've got to the state I feel I'll have to leave home if she comes back. (Caregiving daughter)

Mrs A has somewhat reluctantly come to terms with the fact that due to family circumstances she needs to go into a Home. Her main fear is she may not be able to talk to other residents as they will either be incapable or asleep.   (Social worker, on application form)

As application for admission to an old people's home may represent the last major decision the old person will make, it would seem to merit considerable thought and care. Those who are involved in its making will view it from varying perspectives. Old people must leave behind home and possessions and enter a new life. They may need to escape from loneliness and neglect to comfort and companionship, or their social death may be followed shortly by their physical one.   Relatives, relieved from anxiety or the exhaustion of providing care, may enjoy the freedom to get on with their own lives or may be plagued by a sense of guilt. Professionals involved with the decision may see a hospital bed cleared, problems professionally resolved and an appropriate resource provided, but they too may sometimes wonder whether with more care, time and resources such an irreversible upheaval in the life of an old person could have been avoided.

This book is about these varying and sometimes conflicting perspectives. We begin with the cool detached world of the administrator and policy-maker and with the statistics which influence and reflect their decisions. We turn later (in Chapter 4) to the views and histories of applicants for residential care and of those who look after them. Social workers and other practitioners may find our accounts of the applicants' experience more familiar and compelling. However, before defining more precisely the questions to be considered we introduce the research by outlining the policy and administrative background against which the experiences of applicants and their caregivers has to be set.

Policy background

Between 1961 and 1983 the number of residents aged 65 years and over in Homes provided by local authorities in England and Wales nearly doubled, so that just under a quarter of the gross budget of social services departments is now spent on maintaining a small proportion of elderly people in residential care (CIPFA, 1983). Demographic predictions of a sharp rise in the numbers of very old people in the population by the turn of the century make even more important the question of why old people enter local authority residential care and how they may be prevented from doing so.

It is government policy to keep old people out of residential care and "active and independent in their own homes" (DHSS, 1978; DHSS, 1981). Such a policy is apparently both economical and humane. Most old people want to remain in their own homes (see, for example, Tinker, 1984; Wheeler, 1985), and although a reasonable level of community care can be more expensive than institutional care for some very disabled individuals (Wright et al., 1981), frail elderly people are generally cared for more cheaply outside institutions (Tinker, 1984; Wright et al., 1981). On these grounds the Audit Commission has recently urged the virtues of a policy of community care (Audit Commission, 1983; 1985).

Efforts to implement this policy have focused on increasing the collaboration between services, developing new methods of caring for the frail elderly in the community and increasing traditional domiciliary services. Joint Care Planning Teams and Joint Finance (Hunt, 1983) have been used to further collaboration between health, housing and social services. Local authorities have developed a range of initiatives including alarm schemes, "intensive care" schemes, special sheltered housing, good neighbour schemes and schemes designed to provide "packages" of care tailored to the old person's particular needs (Challis and Davies, 1985; Tinker, 1984). There has been an increase in expenditure on day care for the elderly and in the number of home helps and district nurses (Social Services Committee, 1984).

Nevertheless, although the policy of trying to keep the elderly out of residential care goes back at least to 1958 (see, for example, Goldberg and Connelly, 1982), progress in this direction appears slow, retarded in part by the rapid growth in the number of private old people's homes, and the increase in the number of old people who are over 75 and living alone. Some figures for England and Wales may illustrate the position:

2

* In 1976/7 61% of local authority spending on services mainly intended for the elderly (home helps, aids, meals on wheels, day care for the elderly, residential care for the elderly) went on residential care. The 1982/3 figure of 60% was similar (Social Services Committee, 1984).

* The number of residents in local authority (Part III), private and voluntary Homes rose by 23% from 134.5000 in 1970 to 165.9000 in 1980 (Central Statistical Office, 1982). Part III care refers to the section of the National Assistance Act 1948 which initiated development of local authority residential homes for elderly people who were in need of care and attention.

* In 1960 there were 18.1 residents in old people's homes per thousand population over 65, in 1976 there were 21.5 and in 1983, 22.6 (Bebbington and Tong, 1986). This was an overall increase of 25%.

In these circumstances, the question arises of why an increasing number of elderly people enter residential care despite great efforts to ensure that they need not do so.

The paradox of institutional care

The most obvious explanation for admissions to old people's homes would be that the old people concerned are too frail to maintain themselves in the community. This issue, like many others connected with old people's homes, was first systematically investigated by Townsend (1962). His study like all those subsequent to it showed that the residents in old people's homes are indeed on average older and more mentally and physically frail than the general run of pensioners. Nevertheless, he found that many of his sample of recent admissions to local authority, private and voluntary Homes were surprisingly fit. For example, 70% were able to walk outside the building.

Recent findings have broadly confirmed Townsend's study (see Appendix 1). Thus, although the number of "minimally dependent" people in old people's homes appears to have decreased since 1970, about half the residents are still able to go out (Bond and Carstairs, 1982), and about half have low needs for nursing care (Bowling and Bleathman, 1982; Wade et al., 1983). According to Booth et al. (1983a) only about one in six of a population of Part III residents could be seen as "severely dependent". Moreover, although old people in local authority homes are typically more disabled than old people in the community, at any level of disability there are estimated to be at least five times as many old people in the community as there are in local authority residential care (Bebbington and Tong, 1986).

These findings would be less disturbing if applicants were actively seeking Part III care or if their admission was inevitable for some other reason. On both these points, however, the evidence is negative. Few applicants apparently enter homes because they want to (Barnes, 1980; Shaw and Walton, 1979; Stapleton, 1976; Townsend, 1962) and referrals for Part III care rarely come directly from the applicants themselves. Moreover, social workers generally feel that given adequate provision (including sheltered housing) somewhere between 30% and 60% of those waiting for Part III or admitted to it could be suitably supported in the community (Avon, 1980; Barnes, 1980; Wager, 1972).

3

Explanations for the paradox: some hypotheses

The evidence just given supports the government's policy of community care. The low level of disability of many residents suggests that the policy is feasible, and their common reluctance to enter residential homes that it is desirable. Thus the question remains why the policy is so hard to put into effect.

Existing research suggests a number of possible answers to this question. The first and most important of these concerns relatives. The severely dependent who are maintained in the community generally live with others, usually their relatives (Bebbington and Tong, 1986; Levin et al., 1983). Admission to residential care is more likely if the old person lives alone, has no children and is not visited by relatives (Kay et al., 1962; MacLennan et al., 1984; Townsend, 1962) or if their relatives are under strain or want the old person to enter an institution (Levin et al., 1983, 1985). Other research suggests that the likelihood of an admission may be influenced by an old person's resources. Thus, possession of a home, high social class and high income may make entry to residential care less likely (MacLennan et al., 1984; Wenger, 1984), whereas a poor standard of housing may, in the opinion of social workers, make remaining in the community more difficult (Avon, 1980; Mitchell and Earwicker, 1982).

Other reasons for admission may have to do with the procedures and resources of social services departments. A surprisingly low proportion of those admitted to residential care have been receiving intensive packages of services prior to admission (Avon, 1980; Barnes, 1980). About a fifth may have been known to social services departments for less than a month and two-thirds less than two years (Barnes, 1980). The process of admission may also be somewhat haphazard, being influenced, for example, by the greater number of vacancies for men, the pressures on a particular Home or the "emergency" bypassing of approved admission procedures. Conversely, there is evidence that, in some circumstances, the provision of home help can reduce the likelihood of an old person being admitted to institutional care (Latto, 1984; Levin et al., 1983), that a determined effort to implement social services departments' policy on admission can reduce the number of old people on the waiting list for Part III (Golding and Cooper, 1981) and that a system of case management in which social workers have budgets to "buy in" packages of services tailored to individual needs can keep many very disabled old people in the community (Challis and Davies, 1985).

This evidence suggests that with sufficient, well targeted resources social services departments could reduce admissions to Part III, but efforts to develop community care in these ways are not without problems. Collaboration between services is generally thought to be a prerequisite for community care but it is not easy to achieve. Services differ in the professional attitudes of their staff, geographical boundaries and planning cycles, and respond to differing organisational interests and financial incentives (Glennerster et al., 1983). In general, a high level of home help services in an authority is not associated with a low level of institutional services, a fact suggesting that services are not planned on the assumption that one can be substituted for another (Bebbington and Tong, 1986; Gorbach and Sinclair, 1981). Social services departments are also subject to economic constraints and surveys of frail old people in the community have shown that many receive low levels of service which cannot be regarded as full substitutes for institutional care (Levin et al., 1983; Plank, 1977).

The organisational problems of social services departments over admissions to Part III had been highlighted for us by a telephone survey intended to describe the procedures surrounding decisions on applications in all social services departments in the Greater London Council area (Neill, 1982). The issues with which respondents (local authority headquarters staff) were concerned were primarily administrative and organisational - for example, the length of waiting lists, the procedures for controlling emergency admission and the operation of "swap systems" between Homes and hospitals. The systems for deciding on applications often involved quotas (so many admissions from each area and so many from hospital), or panels representing different interests. Their purposes seemed to be as much to secure "agreement" between different organisational units as to ensure the best outcome for individuals. Other organisational problems included:

* A lack of clear and consistent definitions. Authorities differed over how they defined an application (for example, some only accepted applications from those in immediate need, others also included those who might need a place if further crises arose). No authority kept records of the outcomes of applications, and terms describing the characteristics of applicants (for example, "confused") were typically not defined.

* Disputes over criteria. Hospital staff, general practitioners, social workers and residential staff wanted different things from Part III and disputes arose over the criteria to be applied. Different people were involved in interacting decisions over eligibility (whether an applicant should enter Part III), priority in relation to other applicants, urgency (how quickly a bed should be provided) and placement (which Home was appropriate), and the decisions were not necessarily consistent with each other.

* Variations in procedures and resources. Authorities differed in their procedures for making allocations, in the resources available to provide alternatives to Part III care, in the capacity of their Homes to handle certain kinds of disability and in the numbers of their "difficult to fill" places in "unpopular" Homes outside the authority or in older Homes without lifts.

The question arises of how in this complex and uncertain environment social services departments can ensure that applications for Part III are carefully considered and that policies relevant to applications are steadily developed.

Conclusion

These findings suggest that what we have called the paradox of institutional care has much to do with the conflicting interests of those involved and needs to be understood at two levels. At the level of the individual case, there are the potentially conflicting perspectives of carers, applicants and service providers, with questions of admission influenced by procedures and the resources available to the participants in the decision. At the level of policy, social services departments have difficulty in influencing these decisions because they operate in a sort of fog of war, faced with economic constraints, conflicting interests and lack of information on which to base their policy.

The research described in this book was primarily concerned with the first of these levels. Its central aim was to understand why old people agree (if they do agree) to enter local authority homes and how their caring relatives and social workers view their applications. At the same time the research was intended to be relevant at the second level. To this end we provided information to help a particular social services department develop its policy on admissions, and monitored the developments which ensued. Taken together we hoped that the results would further understanding of why policies on community care are hard to put into effect and what, at a variety of levels, might be done about this.

2 The setting and the project

Introduction

The complexity of the problems with which we were concerned and our wish to combine research with development suggested to us that we should carry out our study in only one authority. Obviously, the advantages of doing this had to be balanced against the difficulty of generalising results. We believed, however, that the main reasons for application were to be found, with varying frequency, in all authorities and wished to gain the depth of understanding that a study in one authority could provide.

Our first task on starting pilot work in the authority in 1978 was to get to know something about it and to understand the problems it faced over Part III admissions. To this end we collected basic statistics on demography and service provision, talked to a wide range of staff, and observed a consecutive series of thirty cases being assessed for Part III. In this chapter we use this pilot work to introduce the authority and some of the problems it faced at the level of administering and developing residential care, and at the level of assessing the individual Part III applicant. As we will see, the problems at these two levels are similar to those identified in Chapter 1. The similarity gives reason for thinking that the research plans outlined at the end of the chapter had a more than parochial relevance.

The authority in which we carried out the research was selected on several grounds. It had coterminous boundaries between the area health and social services districts which it was anticipated would simplify understanding of the organisational and procedural influences on applications for Part III care. The director of the social services department, the assistant director for residential care, the consultant geriatricians and the consultant psycho-geriatrician all expressed interest in the study and were prepared to convey their approval to others working for them. There was a research and development officer in the social services department who was willing to give advice and guidance - and his help proved to be invaluable. A further advantage was that the local authority had recently completed a survey of the elderly (Bird and Kirkman, 1974) and was considering changes in relation to Part III applications (Morley, 1982). In addition, a joint health/social services panel was being set up composed of senior personnel from these agencies.

The authority

The authority was an outer London borough which was demographically and environmentally varied. At its centre, tower block office development provided head office accommodation for insurance and banking enterprises and large department stores formed one of the main shopping centres in south London. To the north and west, small terraced and large Victorian houses accommodated many of the ethnic minority citizens, and at the fringes of the borough, pre-war housing estates and inter-war semi-detached development merged into the neighbouring authorities. The south of the borough contained very affluent areas and large expanses of beautiful green belt countryside. To the south east, there was a high plateau on which had been built a large housing estate. This was regarded as a model development when new, but poor transport, its isolated position and limited employment opportunities had, over time, fostered social and family problems and poverty amongst the community.

As can be seen from Table 2.1, the authority was in general demographically similar to the rest of England although it had a higher proportion of owner occupiers.

Comparison of services provided in this authority and elsewhere in England showed some differences. Broadly, as described in Appendix 1, the authority provided its elderly population with more than average residential care, both in Part III and hospitals, and less than average domiciliary care. The differences were not great and for many purposes may be less important than variations in procedures and relationships between health and social services on which no comparative data exist. Nevertheless, these differences could, in theory, influence our results and so we will compare our findings with those of others wherever possible.

Problems at the administrative level

Our first task in the authority was to understand its services and procedures and see if the issues surrounding Part III application were similar to those identified in other authorities during the telephone survey.

During the pilot phase the researcher met a wide range of people in the local authority and health services. She observed committees at work, interviewed professional, administrative and clerical staff, observed assessments of thirty consecutive applicants, visited institutions and had informal discussion with some applicants and their relatives. This initial work concentrated on problems and was less concerned with the frequency with which these problems occurred or with getting a "fair" picture of the authority.

As in other authorities, geriatric and psychogeriatric in-patients were housed either in very old buildings or in isolated positions - a fact perceived by some staff as reflecting the attitude of the health service towards this age group. Psychogeriatric patients were in a large psychiatric hospital in a remote rural position outside the study

Table 2.1

Social Characteristics of Elderly Population

Characteristics	Study area %	Outer London %	England %
Age			
Persons aged 65 years and over	13.7	15.1	15.0
Persons aged 75 years and over	5.4	5.8	5.7
Persons of pensionable age	16.3	17.9	17.7
Persons living with those of pensionable age who are below pensionable age	6.9	7.3	6.4
Gender			
Elderly women	61.9	60.7	60.4
Marital status			
Elderly women married	35.7	37.4	37.8
Elderly men married	74.2	74.3	73.5
Household composition of persons of pensionable age			
Aged 60/65-74 years living alone	21.9	21.9	22.6
Aged 75 years and over living alone	16.6	17.0	18.1
Living with others	61.4	61.1	59.3
Tenure of persons of pensionable age			
Owner occupied	61.0	58.0	54.0
Rented from Council or Housing Association	23.3	29.0	34.6
Private rented	15.7	13.0	11.4
Amenities			
Pensioners lacking exclusive use of bath and inside WC	6.7	6.1	6.2
Pensioners aged 75 years and over lacking exclusive use of bath and inside WC	8.8	8.6	8.6

Notes:
> Percentages based on "persons" refer to the total population of residents in the area. The "elderly" refers to those aged 65 years and over. "Persons of pensionable age" refers to women aged 60 years and over and men aged 65 and over.

<u>Source</u>: Small Area Statistics for 1981 Census, Tables 2, 29, 32.

authority. Two general hospitals each provided ten geriatric beds but geriatric patients were cared for mainly in a 500-bed geriatric hospital, a former workhouse. Several of the upper wards of the geriatric hospital had no lifts, no balconies and no access to the open air unless patients were carried downstairs by porters. Other geriatric beds were provided in three wards of a small hospital in an isolated position between a railway line and a gas works.

In contrast to the lack of new health service provision for hospital care, the local authority housing and social services departments had been providing new sheltered housing and Part III Homes. During the ten years prior to the study (in the 1970s) six sheltered housing units, giving 229 sheltered housing flats, had been provided by the housing department. Over the same period four new Part III Homes had been opened, providing 173 beds and operating alongside longer established Homes in adapted old buildings. On average per thousand elderly over the period of the study, the authority provided thirty-three sheltered housing units (fifteen with warden and eighteen without) provided Part III care for 16.9 elderly residents and supported 2.8 residents in voluntary Homes. New sheltered housing blocks were scattered throughout the authority and wardens had little contact with each other. Despite the similar architecture of the new Part III Homes, their atmosphere and regime varied, apparently reflecting the management styles of heads of Homes.

Policies in the health, housing and social services sectors of care interacted. The most obvious example of this related to psychogeriatric patients. Over the previous five years national policies of "community care" had been reflected in a decrease in the number of psychiatric hospital beds. One third of the Part III beds were said to be occupied by ex-psychiatric hospital patients and a further 150 ex-patients were said to be boarded out in private households at the time the study started. The waiting time for the two Homes for the elderly mentally infirm was so long that psychiatric hospital social workers had become reluctant to refer old people to them. In the absence of aggregated information, staff in the geriatric hospital assumed that their patients were waiting longer for places than applicants from the community.

The task of planning to overcome these health and social services conflicts fell to the joint care planning team and to managers in the two services. The senior managers of both were accommodated on separate floors in a tower block office building which also contained other local authority departments. There was a common dining room for all staff in the building. It had been anticipated that being under one roof would facilitate communication, but principal officers frequently told the researcher that there was little informal contact between them and others of similar rank in different sections or authorities.

This lack of informal contact hindered collaboration. Some professionals - for example, the community physician and the social services research and development officer - built up fruitful contacts but others - for example, staff in the health authority statistics section and the local authority strategic planning department - worked in apparent isolation. Inevitably, turnover of personnel further disrupted relationships between health and social services especially as there were sometimes delays in filling vacant posts.

When staff in key liaison roles tentatively reached agreement with their colleagues in another service, they did not necessarily have the power to implement these decisions. Some informants were concerned with the complex committee structure through which changes involving health and social services had to be steered, and the different interests (for example, of unions, of consultants and professional groups, and of politicians) which had to be consulted. They also cited the shortage of resources to undertake tasks which might in the long run save money (for example, thorough medical investigation of applicants for Part III). In short, many of the obstacles to health and social services collaboration which others have identified were present in the study area.

Some problems at the level of the individual case

These difficulties in strategic planning were mirrored in the problems frontline workers experienced in obtaining access to long-term residential care. In the health service, community nurses, while committed to community care, resented the control of ambulance drivers over the admission of old people to hospital as "emergencies"; the lack of adequate domiciliary support for the very frail elderly; and the difficulty of getting the agreement of consultants on urgent need for hospital admission. Some general practitioners resented a style of medicine introduced by a new consultant geriatrician who reassessed on a domiciliary visit their referrals for hospital care and made every effort to keep old people in the community. Sisters in geriatric wards were concerned about old people who were considered too frail for Part III but not ill enough for long-term hospital care and about other patients who deteriorated in hospital while waiting for a Part III place.

Staff in social services experienced similar conflicts. In this authority, as in others, assistant social workers did much of the work with the elderly and they expressed concern over the volume of their work, the complexity of some of it, and the pressures on them from professionals with higher status. They also complained of difficulties in obtaining resources. Sheltered housing wardens, who were employed by the social services department, argued that as sheltered housing schemes had all been opened over a short period, a high proportion of their residents had simultaneously become very frail and dependent.

Many conflicts centred on the role of the social services admissions officer who was responsible for deciding who was suitable for care in Part III and who was not. Referring social workers were required to assess applicants prior to referral to the admissions officer and felt that their request for admission should be acted on without a re-appraisal of the situation. Consultants and general practitioners also expected their recommendations to result in action, without question by the admissions officer. Heads of Homes felt that, on occasions, they were expected to take residents who were (or would become) ineligible for Part III care. Such conflicts inevitably led to tactical manoeuvres by professionals. For example, some general practitioners ensured that they referred certain patients to the consultant geriatrician who was more favourable than her colleague to hospital admission.

Some of these conflicts impinged on the patients or clients. Difficulty in deciding whether a problem was medical or social could result in an old person being left in an unsatisfactory situation.

Mrs X is incontinent, increasingly breathless and lives alone. Her daughter and the area social worker feel she is an urgent candidate for Part III care. The admissions officer considers her ineligible because she cannot walk more than eight yards, has heart trouble and is incontinent. The consultant geriatrician has refused admission to geriatric hospital as her heart condition has stabilised and she does not require medical treatment.

At this stage of the project, the researcher wondered how far professionals, in their concern with eligibility for residential care, ensured that applicants fully understood the reason for assessments, that they were fully aware of the far-reaching nature of the decision to enter long-stay residential care, and that they knew the identity of the people to whom they were talking. For example, if the old person was in hospital at application, it was not unusual for two or three people to arrive without prior appointment to assess the applicant, who might then be asked to walk up and down the ward to demonstrate mobility. In these circumstances there was little opportunity for applicants to discuss anxieties or doubts they might have about entering a Home.

At other times, old people made their wishes abundantly clear and refused to go into Part III care but, here too, professionals were not necessarily on the client's side. The admissions officer felt strongly that the explicit wish of an old person should be respected. Nevertheless, the situations of some such potential applicants were "urgent" in that their accommodation was poor and unsuitable, they were confused, wandered out and neglected themselves, or their informal care network had broken down. The usual approach to these situations was that the applicants' wishes should be respected, and they should be allowed to follow their own course of action. The problems of the admissions officer were sometimes increased by conflicts of interest between applicant and carers, as well as between professionals. For example:

> Mrs J's son-in-law telephoned [the admissions officer] about Mrs J, whose husband had been admitted to hospital with a stroke. There is tremendous animosity between Mrs J and her daughter and son-in-law. Son-in-law very aggressive. The upshot was that Mrs J was persuaded to go into Part III against her will in case her son-in-law did anything "dramatic". Case to be reviewed.

Such cases raise issues about the relative power of applicant and carer, ethical issues on the rights of Mrs J, compared with those of her daughter and son-in-law, and bureaucratic or political issues relating to the potential embarrassment to the authority if her son-in-law "did anything dramatic". The situation is complicated by family tension ("tremendous animosity") and an atmosphere of crisis (Mrs J's husband has just been admitted to hospital). A happy resolution to the problem may well depend on the efficiency of various procedures (whether the case of Mrs J is reviewed and if so whether actions have in the meantime been taken which make it difficult for her to return home).

Other cases raised similar ethical conflicts. In some, elderly applicants were apparently becoming "confused" (and hence perhaps not the best judges of their own interests), or the carer was not a relative (and hence perhaps not subject to the same obligations), or the caring daughter was "suicidal" (and hence perhaps absolved from obligations), or the grand-daughter sharing a bedroom with the old person was taking "A" levels (and her interests would not be served by the applicant remaining at home). Some cases raised the moral issue of the potential conflict of interest between an applicant and residents in Part III. For example, the old lady was incontinent or aggressive and the Home could not cope. It was alleged that some admission procedures such as "trial days" were designed more for the benefit of the Home than to increase the choice of the applicant.

Above all, this pilot work raised questions about how far the administrative need to make relatively quick decisions over applications takes account of the wishes of the applicants. The researcher talked to a number of applicants and relatives and then observed discussion of their cases at allocation meetings. In this way she could compare different viewpoints and perceive the way information presented on a case changed in nature and emphasis as it became attuned to administrative requirements. The relevance of information held by home help organisers, ward sisters, or district nurses was sometimes not recognised. Little account might be taken of the applicants'aspirations or strengths. In these ways the essence of the situation seemed somehow to have been lost.

The project and its sub-studies

Despite the problems we identified, we were also struck by the concern which the professionals felt for the elderly, and by their intention to improve standards of care. Determined efforts had been made to provide day rooms and create a homelike and friendly atmosphere in the unpromising setting of former workhouse wards. Social workers, assistant social workers and area officers had an abundance of ideas for improving services, some of which they were trying to put into effect. A new worker had been appointed to support sheltered housing wardens and her work seemed to be bearing fruit in increased willingness by the wardens to accept difficult cases. As already mentioned, an inter-disciplinary panel had been set up by health and social services to consider and resolve a number of issues surrounding Part III care.

This evident goodwill and expertise within the authority combined with our preliminary analysis of the issues surrounding Part III applications to shape the project.

Our first aim was to set the experiences of applicants and their carers in the context of the demands on the authority's Part III Homes and of the alternatives available to applicants as revealed in what happened to those not admitted. Such statistical information seemed to be essential for those planning alternatives to Part III and for attempts to monitor the effectiveness of these alternatives in diverting potential applicants. For these reasons we collected three large sets of statistical data:

* Large-scale application study. Information was collected from a consecutive series of 1053 application forms referring to 970 different applicants and received between June 1978 and May 1981. These forms provided basic information on the applicants and on why their social workers considered they required Part III care, and provided the basis for follow up studies, and more detailed work on sub-samples.

* Outcome study I. All applications in the large-scale study were followed up for at least six months and in most cases for longer to determine the events following the application (i.e. whether applicants had been admitted to Part III, to hospital or had remained in the community; whether, when and where they had died). Transfers between wards within a hospital were not included. However, the nature and dates of all other movements were monitored. These data were analysed to determine the factors associated with these various outcomes.

* *Outcome study II.* 609 applicants in the large sample (99% of those who were alive on 31 August 1981) were followed up through interviews, almost always with a professional worker such as a head of Home or social worker. These interviews provided information on the perceived suitability of the applicant's placement, their physical and mental health, their social activities, visits by relatives and services received. In this way, they provided a picture of the alternatives effectively available to applicants.

Our second aim was to explore how applicants and carers experienced the making of an application. If the process sometimes obscured their wishes and problems, it would be particularly important to examine why, from their point of view, the application had been made and what they felt about it. Practice or policy which ignored these views could hardly be well founded. For these reasons we carried out a:

* *Small-scale study.* In a sample of sixty applications, interviews were held with the applicant, the closest caregiver (defined as the person who most often gave the applicant personal care on a daily basis) and the referring social worker. These interviews provided data on the views of three key participants in the decision, a check on the information on application forms and a variety of more detailed information not otherwise available. The sample was designed to resemble the population of all Part III applicants except that homeless, long-stay hospital patients were omitted for reasons discussed in Appendix 2.

Finally, we hoped that our interviews and statistical information would assist the authority in its efforts to improve the application process, to provide alternatives and to monitor them. We therefore carried out:

* *Development studies.* The research worker helped to foster a number of developments relating to Part III applications during the years of the study, for example, by providing specially analysed information and taking part in working parties. Some of these developments were monitored and some comparisons made between the characteristics of applicants and those of other groups who were in receipt of different types of service.

Data from all these studies have been used to draw conclusions, with each set of data complementing or providing a check on the findings of others and on the observations of the principal researcher. In general, the large-scale data have been used to show the prevalence of problems and the likelihood of particular outcomes, while the more detailed studies have provided "life" and insight into the processes of application.

The book

In our next chapter, we complete our introduction by giving statistical information on the characteristics and problems of all the applicants who requested Part III care during three years. The remainder of the book falls into three main parts. First, we give a detailed account of the views and problems of applicants and their carers and of the way they and their social workers experienced the application process.

Second, we return to all applications made during the study period and report their outcome, and finally we describe the developments introduced by the authority in the course of the research.

Inevitably, there is a tension in the book. The views of applicants may suggest different policy implications from those of carers or professionals; some of the statistical data apparently support a policy of reducing the number of Part III places whereas other data apparently support a policy of increasing it. By bringing together these different kinds of data in one book, and by relating our results wherever possible to those of others, we hope to give a more balanced picture of the underlying dilemmas than would have been possible from one source of data alone.

3 970 applicants: the case for application

Introduction

As we suggested in Chapter 2 the information presented during an application process has to become attuned to administrative needs. Complicated, painful situations and relationships have had to be summarised and to some extent concealed under such terms as "risk", "lack of basic care", "caregivers' problems" and "unsuitable accommodation", and described in such a way that, if necessary, a bewildered, depressed or passive old person can be seen as an "applicant".

To explore these problems, the framework for our study was provided by a consecutive series of 1053 application forms submitted by social workers over the three-year period 1 June 1978 to 31 May 1981. These 1053 applications related to 970 applicants as some people reapplied during the study period. Study of this large group of applications allowed us to capture two essential features. First, and too often overlooked, the context in which the application was being made - for example, were the applicants in their own homes or in hospital, living with others or alone? Second, what was the official basis for the application? What, in effect, were the arguments being employed?

The forms, as it happened, had other uses for us than these. They enabled us to compare our sample with samples drawn elsewhere. They provided a sampling frame for the small-scale study. They provided data which could be used by managers in planning new developments designed to divert potential applicants from Part III. They allowed us to compare the characteristics of applicants with the characteristics of those served by the new developments and hence assess the efficiency with which they were targeted. With the exception of comparing our samples with those of others we leave most of these for later chapters. We begin with one of the basic themes of the report - the context of application and the reasons for it.

The context of the application

Age, sex and marital status

On average over the three years of the study, seven out of every 1000 people aged over 65 in the study authority applied for Part III care. Most of these applicants were very old. Their average age was 82 years and four in ten were aged 85 years or over (see Table 3.1). Women were older and outnumbered men in the sample by three to one but both men, on average aged 79 years, and women, on average aged 82 years, were much older than most pensioners in the community.

Table 3.1

Applicants: Age and Sex

Age group years	Men %	Women %	Total %
	(233)	(737)	(970)@
65 - 74	25	13	16
75 - 84	41	45	44
85 +	33	43	40
Mean age	79.3	82.5	81.7

@ The bases and means include ten men and sixteen women under 65 years.

For both men and women the rate of applicants in the local population rose sharply with age (see Table 3.2).

As women on average live longer than men, did the relative longevity of women account for their greater frequency as applicants? The overall rate of applicants among women, 8.9, was double that among men, 4.5 per 1000 aged 65 and over. However, this ratio of women to men could not be explained entirely by the tendency of women to live longer. As stated, the male applicants were themselves an elderly group, and as shown in the final column of Table 3.2, in each age group women were overall more likely to apply than men.

Note: Throughout the book, the location of the number in brackets at the top of the column or start of a row indicates whether the percentages are based on column or row totals. Within a column or row, percentages add to 100% given rounding errors.

On later tables, tests of statistical significance are presented for the particular contrasts listed under the table. The number of *'s indicates the level of statistical significance that differences as large or larger than those observed could arise by chance in other samples of the same size as this one. The standard convention for referring to this probability has been used:

n.s. = not significant; + = less than 1 in 10 ($p < 0.1$);
* = less than 1 in 20 ($p < 0.05$); ** = less than 1 in 100 ($p < 0.01$); *** = less than 1 in 1000 ($p < 0.001$).

Table 3.2

Average Annual Age/Sex Specific Rates of Applicants

Per 1000 Local Elderly Population by Marital Status

	Currently married	Not married	All
Men aged:			
65 - 74	0.4	6.5	1.6
75 - 84	2.6	15.5	7.0
85 +	14.7	44.0	32.6
All 65 +	1.3	13.7	4.5
Women aged:			
65 - 74	0.4	3.6	2.0
75 - 84	2.2	14.6	11.7
85 +	7.6	38.9	36.5
All 65 +	1.0	13.3	8.9
All persons 65 +	1.1	13.4	7.2

Source: Small Area Statistics for 1981 Census, Table 2.

This somewhat surprising fact could have varying explanations.   In particular, our study produced evidence to support Hunt's conclusion (1978) that elderly men are less disabled than elderly women of comparable age.   However, it was another possible explanation, that elderly men are more likely than elderly women to be married, which proved most interesting.   As can be seen from the other columns of Table 3.2 an old person's marital status had a marked influence on the likelihood of an application for Part III care: half (50%) of the local population over 65 were currently married compared with a mere 8% of applicants.   The first and second columns of Table 3.2 show that after grouping the applicants according to age and marital status, in all groups men appeared slightly more likely than women to apply for Part III care.

The question next arose as to whether we were really looking at the effects of being without a marriage partner or simply those of living alone.   Table 3.3 shows that those living with others to whom they were not married were slightly less likely than those living alone to apply for Part III care.   However, the major difference remains not between those living with others and those living alone but between those living with spouses and those not doing so.

Table 3.3

Average Age-Sex Specific Rates of Applicants* Per

1000 Local Elderly Population Living in Private Households

by "Living Alone" and Marital Status

	Living alone	Living with others		All
		Currently married	Not married	
Rates of applicants:				
Men aged:				
65 - 74	7.0	0.3	1.7	1.2
75 +	24.5	3.0	18.1	9.7
Women aged:				
60 - 74	2.9	0.2	1.4	1.2
75 +	22.7	3.2	18.1	17.2
All pensionable persons	12.0	0.8	9.1	5.4
Local population:				
% of men aged:				
65 - 74	13	80	7	100
75 +	22	65	13	100
% of women aged:				
60 - 74	29	56	15	100
75 +	49	21	30	100
% All pensionable persons	29	32	39	100

* Based on 796 applicants. Excluding 165 applicants in Institution with no other residence or those with no clear household composition and a further nine applicants under pensionable age.

Source: Small Area Statistics for 1981 Census, Tables 21, 32.

Why, after allowing for age and marital status, were men, particularly those living alone, more likely to apply? Overall, men were less disabled than women applicants but information on application forms suggested that bereavement was a particularly important factor for elderly men. Bereavements which had occurred during the previous five years were mentioned in 31% of the applications of widowers compared to only 17% of widows. Typically, social workers described physical deterioration in widowers during a relatively brief period, while they were still suffering the full depressive effect of the bereavement.

Mr A, aged 83, has lived alone since the death of his wife two years ago. He does not bother to cook for himself, has had a slight stroke, and is beginning to get very shaky on his legs. His sight is poor and he feels very depressed.

By contrast, women applicants were more likely to have lost their husbands at an earlier age when they still had the health, the energy and the time to adapt to life alone. This enabled them to carry on with a well-established routine despite increasing frailty.

Mrs B, aged 89, was widowed seventeen years ago ... Her house is old (she has lived there for fifty years) ... It is gas-lit which adds to the risk as Mrs B uses candles when she goes to the toilet at night. Her eyesight is poor and she walks with difficulty.

Residence at application

Applicants differed from other over 65's not only in their age and marital status but also in their residence at the time of application. Forty six per cent of applicants were in hospital, 8% were already in a Home (Part III through emergency admission or a private Home) and 14% were living in the homes of relatives or friends. Overall, only 31% were, at application, living in their own homes, including 9% who were married. Therefore, two-thirds of the applicants were already being looked after by somebody else at the time they applied. In this sense, the typical application appeared to be a request to move from one care setting (including care by relatives) to another (Table 3.4).

The fact that two-thirds of the applicants were already being "looked after" should not disguise the differences between the settings in which they received care. The reasons which lead consultants to press for Part III are not the same as those which influence an exhausted relative to do so.

Differences between settings were reflected in variations in the average age of those applying. The small group resident in private or voluntary homes (including nursing homes) were, on average, two and a half years older (mean age 84.1 years) than were all applicants (mean age 81.7 years). Some were applying because they had become too frail for the Home or were no longer able to pay its fees. At the other extreme, applicants resident in psychiatric hospital were younger on average (mean age 74.4 years) than other applicants - a fact which partly reflects a policy of transferring some long-stay psychiatric patients to Part III when they reach the "eligible" age of 65.

Table 3.4

Type of Residence at Application

Type of residence at application	N	%
	(970)	
Private household		
Applicant's own	302	31
Relation's/friend's	135	14
Hospital		
General	109	11
Geriatric	269	28
Psychiatric	65	7
Residential home		
Local authority	49	5
Private/voluntary	29	3
Other	12	1

Tenure

The fact that so many applicants were (even if only temporarily) in hospital or living with relatives suggested that their decisions were often constrained by the views of others. In this respect it might be expected that applicants who had tenure or ownership would be in a better position to resist most pressures than those who were permanently living in an institution or in someone else's home (Table 3.5).

The follow-up study was to confirm the importance of "homelessness" to the outcome of an application (see Chapter 13). It is therefore particularly significant that nearly one third of the 970 applicants neither owned nor rented a home of their own. Approximately 12% had given up their homes on becoming long-stay hospital patients and 14% to live permanently with friends or relatives. The remainder of this group lived in accommodation which offered no security of tenure. Lack of a home was particularly common among single male applicants, 42% of whom had no home of their own compared to 17% of the married male applicants.

> Mr G (single) worked in the building trade in various parts of the country. Lived with his parents but moved into lodgings when they died. Was admitted to hospital following a stroke and his room given up.

When married men became "homeless" they had usually moved with their wives into the household of sons and daughters. A few others had a long-standing rift in their marriage which meant that they, like single men, were dependent upon the goodwill of landladies.

A further disadvantage faced by applicants was that compared to other old people in the borough they were less likely to have the implicit financial power of owning a home of their own. Out of the 970 applicants, 613 had homes of their own. Most of these lived in rented accommodation, 28% from the local authority and 31% rented privately. Only 22% of applicants with homes were owner occupiers. An additional 114 applicants lived in the households of other people (usually relatives) and of these relatives, 28% were known to be owner occupiers. Therefore, the proportion of applicants in owner occupied homes was clearly far less than the 61% of elderly people in the community who lived in owner occupied property.

Table 3.5

Homelessness and Residence at Application

| | Residence at application | | | |
	Private household	Hospital	Other	Total
	%	%	%	%
	(437)	(443)	(90)	(970)
Applicant has:				
Own home	72	60	38	63
No home of own	26	35	34	31
Not known if applicant has own home	2	5	28	6

We will show later that applicants in the small sample were particularly likely to describe privately rented accommodation as unsatisfactory (see Chapter 9). It was therefore of interest that excluding those in long-term institutional care 26% of the applicants on whom information on tenure was available were living in privately rented accommodation, compared with 18% of the local population over 65. Of the 613 applicants who had homes of their own those who were private tenants suffered most from poor facilities: 22% of them had an outside WC only compared with only 4% of over 65's in the borough as a whole. A further 8% of applicants who were private tenants had to share a WC and 115 were recorded as having no hot water (compared to 4% of those who were owner occupiers).

Household composition

The applicants' marital status, where they were resident at application and their tenure were all related to the composition of their household at their usual address.

Over half the applicants usually lived on their own in the community.

The remainder were almost evenly divided between those who lived with other elderly people only (almost always a spouse or brothers or sisters), those who lived with younger generations (usually sons or daughters) and a group with "other" household compositions (Table 3.6).

Table 3.6

Residence at Application and Usual Household Composition

| | | Usual household composition | | |
Residence at application	Alone	With other elderly only	With younger generation	Other
Private household				
(437) %	58	18	21	3
Hospital				
(443) %	52	13	10	25
Other				
(90) %	33	13	6	48
Total				
(970) %	53	15	15	17

This last group consisted of 165 applicants (17% of the total), most of whom on application had no residence other than a hospital. Of this group, 35% applied from a geriatric, 18% from a psychiatric and 14% from a general hospital. A surprisingly low proportion (13%) were resident in private or voluntary homes. The remainder were living in lodgings or communal group living schemes for the elderly, or had already been admitted to Part III on an emergency basis.

The official case for the application

We now turn from what we have described as "basic information" on the applicants to the "official" reasons for the applications. Social workers based their case for admission on four main planks:

* The applicants' physical and mental health and consequent need for care;

* The capacity and willingness of caregivers to care;

* The suitability of applicants' accommodation;

* The applicants' own attitudes to admission.

It was our impression that in presenting the applicants' case for Part III care, the social workers were influenced by their perception of the decision-making process and their power within it as well as by the setting in which they worked. Thus, hospital social workers had to show that an elderly patient was in a "good enough" condition to cope with more independent living in a residential home. By contrast, social workers based in area offices had to demonstrate that applicants currently living in private households were "bad enough" to require residential care. For such reasons, it was often not possible to decide whether a referring social worker did not know the extent of an applicant's disabilities, or whether they knew but played them down or up to strengthen their client's case. Our method of dealing with the problems of interpreting the information in the forms is described in Appendix 2.

Self-care difficulties and risks

Social workers were understandably concerned with the applicants' standard of "basic self care" (the essential standards of food and warmth) and the risks they faced in their daily lives. For 83% of applicants reasons of this kind were put forward (Table 3.7).

Table 3.7

Basic Physical Care/Risk and Usual Household Composition

		Usual household composition			
	Alone	With other elderly only	With younger generation	Other	Total
Inadequate basic care/risk	%	%	%	%	%
	(514)	(149)	(142)	(165)	(970)
Asserted					
With evidence	44	23	23	17	33
Without evidence	47	62	46	52	50
Not asserted	9	15	31	31	17

Overall: $\chi^2 = 98.88^{***}$, DF = 6.

Asserted v. Not asserted: $\chi^2 = 63.60^{***}$, DF = 3.

With v. Without evidence: $\chi^2 = 35.89^{***}$, DF = 3.

Note:

For the conventions regarding statistical tests, see note on page 17.

For one third of applicants, evidence was given of "lack of care" in the past. A larger group of 50% were described as being "at risk" but no incidents of actual deprivation or danger were reported. To describe an applicant as "at risk" could be a way of galvanising others into activity, for the word "risk" had implications of crisis and a threat of disaster if quick action was not taken. For 17%, social workers reported no lack of basic care or situation of risk. As can be seen from Table 3.7, there was more often evidence of lack of basic care or risk for applicants who usually lived alone.

On application forms social workers presented two broad reasons for lack of basic care. The first related to difficulties with mobility and the other to mental confusion. The meaning of the word "confusion" often had to be inferred, as only applicants applying for a place in a home for the elderly mentally infirm had a psychiatric assessment. Two-fifths of all applicants were described by social workers as having some degree of mental confusion in relation to time, place or people: 17% appeared to be severely confused. A further 22% were apparently "occasionally" confused, a phrase which covered a range of conditions. Some applicants were described as having lapses of memory about some issues but not about others. Others were reported to have experienced a recent shock such as a bereavement, a stroke or surgery after which a degree of disorientation had been noticed.

"Mobility" problems also varied in severity and in the precision with which they were described. Over two-thirds (72%) of applicants were said to have difficulty in climbing stairs, 24% used a zimmer frame and 4% were confined to a wheelchair. Applicants who were said to be confused were less likely than others to have mobility problems. As Table 3.8 shows, nearly half the applicants had problems with mobility but not with confusion.

Table 3.8

Confusion and Mobility

Mentioned problems with:	%
	(970)
Mobility only	46
Confusion only	19
Both	21
Neither	14

Two-thirds of the applicants were reported to be suffering from physical illness, mainly the common difficulties of the elderly such as arthritis, cardiac conditions or strokes. Like problems with mobility, physical illness was less often reported when an applicant appeared to be confused.

Careful examination of the 14% of applicants who had no reported problems with mobility or confusion suggested that their applications arose from varying circumstances including homelessness, physical illness, frailty, stress within their care network, and the need to relieve a hospital bed. About a quarter of the applicants whose only residence was a hospital bed apparently did not have problems with confusion or mobility.

One in three applicants were also said to suffer from visual handicap or deafness. Only 3% of applicants were totally blind (nearly half of these lived alone), but, as we shall see from the small sample, the problems of the visually handicapped could also be severe. On the basis of interviews with the small sample (Chapter 5) it seems probable that application forms almost certainly under-represented the prevalence of sensory difficulty and in particular loss of hearing (reported on 17% of applicants). Only 3% were reported to have other problems such as difficulty with speech but the impression was gained that expressive loss following strokes, although not unusual, was not always recorded on forms.

As a consequence of their physical ill health, poor mobility, visual handicap or confusion, most applicants had difficulties with one or more self-care tasks (Table 3.9). "Confusion" was particularly associated with incontinence and mobility problems with an inability to climb stairs. Some types of self-care difficulty (for example, inability to wash, dress, eat or go to the lavatory unaided) were particularly severe in their demands on caregivers or services. However, such difficulties were far less common than problems with mobility or cooking. Thus, although most applicants were said to have difficulty in preparing meals (89%), only 8% were said to have difficulty in feeding themselves.

As we will find in the small sample, there were considerable differences between applicants in the extent of their self-care difficulties. Roughly a quarter had no more than one such difficulty, but at the other end of the scale, a quarter had at least four. Those who had problems with dressing themselves commonly also had problems with getting in and out of bed or managing independently in the lavatory.

A further interesting feature of Table 3.9 is that the old people applying from hospital appeared to be, in certain respects, less disabled than those applying from the community. Although patients in the psychiatric hospital were younger and more physically active than those in the acute or geriatric hospitals, comparisons without this more active group did not change the overall trend. The explanation for this finding is unclear. Hospital patients may have benefited from a programme of rehabilitation. As we have already said, hospital social workers may have tried to play down the difficulties of hospital applicants in order to show that they were "good enough" for Part III. Some hospital applicants may simply have been in certain respects fitter, and their applications precipitated by their position in hospital.

Carers' problems and caring networks

Nine out of ten of the applicants not in long-term institutions were said to have current or recent contact with relatives or friends, and 64% made applications which were associated with problems of their caregivers. These problems were predominantly of two broad types. First, caregivers had personal or work responsibilities which conflicted with those of caring for the elderly person. Following Isaacs et al. (1972), we saw this group as facing a "dilemma". Secondly, there were the physical and emotional strains of caring. We called this group "tired".

Overall, 39% of the applicants normally resident outside an institution had caregivers who appeared to be facing a dilemma or stress. This applied to more than half the applicants who lived with people of a younger generation. However, 39% of the applicants living alone also had caregivers who were facing some dilemma of divided responsibilities or stress.

One fifth (19%) of the applicants were coded as having "frail or tired" caregivers. As can be seen from Table 3.10, this applied to half

Table 3.9

Self-Care Difficulties and Residence at Application

Residence at application

Self-care difficulties	Private household %	Hospital %	All applicants %	χ^2 (DF = 1)
	(437)	(443)	(970) +	
Types of difficulty				
Preparing meals	83	96	89	27.51***
Climbing stairs	71	75	72	1.54
Walking	59	35	47	47.77***
Dressing	32	26	29	3.50
Washing	37	17	27	35.57***
Getting in/out of bed	26	14	21	16.98***
Using WC	16	14	15	0.95
Feeding self	12	4	8	16.48***
Number of above difficulties				
0 - 1	25	26	26	
2 - 3	41	55	47	
4 and more	34	19	27	
Mean	3.1	2.5	2.8	

+ Includes 90 applicants with "other" residence at application for whom mean number of difficulties was 2.8.

Number of Difficulties

Distribution: $\chi^2 = 27.74$***,   DF = 2.

Mean: t-test = 5.11***, DF = 819 which allows for significantly different variances and the appropriate degrees of freedom.

the applicants who lived only with other elderly people and much less frequently in other households.

In general, most applicants appeared to have caregivers who were available and willing to care. The problems arose not from rejection but from exhaustion or incompatible demands.

Table 3.10

Main Problem of Caregiver and Usual Household Composition

(excluding applicants with no residence other than an institution)

Main problem of caregiver	Usual household composition				
	Alone	With other elderly only	With younger generation	Other	Total
	%	%	%	%	%
	(514)	(149)	(142)	(38)	(843)
Dilemma/stress/preoccupation (e.g. with employment)	39	28	56	18	39
Illness/frailty/tiredness	13	49	12	24	19
Rejection of applicant	2	6	13	11	5
Impending move/overcrowding	3	5	10	3	4
No problem reported	18	4	5	16	13
No informal caregiver/ caregiver died/ insufficient information	25	8	4	29	19

Overall: $\chi^2 = 209.40^{***}$, DF = 15.

The problems of caregivers interacted with those of lack of basic care or risk. Two-thirds of the applicants who were said to lack basic care or to be at risk had caregivers whose difficulties were also presented as reasons for the application. Many of the caregivers were looking after old people as physically or mentally dependent as any found in institutions. Of the 167 applicants who were reported to be "severely" confused, 29% were in the psychiatric hospital at application but almost as many (22%) were being cared for in the private households of informal caregivers (Table 3.11).

Despite such severe problems, many caregivers had not received help from domiciliary services. Table 3.12 shows that health or social services had been deployed to 61% of the 843 applicants who usually lived outside an institution.

However, 90% of these 843 applicants had been in contact with relatives or friends including 33% who had been sustained by these informal caregivers only (compared with 4% by statutory services only).

Household composition at their usual residence was strongly related to whether or not applicants had received the three main domiciliary services (home help, meals on wheels, district nurse). One or more of these services (Table 3.13) had been supplied to 70% of those who usually lived alone, to 51% of those who lived with other elderly people, but to only 31% of those living in the household of a younger generation. Thus in this sample, as in others, services seemed to be deployed less to support caregivers than to substitute for them.

Table 3.11

Type of Residence at Application and Confusion

| | | | Applicant was: | |
Type of residence at application		Apparently alert	Occasionally confused	Severely confused
Private household				
Applicant's own	(302) %	63	23	14
Relation's/friend's	(135) %	60	19	21
Hospital				
General	(109) %	71	18	11
Geriatric	(269) %	58	24	18
Psychiatric	(65) %	49	23	28
Residential Homes				
L.A.	(49) %	47	27	27
Private/Voluntary	(29) %	66	24	10
Other	(12) %	(10)	(1)	(1)
Total	(970) %	61	22	17

Overall: $\chi^2 = 23.46^{***}$, DF = 14.

Home help was the service most commonly provided, particularly to applicants who had been living alone. Overall, home helps had been provided to 50% of applicants, meals on wheels to 31% and the district nurse was visiting 26%. Only the district nurse was as often deployed to applicants living in family groups which included younger generations as to those living alone or only with other elderly people.

Table 3.12

Care Network and Usual Household Composition

(excludes applicants with no residence other than an institution)

	Usual household composition			
Care network	Alone	With other elderly only	With younger generation	Total
	%	%	%	%
	(514)	(149)	(142)	(843) +
Informal only	21	54	61	33
Social and health services only	6	-	-	4
Both	68	46	39	57
Neither	6	-	-	6

+ Includes 38 applicants with "other" composition.

Any social or health service v. None (None = Informal Only + Neither):

$$\chi^2 = 78.56^{***}, \quad DF = 2.$$

Accommodation: suitability and self care

Accommodation was classified as "suitable", "unsuitable" or "detrimental". The information on which this coding was based was of variable quality. Hospital social workers did not necessarily visit applicants at their home address before making a Part III application. Some social workers felt that accommodation problems were outside their remit or power to resolve and had little to say about them. Where accommodation was suitable, social workers did not always record this fact.

Despite these limitations, 32% of applicants who had homes of their own were coded as living in accommodation which was either detrimental (9%) or unsuitable (23%). These judgements were clearly related to the applicants' physical abilities. Applicants who were physically ill, had difficulty with four or more self-care tasks or who had to use a walking aid or a wheelchair were all more likely to be coded as living in unsuitable accommodation.

Not surprisingly, there was some relationship between incontinence and the situation of lavatories, a relationship which emphasises the importance of the finding earlier in this chapter that an unusually high proportion of applicants had outside WCs only. Of applicants with an

30

outside lavatory only, 19% were said to be incontinent and 21% to have difficulty in using it. By comparison, only 11% of applicants who had inside lavatories were said to be incontinent and 15% to have difficulty using them. Although outside WCs might sometimes be more accessible than those upstairs, the journey to some could be cold and hazardous.

Table 3.13

Main Services and Usual Household Composition

(excluding applicants with no residence other than an institution)

	Usual household composition				
Services received by applicant	Alone	With other elderly only	With younger generation	Total	χ^2 (DF = 1)
	%	%	%	%	
	(514)	(149)	(142)	(843)+	
Any of:					
Home help	64	35	15	50	117.79[***]
Meals on wheels	40	20	10	31	54.64[***]
District nurse	26	31	24	26	1.98
None of the above	30	49	69	41	74.42[***]

+ Includes 38 applicants with "other" composition.

Attitude and mood of applicants

It was interesting that in 25% of application forms there was no record of how the applicant felt about the prospect of entering residential care. However, any evidence on this subject in the forms was coded. On this basis 28% of applicants were coded as having a positive attitude towards the prospect of entering Part III and 26% as having accepted the situation. In 16%, applicants were coded as reluctant and in 3% as against the idea of entering Part III.

The applicants' attitudes to the prospect of residential care had to be viewed against a background of social isolation, anxiety and depression. Table 3.14 shows that most (70%) applicants were described as isolated to some degree and 44% were described as either anxious or depressed about their current situation. Depression was attributed more often to applicants resident in private households at application (30%) than to those in hospital (18%). Applicants who usually lived alone were more often described as depressed (28%), but so too were 20% of those who usually lived with other people. Only one in five applicants were coded as neither anxious, depressed nor isolated. Although these codes were not based on hard data, they underlined serious questions about the quality of the applicants' lives.

Table 3.14

Anxiety/Depression and Social Isolation

	Anxiety/depression		
	Either/both mentioned	Neither mentioned	Total
Social Isolation	%	%	%
	(425)	(545)	(970)
Great	41	19	29
Some	37	45	42
None/no mention	22	35	30

Overall: $\chi^2 = 57.30^{***}$, DF = 2.

Trend: $Z = 7.06^{***}$, DF = 1.

Conclusion

As our study was conducted in one authority only it was important to determine whether our findings were typical. In general it appeared that they were. The average age of our applicants closely resembled that of applicants reported elsewhere as did the proportion of women applicants (Avon, 1980; Plank, 1977; Wager, 1972). Just over half our applicants lived alone, a proportion very similar to that found in other studies (Avon, 1980; Golding and Cooper, 1981; Stapleton, 1976; Wager, 1972). The proportion of applicants who were in hospital was, however, rather higher (46%) in our study than in national surveys of residents where the range is 30%-36%. This difference may arise in part because we excluded transfers between Homes from our calculations. For example, Bebbington and Tong (1986) reported that 34% of Part III residents in a national sample had applied whilst in hospital, but when inter-Home transfers are excluded, this proportion rises to 41%.
The sample resembled others in terms of the reasons for the application as well as the contexts in which they were made. Risk and physical frailty were stated to be important in the great majority of cases (Mitchell and Earwicker, 1982; Wade et al., 1983), although in ours as in other studies many of the applicants were not severely disabled. The proportion of cases in which informal carers were said to have problems was similar in other studies (Avon, 1980; Wade et al., 1983). In relation to "unsuitable accommodation" and homelessness, however, there were differences between our study and those of others,

with reports of unsuitable accommodation varying from 5%to 50% (Avon, 1980; Golding and Cooper, 1981; Wager, 1972) and of homelessness from 7% (Wade et al., 1983) to 25% (Townsend, 1962). It should be remembered, however, that we defined "homelessness" as lack of tenure and our figures for applicants who were not living anywhere except in an institution would be close to those of Wade.

In terms of services, there were close similarities between our own and other samples in the proportion who had received a home help (around one half) and the proportion who had had a district nurse (20%-25%) (Avon, 1980; Golding and Cooper, 1981; Plank, 1977; Wager, 1972). There was more variation (51%-31%) in the proportion who had received meals on wheels (Bowling and Salvage, 1984; Golding and Cooper 1981; Plank, 1977; Wager, 1972). In this respect, our sample (31% of whom had received meals) were at the lower end of provision. Like ourselves, Wager (1972) reports considerable variation in the provision of services to applicants living alone compared with those living with their married children. In this respect, his sample were even worse off than ours for no applicant who lived with their children in Wager's sample had had a home help but 15% in our sample had.

Standing back from the data, two broad and very different kinds of reason for application can be seen. In the first place, there were the official reasons for application - the old person was at risk, or the caregivers were under stress, or the housing was poor. Second, and often unrecognised explicitly in the application forms, were "contextual reasons", for example, applicants were much more likely to be in hospital, less likely to be married and less likely to own a home of their own than the general run of old people in the authority. In two-thirds of the cases they were not "in their own place" when they reached the point of application.

In the next two parts of this book we will follow these twin themes of the "official" and the "contextual" reasons for applications. We will show, for example, that when looked at in detail the official reasons of risk or lack of basic care often reflect less serious and more remediable problems than might appear, and that they are seen differently by different participants in the application process. We will show also that the outcomes of applications had more to do with the context in which the applications were made than with the official reasons for it. We will suggest that the existence of these two kinds of reason may have contributed to the difficulty the authority had in targeting new developments to potential applicants; those served by such developments might indeed be "at risk" but not in a context where an application was likely. In this way the distinction between "official" and "contextual" reasons has a major relevance to the explanation of the paradox of institutional admission to which we referred earlier.

All this, however, is to anticipate our argument. We turn next to the detailed study of the small sample of applicants, caregivers and social workers on which much of this argument is based.

4 Introducing the small sample: the past and the present

Introduction

About such a group as the old people in our study Norman (1980) writes, "What they might like to do and what is physically or financially possible diverge .... However there are ways in which society further restricts this narrowing range of choice by imposing on elderly people forms of care and treatment which are the fruit of social perception, social anxiety, convenience or custom rather than inescapable necessity." The extent to which such constraints on their autonomy applied to the applicants in this study was an underlying theme of our work. Furthermore, the old people we were perceiving as "applicants" were each perceiving themselves as uniquely human and we have tried to incorporate some of this dimension in our discussion.

In this section we do so by considering data from interviews with social workers, applicants and caregivers in a small sample of sixty cases which was reasonably representative of the large one and drawn in such in way that half the old people were applying from hospital and half from the community, and in each of those settings half normally lived alone and half with others (for details of method see Appendix 2).

As each applicant was drawn in the sample, permission was sought from the referring social worker for the interviews to proceed. Social workers were also asked for their opinion of the identity of "the closest" informal caregiver (defined as the person "who gave the applicant most personal care on a daily basis").

Letters explaining the purpose and confidentiality of the interviews were sent to applicants and to their informal caregivers, appointments were offered and an opportunity given for these to be confirmed or refused. Interviews were attempted with all applicants in the sample including those reported to be confused. In only one case was it impossible to obtain any degree of rational response, although with six others memories were selective especially about recent stressful events.

No applicant refused the interview and many made an "occasion" out of it. Several had taken particular trouble with their appearance, some

34

had brought out the best china and insisted upon the interviewer having tea; others took the opportunity to give vent to their anxieties and distress about the situation in which they found themselves.

Interviewers often mentioned the sense of humour and vitality shown by applicants. Even those who seemed depressed at the start of the interview showed flashes of humour as the conversation proceeded. For example, one old lady, now blind, severely disabled and housebound roared with laughter when she heard the sound of her own recorded voice:

That's not me is it? Not my voice - ain't I dreadful?

In this chapter we are concerned with the applicants' perceptions of their past lives and ability, of which the teacups were a symbol. We also examine how in the old people's eyes their circumstances had changed, and the implication of these changes for their morale.

The past

Although professionals in the health and social services may perceive applicants primarily as people with problems, the applicants were more interested in themselves as people with histories. These histories included their roots in a locality, the families they had raised and their adult experiences in both employment and leisure. The contrast between their past achievements and the limitations of the present affected both the reasons for which they applied for residential care and their attitude to this decision.

Roots

Most applicants considered that their personal roots were in the study authority and three-quarters of those who still had homes of their own, or who had recently relinquished them, said their roots were in the borough. Half who still had homes of their own had lived in them for longer than twenty years. Most had first moved in long before retirement age and, in some instances, when they themselves were parents of young children. Several had been born in the borough - two in the same house in which they still lived. Three-fifths of the applicants resident in another person's home had been there for more than ten years.

Roots usually related to particular localities within the borough, some of which were quite small geographical areas. Other parts of the same authority could be experienced as socially alien and bewilderingly unfamiliar. Such allegiance to "the place where I belong" had implications for placing applicants in Part III Homes outside their "own" localities where a visit to a particular pub or a familiar row of shops was not possible.

Applicants who lived in the household of others less often had their roots in the study authority. Over half had moved into the authority from elsewhere - usually after retirement - either to be near or to live with their relatives. Some still had vivid memories of the effects of this upheaval. The security of "belonging" did not refer only to close personal relationships but to familiar sights, sounds, the smell of the air, local traditions and the pace of life. Whereas such considerations may not be overriding, they were important to applicants.

Elderly people who had known each other since they were young - either friends or relatives - seemed to have a special quality in their relationships. Past hostilities often survived, but so too did mutual memories of the wholeness of appearance from youth to age, the roots of personality and the changes wrought by events over time. The quarrelling of elderly siblings or couples appeared uninhibited, with little concession to frailty or age. Interviews with these applicants indicated the importance of such long-standing relationships and the impoverishing effect on an elderly person when the last person who knew them when they were young died. The death of a sibling or long-standing friend was mentioned by several applicants as an important landmark in their personal history. Some applicants no longer had friends or relatives alive who remembered them in their more active, youthful years and therefore they were now the sole custodians of memories of their past.

Family

The sixty applicants had brought up relatively small families - certainly smaller than those from which most of them had originated. Seven had been childless and fourteen had had one child only. The applicants who had been married (including the childless) had had an average of 1.9 children, and the number of children now available to them was smaller still.

Five widows mentioned the death of one of their children. The distress expressed over these bereavements conveyed the shock experienced by a parent (of whatever age) when a "child" (of whatever age) dies. Nine other applicants had experienced long-standing separation from a child. In most cases this was because adult children had either emigrated or moved too far away for personal contact to be easy or regular. Two applicants had become estranged from their children following a divorce or separation many years previously.

Three applicants had travelled abroad within the five years prior to their Part III application hoping to find security with their emigrated children. One couple had gone to live with sons in New Zealand and had sold their home and possessions in order to do this. Another applicant had gone to Canada for an extended stay with her daughter. When these arrangements had failed they had returned to England. In each case, the health of these applicants quickly deteriorated and within five years they had made an application for long-stay residential care.

For applicants, one result of having had few children was that they did not now have many grandchildren. Nevertheless, when asked what they would most miss on admission to Part III care, all who were in contact with their grandchildren said they would most miss seeing them so often. Those who lived in the same household with grandchildren said they would miss "seeing them grow up" and "having them pop in to see me when they come home from school". Fear of losing this close and spontaneous contact was given greater priority by some applicants than anxiety about losing their own independence.

Adult life experiences

Most applicants had been born around the time of Queen Victoria's death, had been young people in the First World War and adult in the Second. Women applicants were on average older than men and more likely to be widowed. When they described their husbands' service in the armed forces, they were often referring to the First World War, whereas men applicants described their own experiences in the Second. The Second World War to women meant their sons being called up or, in two cases, being killed.

Reports of reactions to such past crises could increase understanding of response to the current one. A daughter recalled how her only brother had survived a prisoner of war camp but was killed in an accident on the journey home. She described her mother's reaction:

> We all went to pieces but she never broke down.

The contained attitude with which this old lady had repressed distress during other crises in her life was still apparent at the time of application.

War had also influenced the variety of employment experienced by women applicants - two had been nurses (one serving in Ceylon and India), others had been in the land army, in a munitions factory and a "clippy" on the trams. A few applicants had moved into the study authority because they had been bombed out of their previous homes in other parts of London.

Apart from their war-time experience, nearly half (nineteen of the forty-three women applicants) had had long-term paid employment. All except one (said to be mentally handicapped) of the single women had worked, as had ten of the thirty applicants who were now widows. Commonly, their usual employment had been in occupations traditional for women. Nine women had been "in service", done daily cleaning, worked in a laundry or taken in washing. Several were proud of their work record, and described how they had "looked after" Lord ... , or had cleaned the local police station for twenty-five years.

Only one male applicant had never been employed (he was regarded by his family as mentally handicapped). The previous occupations of most men applicants had been in unskilled or skilled manual jobs. Two men had had their own businesses (one selling used cars and the other in "rags"), another had worked abroad for many years as a senior mechanical inspector of railways. Typically, employment for unskilled men had involved travelling to where the work was and several mentioned this. It meant that they had had to be away from their homes for long periods ("but the money was good"), and this could influence their children's later attitudes to caregiving. One daughter who now (unwillingly) had her father living with her, recalled the unemployment in Ireland between the wars, and said:

> He was always over here [in England] working - we hardly knew him as kids. It was mum who bore the brunt. It was her we were close to.

This daughter would have more willingly cared for her mother had she lived than for her father, whom she felt she hardly knew.

Activities and interests

The applicants' previous leisure activities had mainly been centred on their homes or, for some of the men, in the pub. Few described themselves as having had "hobbies". Reading was the most popular passive pastime and going for a walk and talking to people had been the most popular active one. One man in hospital escaped from the tedium of his life through reading and said:

> Books are like music - if you like a piece you can hear it over and over again.

37

Two applicants were prolific letter writers. Leisure activities of applicants in their more active years had also included cycling, darts, billiards, table tennis, going to dances, gardening, playing cards, doing the pools and playing the piano. Although most applicants watched television, they seemed less enthusiastic about this than about more gregarious activities. Some applicants had been to pop-in centres or clubs after their retirement and had enjoyed these. However, attendance had depended upon their ability to make the journey independently.

Women applicants tended to describe themselves as having been more socially active than their husbands:

> I'd always go to the shops for him while he was fiddle fuddling around at home. He never had time for the neighbours.

Also, several applicants expressed pride at their lifelong independence:

> We never had no help from nobody.

The process of change

Applicants' past lives had been characterised by hard work, self-created interest and activity. This reinforced the bewilderment of some about their current disabilities:

> I can't think why I'm like I am now - I've always been so active.

Except for seven applicants who had poor memory of their previous lives, all applicants could recall the events which had started the decline from their active independent past to their circumscribed, difficult and dependent present. One third related their initial difficulties to loss, a further third to illness or disability and the rest to other factors such as developing conflict between themselves and their caregivers or their lack of caregivers. One third of applicants said that difficulties leading to their application had occurred in the previous year, a further third between one to four years earlier and the rest longer ago.

Loss

Loss through death had started a downward spiral of events for one in three applicants and three-quarters of these bereavements had happened between two and ten years prior to the application. Typically, applicants said that they had managed fairly well during the year following their bereavement but that after this their daily lives had become increasingly difficult for them. For several, depression following grief was increased by other traumatic events such as physical disability.

For example, a man whose wife died had a stroke and was transferred into a sheltered housing flat within a year of his bereavement. He felt the move had been forced on him too soon. During it he had lost the only photograph he possessed of his wife.

> I haven't got even a photo of her. Sometimes I can't picture her face. I'd like to have chatted to people who knew her. It's made

38

my mind go to pieces - I haven't felt mentally in control since - my head has gone.

This wish to share memories of people who had died with others who had known them was mentioned by other bereaved applicants. As suggested by the findings in the large sample, the bereavement of men was particularly relevant to their application. One man sobbed uncontrollably when he first mentioned the death of his wife four years previously. Men applicants expressed desolation following their bereavement and they also seemed unable to cope with the practical tasks of living alone, such as cooking, washing their clothes and, most of all, managing their money.

Most of the losses which were described had involved the death of a spouse, but relatives or friends who moved away were also mourned as if they had died. There were other types of loss also. Following the death of her pet dog one applicant had become housebound (for she no longer had need to go out twice daily), increasingly arthritic and at application required help with almost every self-care task.

Confused applicants or their caregivers also cited precipitating difficulties of loss. For two applicants bereavement had been followed by severe and sudden disorientation. The only son of another had committed suicide whilst on holiday six years previously and at interview she was continually saying:

My son will be coming to see me - I have got a son, haven't I?

Another applicant had experienced the sudden death of her husband after which she walked the streets during the night searching for him.

Loss of a familiar environment and "roots" was also said to have had serious repercussions for some. One applicant, who had been brought from Ireland by a well-meaning son to the unwilling care of an overburdened daughter, said he just wanted:

To go back to Ireland where I'd have my own sort of people around me.

Another old lady had been moved a shorter distance - from the East End to a flat near her daughters. The daughters had not realised that in the years since her move this old lady had returned to the East End daily until she was found wandering, lost and confused, and was eventually admitted to a long-stay psychiatric ward.

Illness or disability

Around four in ten applicants attributed the start of their difficulties to illness or physical disability which had placed limitations on their independence and social contacts. Most applicants complained less about their self-care struggles than about their feeling that they had little to struggle for. Similarly, they complained less about physical pain than about the monotony of having to expend so much of their time and energy simply on maintaining their own basic care.

In the view of applicants, some types of disability were more important than others and much depended on the nature of their previous interests and activities. For example, a man who loved gardening was frustrated, irritable and depressed when two stiff arthritic hips prevented him from bending and he had to watch his garden go wild.

The most important physical loss, however, was loss of sight, which was sometimes accompanied by loss of balance. Two-fifths of the applicants described unprompted how fond they were of reading and over half of this group had been prevented from doing so because of increasing visual handicap. Deteriorating sight had also prevented women from continuing to sew or knit. Inability to do simple tasks like telling the time, or to know when the gas stove was alight or food hot was a continual source of frustration and depression which led to further anxiety about what would happen in future if their sight became even worse.

It seemed that volunteers to transport these very old people to social centres or even to church could be hard to find. Some applicants who had previously enjoyed going to pop-in or community centres were no longer able to make the journey. Their absence was seldom followed up. A blind lady, now living alone, had been regularly to a community centre for several years until she was 80 years old.

> With my sight going and my legs getting tatty, I can't get there now. We used to have some nice social afternoons there.

A number of applicants thought that becoming housebound had been a major factor in eroding their will to cope. More than anything else, this had increased their isolation, lowered their morale and made them aware of their physical disabilities and pain. In their usual address, twenty-nine applicants (48%) were housebound to the extent that they felt unable to go out alone and seldom did so. A further fifteen (25%), although they occasionally went out, were confined to their homes for most of the time. Surprisingly, two out of three of the applicants who usually lived with younger caregivers hardly ever went out of their homes.

Despite living with their families, applicants could be both physically and socially isolated, especially those who spent their lives confined to upstairs bedrooms because these were on the same level as the lavatory. One applicant who lived upstairs in her daughter's home had not bothered to dress herself for over three years because there was nothing to get dressed for - until a district nurse (ordered by the GP) made her dress. She was said to "blossom" when she was eventually admitted to hospital. On some occasions this isolation was related to conflict within family groups.

Becoming housebound had, in most cases, happened gradually. Commonly a fall, deteriorating vision or diminished confidence through "wobbly legs" had decreased the frequency of journeys out, which in turn had further diminished self confidence to attempt them. One man described the experience of becoming housebound:

> I can't understand why I should go like it - I used to go out to the shops every day. Now it's about once a week. About three months past I got as far as the top of the drive and went down on the floor. My legs went wobbly. I've had that wobbly feeling two or three times - it lasts about two or three hours. I daren't trust myself to go out anywhere.

Since becoming semi-housebound, he was more aware of his disabilities and had lost interest in other activities for he continued:

> I can see straight in front of me but not out at the sides. The letters come now and I just read them and stick them on the shelf. I used to read the papers but now I only look at the sporting pages.

I used to go up to the pub. My right ear is terrible now - it got bad when I loaded guns with big shells in the war but it was never looked into because I never bothered.

Little action to prevent the elderly becoming housebound was evident. Domiciliary services were often aimed more at maintenance of life within the home than at improving its quality outside. Provision of services such as meals on wheels or home helps could further decrease the need to go outside. Although neither his ear, his sight nor his "wobbly" legs had been investigated, the applicant just described had been provided with a home help. "My home help gets my shopping and pension now."

Other reasons: conflict in relationships

Around one quarter of the applicants attributed the start of their difficulties to conflict with relatives or friends - often those with whom they lived. This had had repercussions on the mood and morale of several applicants who were interviewed, and was reflected in the fact that over two-fifths of the sample said that they felt a burden to their caregivers. In nearly all these cases the caregivers agreed that the applicants had probably come to feel this.

Applicants with no informal caregivers

A few applicants had no relatives or friends and so their application had been influenced by lack of relationships rather than by conflict. For ten applicants (a third of those living alone) the closest caregiver who could be identified was a "professional" such as a sheltered housing warden, a day centre worker or a home help. One other applicant had no contact either with relatives, friends or professional persons. Most of these especially isolated applicants were described as very lonely, depressed and distressed by the Part III application.

The two exceptions were one applicant who was very confused and another who was a colourful, alert and mobile ex-actress who was continually in debt. The sheltered housing warden, her closest caregiver, considered that long-stay residential care was inappropriate for her, but the warden felt that she had neither the status nor power to express her views.

The "professional" caregivers who were interviewed about these applicants sometimes had very tenuous links with them. The closest relationship was between a home help and an applicant whom she visited twice a week. The other professionals had little intimate knowledge of the applicants and most were unaware that theirs was the closest relationship currently available to these isolated people. A sheltered housing warden said of one applicant that she "saw him about most days" and a day centre worker had lost touch with an applicant for some months during a hospital admission.

A major repercussion of this isolation was the absence of an advocate. These old people had to fight for themselves and all except one lacked the physical strength or emotional conviction to do so. They were a particularly vulnerable and powerless group.

41

The present

Mood and morale

Words like "loneliness", "isolation" or "depression" appeared frequently on application forms and were used to cover a wide range of circumstances - from bereavement to boredom. Both application forms and interviews showed that many applicants' lives lacked companionship, a feeling of being involved or wanted. Poor environmental conditions, struggles with self-care tasks and becoming housebound further diminished the quality of their lives.

There were three areas of questioning which most often produced spontaneous descriptions of how applicants perceived their isolation. First, when asked about their past lives, applicants often compared past relationships with the present ones. For example, when describing his problems and loneliness, one isolated widower's voice was a depressive monotone. He insisted upon relating his memories of returning from armed service abroad and while doing so his voice contained a lilt and communicated the vitality and enjoyment of memories of people who were fond of him. On discharge he went to find his wife:

> They didn't know I was coming. Her sister opened the door "Hello George where have you come from". "I've come from Italy". 'May [his wife] has gone away to her sister's place - come and have some tea with us." When I went there, May was in the scullery with her other sister. When she heard my voice she couldn't stop cuddling me. Her brother was in bed and I went and sat on the edge of his bed so I could see his face when he woke up.

Others also needed to show that their current lack of family and friends did not imply a past in which they had been unable to make affectionate relationships.

Secondly, when asked about their activities and self-care difficulties during different periods of an "average" day, applicants placed greater emphasis on the times when they felt especially lonely or fearful than on their practical problems.

Finally, direct questions were asked about the whereabouts of relatives or other people who were alive and about the contacts which applicants had with them.

Around one in four applicants had elderly relatives or friends alive but could no longer travel to see them. Some of these relatives or friends were in distant parts of the country but most lived in or around London. Sometimes contact had lapsed as a result of depression or lack of effort:

> I've got a brother in Wales or I think I have. I don't know whether he's dead or alive. Somehow I can't write letters since my wife died.

Other contacts were difficult because of frailty and lack of transport. When invited to dream about what they would do if they had enough money to call a taxi when they wished, a typical response was:

> I could go to see my sisters in Peckham - that would make all the difference." [This would have involved a journey of about seven miles.]

The apparent importance to such very old people of being enabled to maintain occasional personal contact with others of their own generation cannot be over-emphasised.

Other replies included descriptions of the quality and nature of regular visits:

> He only pops in for ten minutes to see how I am - I know he is very busy.

Two types of isolation were expressed. The first arose from physical constraints and becoming housebound. For example, talking to people could depend upon being able to get to the front gate.

> I can't get down the steps to sweep the path out there now. I haven't seen the neighbour next door for months. She keeps herself to herself and only talks if I'm at the gate. I don't ask her to do nothing.

Lack of social contacts could atrophy social skills so that a sort of agoraphobia becomes evident amongst some housebound applicants.

> She [a neighbour across the road] is always asking me over for a cup of tea - but I can't do with that sort of thing now. You get out of the way of it - mixing with people.

The view from the window had become important to housebound applicants and the activities and enjoyment of others was sometimes described, especially by those living alone, as increasing feelings of isolation:

> I can't abide weekends. It's too noisy - too many people walking past the window laughing and talking.

Minor disruptions became magnified. One housebound man (who was not on the telephone) led the interviewer to an envelope which was placed by a clock in a prominent position in his room. This letter had been there for several weeks and represented the focus of his anxieties.

> My pension worries the life out of me. I had this letter - they've stopped some money. They say Dr X hasn't written about my diet. I can't sleep thinking what to do about it. I don't know how I shall manage with the winter coming.

Worry had immobilised this old man for he had neither written to his doctor to ask for the appropriate letter to be sent nor had he contacted the social security office.

Three caregivers regularly pushed applicants out in wheelchairs as they felt that this was an important way of alleviating the applicants' depression. All had manual wheelchairs and all complained of the physical stress of pushing them. One said that she had been told about a luncheon club to which her elderly mother could go. However, no transport was available to take her, and her husband used the car for work.

> I think mum would have enjoyed it as she would have met other people and it would have been a change for her.

However, this daughter said that the luncheon club was:

Two hills away - I didn't feel I could push the chair that far.

Perhaps the applicant's wheelchair, like many others commonly issued, did not have brakes quickly accessible to the person pushing, which made coming downhill especially hazardous.

In other cases a supporting arm or a wheelchair (and somebody to push it) would have enabled outside contacts to have continued for longer. Some caregivers had been puzzled when an offer of a car trip was turned down. Descriptions of an applicant's incontinence in other parts of the interview and the apparent absence of incontinence pants and pads made it possible that such a refusal of outings might arise from an applicant's fear of "accidents" in the car.

Feeling a burden on their caregiving relatives resulted in some applicants becoming depressed and inactive despite being physically able. For example, a man who had recovered from a stroke gave up his home to move in with his son but then realised that his presence proved intolerable to his daughter-in-law. At application he was described as "just sitting all day and staring at the wall". When offered day care he showed he was able to get onto a bus unaided and was probably capable of living independently in a home of his own.

Applicants were not asked whether they had thought of suicide. Nevertheless, the subject came up and the wish for death was particularly apparent amongst those applicants who felt unwanted by those around them. Three had attempted suicide.

One of these lived alone, had Meniere's disease and was on hostile terms with her only son and his wife. She took an overdose a few hours before her son was due to call. The second had slashed her wrist and it was unknown whether this was due to her sudden bereavement, feeling unwanted by her only son or her previous mental illness. The third, and most serious, suicide attempt was by an applicant who had cared for her older sister in derelict and damp surroundings since her own widowhood six years earlier. She had diabetes, deteriorating vision, and had been told that a gall bladder operation was not possible for several months. She felt her GP was irritable with her when she constantly summoned him because of her intense pain. This applicant took a massive overdose, was admitted to hospital only just in time to save her life and was operated on for removal of her gall bladder a few days after her hospital admission.

Conclusion

As we have seen in this sample, the applicants' histories were varied and their views of themselves extended beyond the problems outlined on the application forms. Most had lived in the same locality and sometimes in the same house for many years. As they perceived their situation, their applications had arisen through a process which often involved loss, increasing physical difficulties and conflict with relatives. The significance of these events went wider than the difficulties of managing personal needs. Becoming housebound, for example, meant not only dependence on others for some of the necessities of life, but also curtailment of activities which had made life worth while.

In these respects our findings, although based on the retrospective accounts of applicants, are supported by those of others. There is increasing awareness of the inter-relationships between severe life events, poor physical health, major social difficulty and depression

(Millard, 1983; Murphy, 1982). Other studies have also drawn attention to the connections between loneliness, depression, physical disability and care networks (Jones et al., 1985; Post, 1972; Sinclair et al., 1984). Bereavement and the repercussions of unresolved grief, especially in men, have been recognised (Parkes, 1969, 1972). The extent to which available professionals, such as general practitioners, are able to detect and arrest a process of deterioration is important (Cartwright, 1982). In our sample there was little evidence that they had been able to do so.

If social services departments are to intervene in these problems, they must be interested in the applicant's abilities as well as disabilities and be concerned to improve the quality of his or her life as well as its maintenance. They must also target their efforts at the events or processes which apparently lead to deterioration in quality of life - loss, becoming housebound, conflict with relatives. Thus, they may seek to:

* Develop schemes, in liaison with other agencies, to maintain the morale of elderly people, particularly those which enable the housebound to go out.

* Extend and modify the role of home helps to provide both practical support in the aftermath of a bereavement and encouragement (especially to bereaved men) to acquire domestic skills. (A small weekly group of widowers in which they learnt from a home help to cook, wash clothes and work out their weekly budget might be worth trying.)

* Recognise the need for the bereaved to talk about the dead person, for example, by developing counselling schemes for the recently bereaved, to which GPs could refer.

These examples leave out the crucial role of relatives in preventing or hastening deterioration in morale in the old person but to that we return in a later chapter.

5 Problems of caring: basic self care

Introduction

As we have described, the applicants saw their physical deterioration as one of the key determinants of their present state. In this chapter we consider the physical and mental disabilities suffered by applicants and examine the degree to which these contributed to "lack of basic care" being given as a reason for the application. We will examine in detail the particular problems which applicants faced at different times of the day, drawing implications for service provision, and we will compare the applicants' views on these matters with those of their informal caregivers and referring social workers.

Method

Applicants and their caregivers were asked questions about "any particular disabilities or health problems". A checklist was used to record descriptions of the nature of each difficulty, and respondents were asked to rate it as constituting either a severe/frequent problem, occasional problem or no problem. The checklist included questions on sight, hearing, speech, mobility, dexterity, balance, incontinence, memory and pain (including severe discomforts such as persistent irritation).

Applicants' sensory and physical disabilities

Sight

On application forms of both the large and small samples, few applicants were described as completely blind, but some visual handicap was reported in 19% of the large sample and 16% of the small sample. However, in interviews, half the applicants and two-fifths of the caregivers said the applicant had some problems with vision (Table 5.1). Thus, in three-fifths of the small sample either or both applicant and caregiver said the applicant had a problem with visual handicap.

Some visual losses arose from diagnosed conditions such as cataracts or diabetes but others had not been medically investigated. Blindness seemed to present fewer problems in self care than did partial sight. Possible reasons for this included the fact that most blind applicants usually lived with and were cared for by others, had been visually handicapped for a long time and had acquired appropriate equipment such as braille clocks or talking books. Partially sighted applicants seldom had this range of aids and were often struggling alone with a strange situation of sudden or steady deterioration of vision (for example, through cataracts).

Table 5.1

Disabilities of Applicants as Reported by Applicants and Caregivers

Disability to do with:	Reported by		
	Applicant	Caregiver	Either
	%	%	%
	(60)	(56)	(60)
Balance	61	70	78
Mobility	59	70	76
Memory	42	54	60
Sight	49	39	59
Incontinence	15	45	53
Dexterity	40	27	47
Hearing	35	36	46
Speech	2	7	7

Note:

Please note that this and all subsequent tables in Chapter 5 are based on data from the Small Scale Study.

Hearing

On application forms of the large and small samples hearing loss was reported on 17% and 12% respectively. In interviews with the small sample one third of applicants and one third of caregivers said loss of

47

hearing was a problem. In nearly a half of the small sample either or both applicant and caregiver said the applicant had a problem with hearing.

Speech

Difficulties with speech arose most commonly from expressive loss following strokes and were reported in around 3% of the large sample and 7% of the small.

Disability in speech, hearing or sight were obviously crucially important elements in communication both during the decision-making process and in establishing new contacts upon admission to Part III care.

Mobility

On application forms of the large and small samples, problems with mobility were reported on 68% and 74% respectively. In interviews with the small sample three-fifths of applicants and two-thirds of caregivers said limited mobility was a problem. In three-quarters of the small sample either or both applicant and caregiver said the applicant had mobility problems. A similar proportion described problems with balance.

Restricted mobility arose from a variety of causes, such as breathlessness due to chronic bronchitis or heart disease, dizziness or loss of balance or lost sensation or strength in limbs after strokes or fractures. Arthritis, which disabled applicants in various ways, was recorded on application forms of 19% of the large and 27% of the small samples.

Loss of mobility was not necessarily associated with problems with the applicants' legs. Stiffness and weakness in arms or a sudden deterioration in vision had seriously affected the ability of some applicants to move from one place to another. One arthritic old lady, for example, had a zimmer frame but one of her arms was too stiff to lift on to it. Another could reach the zimmer with her hands but any pressure on it whilst walking caused acute pain in her elbows and shoulders. A man who had become nearly blind after surgery could still move confidently around his flat but could not steer a straight course along a pavement. (He had not received mobility training nor was he likely to.) The three symptoms which applicants most often associated with restricted mobility and difficulty in basic care were loss of balance, stiffness and visual problems. These three, together with confusion, presented the biggest problems to applicants in relation to self-care tasks.

Dexterity

Nearly two-fifths (38%) of the applicants said they had problems with dexterity, but this had been noticed by rather fewer (27%) of their caregivers. Loss of flexibility, pressure and sensitivity in hands or fingers is a less obvious disability than is a loss of mobility or balance and was not systematically reported on application forms.

Incontinence

In the large sample, there was mention of incontinence on 11% of application forms. In interviews with the small sample, however, one in six applicants and nearly half the caregivers said that the applicant was incontinent. This meant that in over half the cases either or both applicant and caregiver said that the applicant was incontinent, and that this problem was mentioned by three times as many caregivers as applicants. Although incontinence was reported three times more often by caregivers than by applicants some caregivers described an applicant as "incontinent" when they were only recalling an occasional accident.

Also, the strong smell of urine which interviewers noted on some applicants who maintained that they had no problems in this direction did not necessarily mean frequent incontinence, but could be under-clothing, chairs or carpets which had been allowed to "dry out" without being cleaned. Living with this smell might have resulted in applicants being unaware of it whereas it troubled their caregivers. Those applicants who said they were incontinent often linked this to their mobility and to where their lavatory was situated. The comment, "sometimes I can't get there in time", could mean they regarded the problem as concerned with their legs or inconvenient stairs, not with their "waterworks".

Confusion

On application forms of the large and small samples severe confusion was described on 18% and 13% respectively and "occasional" confusion or lapses of memory on a further 23% and 18% respectively. It was important to recognise that memory loss was not necessarily the same as confusion. The ambiguous use of the word "confusion" to cover a wide range of conditions described on application forms indicated the need for sharper assessment and screening techniques (Levin et al., 1983).

In interviews with the small sample the word "confusion" was not used in a question to applicants or to caregivers but both were asked, "How is the applicant's memory these days?" In three-fifths of the small sample, either or both applicant and caregiver said that the applicant had some problems with lapses of memory. There was some disagreement between applicants and caregivers. Three in five applicants said they had no problems with their memory but a half of the caregivers said the applicant did have a problem with memory and for 37% of applicants, caregivers rated memory loss as severe.

Applicants who said that their memory was failing frequently expressed agitation, distress and anxiety about this, voicing feelings of frustration, fear and vulnerability:

> I forget - I can't remember - not recently. Things get on my mind. I try to fathom them out and can't.

This applicant lived alone and, during recent years, had experienced the death of all her sisters, cousins and other close relatives. Now her closest caregiver was a neighbour who, although she had known her for twelve years, remembered her only as old. The emotional isolation of this applicant and others like her arose not only from the bereavements she had experienced but also from feeling that the mental images of important people and landmarks in her life were slipping away from her. Some applicants wished to forget less pleasant memories. One man, bereaved, living alone and feeling depressed said, "I remember what favours me." He could remember his childhood vividly but then added, "these days aren't interesting - they're not worth remembering." Applicants forgot where they put things about the house, and names of people, events and dates which were important. This upset and frightened them. A few said they did not always recognise the faces of people they knew. Shocks (such as bereavement), change (such as rehousing), or hospitalisation were also mentioned as precipitating lapses of memory. An applicant in hospital said she "lay awake all night thinking about home and trying to remember where the furniture and everything was".

Attempts to understand where they were and how they had come to be there pre-occupied confused applicants. For example, one was already in a Part III Home at interview. Halfway through a largely meaningless conversation she suddenly said to the interviewer:

I'm never going to get out of this place, am I?

Pain

In contrast to most surveys of the elderly, we enquired into the presence of physical pain or discomfort. Whether or not an applicant regularly experienced pain was seldom reported on application forms but in response to a direct question in interviews, "In your ordinary day-to-day life are you in pain at all?", 7% of both applicants and caregivers said the applicant was in frequent or severe pain, 30% of applicants and 25% of caregivers said applicants were in occasional pain and 15% of applicants and 18% of caregivers said applicants experienced "mild" pain. Therefore, half the applicants interviewed described painful conditions. From some applicants' descriptions of their struggles with self-care tasks, it seemed that even pain described by them as "occasional" could be severe enough to keep them awake at night or make some times of the day miserable.

Attitudes to health and recovery

Applicants, caregivers and interviewers rated the applicants' general health on a four-point scale: very good, average, so-so/poor or bad. One fifth of applicants and a similar proportion of caregivers described the applicant's health as "very good". The majority of applicants and caregivers (58% and 53% respectively) said the applicant's health was "average". "Poor" health of applicants was reported by 8% of applicants and 12% of caregivers and bad health by 10% of applicants and 17% of caregivers.

Therefore, although most had some physical illness or disability and half had some pain, only one in five applicants described their general health as below average, so-so/poor or bad. Like other samples of elderly people (Hunt, 1978), most applicants were optimistic about their general health and compared it to a stereotype of "people their age". "I'm very good for my age." Other applicants distinguished their general health from particular parts of their body which were being a problem to them. "I'm all right in myself - it's only my leg." In most cases, their informal caregivers agreed with the applicants.

Applicants in hospital were asked if they expected their health to get back to normal and more than half did. Only one in ten did not expect a reasonably full recovery. The informal caregivers of these applicants, however, were less optimistic. Only a quarter expected the applicant to return to normal health and nearly a half considered this unlikely.

In general, the applicants interviewed distinguished between acute and chronic illness. For acute illness, they expected treatment, rehabilitation and recovery. Most appeared philosophical about chronic pain and disability. This attitude towards themselves contrasted with the more pessimistic assumptions of their caregivers and social workers.

Views on basic care

On application forms, the inability of applicants to provide basic care for themselves (the essential standards of food and warmth) was recorded as a predominant reason for their need for residential care. We wished to explore this issue in some detail, not only because of its importance as a reason for application but also because of the obvious implications for service delivery. After questions on specific physical disabilities, the interviewers directed the attention of applicants and caregivers to the implications of these on the applicants' self-care ability in an "average" day in their usual residence. Interviewers were asked to note whether weekends were different in care terms and what happened when the usual caregiver was ill or away. A checklist of various periods of the day was used and questioning started with applicants being asked the time they usually got up, how they got out of bed, dressed, made a meal and so on. It ended with an enquiry about usual times of going to bed and how well they slept.

Applicants, caregivers and social workers were asked, "Have these difficulties with health and basic care anything to do with your decision to apply for a home?" Over half (56%) of applicants (excluding the small number who were severely confused), 58% of social workers and 83% of caregivers considered that difficulties with basic self care were definitely or probably a reason for the application. The contrast between caregivers and applicants was particularly strong among those applicants who lived with others. Here, seventeen caregivers out of twenty-one said that problems with basic care were definitely a reason, whereas only eight applicants in the same group said the same. All fifteen relatives who visited to care thought the applicant lacked basic care but only eight applicants in this group agreed.

One reason for this variation in opinion between applicants and their closest informal caregivers arose from different definitions. With respect to "lack of basic care" for example, four out of five caregivers considered that applicants lacked basic care, but during discussion, younger caregivers especially revealed personal standards for basic care different from those described by applicants. Irregular washing, dust and muddle and, above all, smells of stale urine were, to some caregivers, clear signs of self neglect. Applicants (and to a lesser extent the social workers and interviewers) did not regard a degree of smell, dirt and confusion as necessarily constituting lack of basic care. When applicants and caregivers lived together, the caregivers were naturally more conscious than the applicants of the difficulty of providing a reasonable standard, since it was they, in most cases, who had to do the work. Furthermore, unlike some elderly applicants, caregivers were more likely to have an unimpaired sense of smell.

Applicants' views

The thirty-two applicants who described themselves as lacking basic care or the ability to look after themselves adequately were studied in more detail for indications of which types of disability or sensory loss had influenced this opinion. As can be seen from Table 5.2, applicants who considered they lacked care more often also reported that they were physically ill. They described how, during a bout of illness (for

51

example, bronchitis) they had felt helpless, weak and incapable of looking after themselves. Other differences between the two groups did not arise to the extent which might have been anticipated. The remaining disabilities listed in Table 5.2 were inconvenient, but ways of coping with them could be learnt. In general, with the exception of poor balance and falls, they did not result in unexpected crises.

Applicants who thought they lacked basic care more often reported difficulty over getting up in the morning (78%) than those who considered their care adequate (50%). As might be expected, higher proportions of those who had difficulty with their own basic care found specific self-care tasks difficult (for example, washing, dressing, cooking, going to the WC). More careful analysis, however, suggested that those whose self-care difficulties were not a reason for application fell into two groups - the comparatively fit and the severely disabled who were already being looked after by others.

Table 5.2

Characteristics Reported by Applicant and Applicant's

View of Need for Basic Care as a Reason for Application

Characteristics reported by applicant	Applicant considered need for basic care:		
	Was a reason	Was not a reason	Total
	%	%	%
	(32)	(28)	(60)
Housebound	84	61	73
Lacking balance	69	54	62
Poor mobility	69	43	57
Physically ill	69	29	50
Visual handicap	53	43	48
In physical pain+	44	32	38
Lacking dexterity	47	29	38
Poor general health	28	11	20
Incontinent	9	18	13

+ Excluding mild pain.

Extent of self-care difficulty

From the point of view of service delivery it was important to determine whether the sixty applicants were generally dependent (in that they needed help for several tasks throughout the day or night) or whether they had particular problems with specific tasks or events which occurred at particular times but at other times could look after themselves.

A content analysis (Table 5.3) of all interviews on each applicant with regard to their self-care difficulty, the help they needed and the help they received showed that:

* One third of both applicants living alone and those living with others were independent with regard to self care. Their difficulties arose from a variety of social causes including in some cases difficulty in managing their money.

* Half of all applicants experienced problems with specific tasks at particular times but such difficulties were more common among those who lived alone (67%) than among those living with others (37%).

* A minority (17%) were regarded as generally dependent because they needed extensive help on a regular basis. All of this latter group were (or had been) living with other people and over half of them were severely confused.

Table 5.3

Degree of Applicant's Self-Care Difficulties and

Applicant's Usual Household Composition

| | Usual household composition | | |
Applicant's self-care difficulties:	Alone %	With others %	Total %
	(30)	(30)	(60)
Arose over specific events or at particular times	67	37	52
Were part of applicant's general dependency	-	33	17
Did not arise - applicant independent over self care	33	30	32

The distinction between the groups of applicants who were generally dependent, who required help with specific tasks or who were independent can best be illustrated by three examples:

Generally dependent (17% of the sample)

An elderly husband caring for his "generally dependent" wife said:

> I take her a cup of tea about eight o'clock and lay all her clothes
> out for her. She tries to dress herself but she puts her shoes on
> before her pants and trousers and then can't get them over the top
> so I usually have to undress her and sort it all out. Usually
> she'll wash herself but I have to tell her where to go. I have to
> show her where the lavatory is and make sure she's wiped herself
> properly. She tries to help herself and me, but can't. She won't
> leave my side. She'll often say she's going to do the potatoes for
> dinner after we've had tea, forgetting that we had a meal at
> lunchtime.

Having a "generally dependent" wife meant that this old man felt
constantly "on duty" throughout the day and night. (Such situations are
more fully discussed by Levin et al., 1983.)

Difficulty with specific tasks (52% of sample)

A daughter living with her 96-year-old mother said:

> My husband takes her in a cup of tea about seven o' clock. She's
> been getting up later and slower in the last couple of years so now
> I take her breakfast in bed. She washes and dresses herself but we
> help her bath once each week. She doesn't do any cooking because I
> cook for all of us but she'll make herself a drink if we're out.
> She's got cataracts and can't see all that well but she can see TV.
> She's a bit unsteady but manages with a frame. She's incontinent
> when she has "an accident" but that doesn't happen often. I can't
> remember the last time she went out. It must be months or even a
> year ago. She'd like to go but she wouldn't manage alone and we're
> all out at work. She does go to stay with my brother for a holiday
> each year.

This daughter and her family had natural breaks from their caregiving
responsibilities throughout the day because for much of the time her
mother could cope unaided within a suitable environment.

Independent in self care (32% of sample)

A man, aged 80, was cared for by a much younger wife who had applied
for him to enter Part III without his knowledge and while he was in
hospital. Marital stress was acute.

> I haven't got a particular routine. I usually stay at home while
> the wife goes out visiting - I only go with her if she wants me to.
> I can wash, dress and shave but I don't dash about here, there and
> everywhere like I used to. Now, since my operation, I've got a
> catheter and bag but I manage that all right. I can manage the
> stairs and most things. I just take my time. I enjoy reading and
> read on and on. As long as I've got a book and something to eat,
> I'm all right. I do as I'm told and keep the wife agreeable.

In care terms this husband was completely independent of his wife.
The stress between the couple arose from marital conflict and not from

caregiving responsibilities.

In a few cases, difficulties had arisen over money. Such financial problems sometimes arose for widowed men, or old people who were mentally handicapped or who had become institutionalised and were unused to handling money. In six cases such problems seemed to the interviewer to be contributing to Part III applications which could have been prevented.

Specific difficulties during an "average" day

The applicants and their caregivers were asked how the applicants managed specific self-care tasks through a "normal" day at their usual address.

Getting up

Elderly people, when in bed, are in an especially vulnerable state for they are without false teeth, spectacles or hearing aids. Two-thirds of the applicants described difficulties over getting up - a process which involved a variety of activities. The first task in the morning, especially for those living alone, was to decide what time it was. Some commonly mistook the time and got up in the middle of the night by mistake - not necessarily because they were confused but because they did not have a clock which they could see. The impression was that most did not have a night light or a torch either. One applicant, who had mistaken the time on dark winter mornings for years, had recently bought "a blind clock" (at her own expense) and now was able to tell the time without her glasses. Several applicants said that they feared the dark. Therefore, before labelling disorientation over time in the mornings as confusion, it might be as well to check, for example, that such old people have a large illuminated clock which they can see without their spectacles.

Getting up times

The time when the difficult phase of getting up usually began had implications for service provision to maintain elderly people in their own homes (Table 5.4). Half of the applicants in the sample were in hospital and it was difficult for one in four of these to recall what time they usually got up when in their own homes.

Most applicants had definite getting up times and, despite their age and frailty, appeared to continue to get up at similar times to their lifelong patterns. Thus, two of the more mobile men still got up at 5.00 a.m. (the time they had previously gone to work). They went out to buy a newspaper which they brought back to bed with a cup of tea because this was the warmest place to read. On average, applicants who were (or had been) living alone got up at least an hour earlier than those who lived with other people. Nearly half of those living alone were up by 7.00 a.m., and a further quarter were up by 9.00 a.m. Applicants who said they lacked basic care and had difficulty with self-care tasks had a similar pattern of getting up times which meant that if services were to be provided to help with getting up, they would have to be early.

Applicants who usually lived with relatives got up later: only a quarter got up before 7.00 a.m., and one third did not start to get up until after 9.00 a.m. Sometimes, this was because applicants chose to linger in bed but more often it was to fit in with the household regime. From the descriptions of caregivers, early mornings could be fraught times with husbands and adolescents going off to work and applicants were requested (or instructed) to stay in bed until the activity had died down. A wife, hostile to her disabled husband (the applicant), said:

> I let him get up in his dressing gown to have his breakfast - then I make him go back to bed while I get on.

Getting out of bed

Most applicants were able to get out of bed unaided although some found this difficult and painful. "Somehow I manage to roll out of bed," said one arthritis sufferer. Monkey poles or grab rails or even a piece of rope tied to the bottom of the bed which might have helped as a leverage to stiff, weak limbs were not spontaneously mentioned by applicants or caregivers and we are certain that few, if any, had such aids.

Table 5.4

Applicant's Usual Time of Getting Up and Going to Bed

and Usual Household Composition

	Usual household composition:		
	Alone	With others	Total
	%	%	%
	(30)	(30)	(60)
Getting up times			
7 a.m. and earlier	47	23	35
Between 7 and 9 a.m.	27	30	28
Later than 9 a.m.	7	33	20
It varies	20	13	17
Going to bed times			
Before 8 p.m.	20	7	13
Between 8 and 10 p.m.	30	47	38
Later than 10 p.m.	23	17	20
It varies	27	30	28

Standing up was much more difficult. As one applicant said "I have to push on to the bed in the mornings to get my balance." Many described feeling "shaky", "hazy", "dizzy", "tottery", "breathless", "slow", when attempting to stand, dress, wash or cook. "Wobbly legs" or "legs giving way" exacerbated the fear of falls in the early morning and made every action (and particularly going down stairs) especially hazardous.

There were also frequent descriptions of accentuated early morning problems with dexterity including loss of sensation in the tips of fingers or less strength to grip. Pain and stiffness were described as worse in the morning. Getting dressed could be a long and tortuous business for some applicants which could take one to two hours. There were problems over dizziness when bending down to pull on shoes, over fingers too numb to do up buttons or zips, while stiff shoulders made it difficult to pull clothes over heads or comb hair. "I have to bend right down to get my dress over my head," said one woman with arthritis.

Difficulties related to loss of balance, dizziness and numbness were mentioned far more frequently by those living alone. Applicants who lived with others had people to compensate for their difficulty or mask it. Other problems which could contribute to these early morning difficulties include inappropriate medication, damp and unheated bedrooms, and a re-awakening of depression and loneliness making for reluctance to face the day.

When I wake up I wonder if it's worth it.

An early morning cup of tea

The first cup of tea of the day was very important to these applicants. Most younger caregivers who had applicants living with them took their relatives a cup of tea in bed and the elderly people who lived together gratuitously told the interviewer who made the early morning tea. Usually, it was the husband who made the tea for his wife (a habit that may have survived from the days when the husband went to work). One old couple whose son had fixed up kettle and tea-making facilities by their bed described sitting in bed in the early morning and drinking their tea as one of the best times of the day. Some elderly people who lived together and felt shaky in the mornings started the day by squabbling over who was to get up first.

For those living alone, the struggles to get up seemed largely in order to make a cup of tea. As one otherwise uncomplaining lady with severe arthritis said, "I often wish there was somebody here to bring me a morning cup of tea." Two applicants had caregiving neighbours who fulfilled this need. One neighbour was a tenant in the flat below and the other lived next door. This latter neighbour woke her husband and son, made them tea and brought a cup into the applicant in bed. She helped her out of bed and then returned to cook breakfast for her family. After an hour or so when they had gone to work this neighbour returned to the applicant. She helped with any residual problems over dressing (such as tying shoe laces or doing up buttons) and saw her safely down stairs where she was then able to cope at her own pace. One other applicant had a district nurse every morning and evening but no other applicant living alone had help in the early morning.

Washing

The main problem mentioned with washing was standing. "I get dizzy when

I stand to wash or cook." Washing also seemed to be related to isolation. One man said he washed and shaved twice per week - on the days his home help was due to call. As he said, "I don't bother with it - after all I'm not going anywhere am I? And nobody's going to come here?"

Cooking: lifting and carrying

Two-thirds of the applicants described difficulties over cooking. This activity also involved standing. It was particularly difficult for the visually impaired who said that they did not always know when the gas ring was alight and so they waved their hands over the top of the flame and had sometimes burnt themselves. One blind applicant had braille controls on her cooker but few of the partially sighted had adapted cookers. One visually handicapped lady said that because she could never tell when food was hot enough, she tasted it and so she often burnt her mouth. Gas cookers were also used to heat rooms - by lighting the oven and leaving the door open.

Apart from a general disinclination towards food and unnecessary effort in the morning, the main problem over cooking was in lifting and carrying. Fears of lifting hot pans off the stove were expressed. One old lady who was brought cooked meals by her family which they left heating on a pan of water explained that she seldom ate these because she could not lift the plate off the pan without spilling it and scalding herself.

Carrying, especially breakables like crockery, with two hands was a problem for immobile applicants. "If I carry something with both hands I fall over." Many lacked the strength in one arm to carry single-handed ("it shakes") and yet they needed the other hand free to use a stick or to hold on to furniture to keep themselves steady. "I need to hang on to the chairs in the mornings." For others, cutting food was also a problem and in these circumstances help from others in the household (however elderly or disabled they were) could save much frustration.

Appetite and meals

Although some applicants said that they were not interested in food ("not hungry") most said that they had good appetites and ate adequately. Their caregivers frequently did not agree with this statement. It is estimated that between 3% and 7% of elderly people suffer from clinical malnutrition (DHSS survey quoted by Thomas, 1985) but with the provision of meals on wheels, the nutrition of most elderly people is said to be adequate. However, comments from some applicants indicated that their diet was at best monotonous and at worst inadequate. A widower living alone knew what his weekly shopping bill would be because he always bought the same (via his home help).

> I always feel groggy in the mornings. I get up and make myself a cup of tea and sometimes I have a biscuit or a bit of toast with it. My meal comes about eleven o'clock and I have that as soon as it comes. I have a cup of tea about four and then a bit of supper at eight. Then I undress and get ready for bed. I get her (the home help) to buy a packet of ham on Tuesdays for my suppers. There's four slices in the packet and that lasts me four days. Sometimes I throw half of it away. On Friday she gets me a packet of pies (two pies in a packet eaten cold) for the weekend - I don't eat much -

don't feel like it - don't feel hungry."

Some caregivers said that when they cooked for and ate with applicants, the applicants ate heartily and enjoyed their food.

A few caregivers said their relatives habitually opened tins and ate the contents cold - soup or tinned baked beans. Only two in five of those applicants who lacked basic care and were living alone had meals on wheels. Four other applicants said they had tried and discontinued meals or had refused them out of hand. "Did not like the taste", "tasteless", "too expensive".

Getting to the WC

About half the applicants interviewed described difficulties in getting to the toilet. Commodes had been provided for most whose lavatory was on a different floor and who found it difficult to climb stairs. However, the problem of emptying commodes remained. One severely arthritic applicant used her commode downstairs but as she could not bear to have it unemptied in her living room, she then crawled upstairs to her lavatory to empty it, pushing the commode bucket up the stairs in front of her. Coming down with the empty bucket was even more hazardous. Other applicants waited for relatives or home helps to arrive. With one exception, neighbours or friends did not empty commodes and one neighbour said that this was one job she could not bear to do. Some applicants almost certainly put urine down the sink or an outside drain if they had one. In some ways this was logical. Why struggle upstairs to flush urine into a pipe which then runs into the same sewer at ground level? However, the need to use commodes and take these measures seemed a humiliating experience to some applicants who were struggling to maintain the standards they had lived by in the past.

The afternoons

In the afternoons several applicants said that they felt better - "more like myself". Some said that they would hope for "something to happen" like a visitor who would sit and talk or a trip outside but "it" rarely did. In this respect, there seemed little difference between weekends and weekdays.

Going to bed

Some applicants living alone (who got up earlier) chose to go to bed later than those who were living with other people. However, half of all applicants were in bed by 10.00 p.m. The late-night film on television was mentioned by several, especially those who lived alone. If it was a "good film" they would stay up to watch it and there seemed to be a fair amount of dozing off. This meant that they sometimes dozed in their warm chairs for the rest of the night. Although getting undressed and into bed presented the same problems in reverse as getting up, there were fewer complaints of difficulties at night. Apparently, applicants were less unsteady and dizzy then and possibly, also, they and their rooms were warmer at night than in the morning.

Three elderly couples, who said that difficulty in looking after themselves was a reason for their application, slept regularly on chairs in their living rooms (although one couple did have one single bed which they used in turns). They did this because it was warmer than getting into a cold bed (in an unheated bedroom) and because it was easier to get up from a chair to go to the lavatory.

Variations in views

Variations in opinion between caregivers and applicants about lack of basic care reflected similar variations over other issues, such as the presence of visual handicap, hearing loss or incontinence. Overall, the views of caregivers corresponded more closely with those of the social workers than of the applicants. Such variations throw doubt upon the degree to which opinions of applicants were accurately reflected on application forms. If the views of applicants differ from those of their informal and statutory caregivers, whose view should prevail?

Similarly, the discrepancy between social workers and caregivers over the frequency of incontinence may have reflected the social workers' reluctance to enquire about a symptom which could, if frequent, render a client ineligible for Part III. Different interpretations between settings could mean that a ward sister might not consider a patient "incontinent" if he had a bottle by his bed which he could use in time whereas the same man would be regarded as incontinent in a Part III Home - where he would not have his bottle nearby.

Applicants and their caregivers expressed similar opinions about the applicants' difficulties with sight, hearing and speech and about their problems with balance and mobility. By contrast, more applicants than caregivers described problems with dexterity. Unlike incontinence, these difficulties and sensory losses constitute a personal disability to the sufferer but are not usually a social disability to those around him.

Conclusion

Two major findings stand out from this chapter. First, detailed questioning revealed a higher level of disability than suggested by the application forms. Second, despite these difficulties, most applicants were not so disabled that they could not look after themselves. A minority were well able to do so. Most faced particular problems in tackling specific self-care tasks; only a small group were "generally disabled". In these respects our findings, although perhaps more detailed than those of many studies, were in keeping with the research quoted in Chapter 1 which shows that few of those applying for or in residential care are in need of the sort of intensive care which can only be provided on a twenty-four-hour basis.

The implications for practice seem clear. Social workers should have a detailed knowledge of applicants' specific self-care problems and the times these occur. They also need to take account of the impact of the problems on caregivers, particularly when the applicant is "generally disabled". Before these old people embarked on the fundamental change of entering residential care, some simple remedies based on detailed and practical, functional and medical assessments might have been offered. Earlier pooling of expertise might facilitate attention to the condition which gives rise to need (for example, loss of balance may indicate need for medical assessment, chiropody or review of diet as well as an aid).

The first need was for simple aids such as large clocks and night lights and more grab rails, monkey poles and other items for support and leverage. Ramped surfaces adjacent to cooking stoves, trollies or an adapted basket on wheels might facilitate moving crockery, hot pots or food from one place to another. Some solutions required the services of an occupational therapist, an imaginative handyman and a needlewoman, together with sensible (and cheap) shopping for clocks, electric wire, stools, grab rails, velcro tape, guard rails and holders to keep dishes steady. Above all, braille or other controls for gas cookers seemed essential for the visually handicapped.

A second need was for changes in the types of services and in their timing. If more very old and frail people are to be maintained for longer in their own homes, the self-care problems which arise in the early mornings and, to some extent, at night may require a different type of service. The help required by most applicants at these times did not demand the skilled services of a nurse but the reliable and regular assistance of a care worker who lived close at hand.

A third need was for adapted furniture and accommodation. Some old people were sleeping all night in the chairs they had occupied for most of the day, with resultant medical implications. Living and sleeping in one room possibly ensures continued warmth at night but this implies the need for more properly designed bed chairs which would not result in pressure sores and swollen ankles. More help might also be needed to enable such applicants to wash, change their clothes and move during the day so that soreness from stale sweat or urine or becoming fixed into a sitting position could be avoided.

It is perhaps surprising that economic ways of installing downstairs lavatories on a large scale have not been devised. The present design of commodes was unacceptable to many applicants interviewed.

Whereas some day-care facilities might greatly have benefited some of these applicants, the descriptions of the struggles of some in the morning suggested that any transport that arrived before noon was unlikely to be fully utilised. It was in the afternoons and early evenings that many applicants felt physically better and receptive to outside activity and stimulus.

Such solutions may not be easy to provide. At least one report (Keeble, 1979) has documented problems of supplying aids and adaptations and described unclear definitions of responsibility between health and social services, shortage of transport and storage space, and inadequate procedures for reviewing existing aids and adaptations to ensure they remain safe. Our concern here is not to minimise these problems but to show the importance of overcoming them.

6 Problems of caring: risk

Introduction

"Risks" of various types were given as one reason for the need for residential care for 83% of the 970 applicants in the large sample. Various types of risk were described, the most common being falling for the physically frail, and fire and wandering out for the confused.

Although it is agreed that many old people are "at risk" there is less agreement on the extent to which they should be free to decide to live at risk. Brearley (1982) comments: "Many of the things we do for people in our attempt to remove or reduce the risks in their lives actually create risks". Norman (1980) points to similar anomalies: "Society is not consistent in the risks it allows and those it attempts to defend itself against ... Mountain climbing and pot-holing continue in spite of grumbles about the cost of rescue ... yet paraplegics are often prevented from using public buildings because ... they might not be able to escape ... Society treats people in institutions differently from individuals in their own homes who are not compelled to have even a fire extinguisher at hand, yet fire officers impose crippling demands for precautions in old people's Homes". It seems right that high standards should be applied to institutions, but regrettable that more safety devices are not available for old people in their own homes.

As Norman and others point out, at one extreme some risks are highly regarded; skills are developed to respond to them and they are associated with physical fitness and virility. At the other extreme, a total inability to tolerate risks is regarded as mental illness and is given labels such as "phobia" or "panic". In general, taking risks is an intrinsic part of life and a consequence of human mortality. If they are able to perceive danger and act accordingly, it is generally accepted that people have a right to decide which personal risks they choose to take and which to reject. However the situation with regard to risk faced by the old people in this study was not simple or clear-cut. On the one hand the dangers they faced in their daily lives could be exacerbated by hazards in their environment (such as cold, damp, inconvenient stairs), by their own physical frailties (such as stiff, painful limbs or poor vision) or by increasingly slower reactions. On the other hand, the freedom to make decisions about risk could all too easily be removed from these very old people who could be regarded as "like children" in their need for protection, so that decisions were taken on their behalf.

In this chapter, we use the small sample to explore how this situation came about. We look first at the differing ways in which applicants, caregivers and social workers regarded risk, then at what led applicants to be concerned about risk and finally at other factors such as ways of summoning help in an emergency.

Method

As well as being questioned generally about accidents, illness and related worries, applicants and caregivers were asked specifically about falls, medical emergencies, fire and violence. These four types of risk were selected on the basis of a preliminary survey of applications before the interviewing began. For each type of risk, applicants and caregivers were asked whether an accident had occurred, what happened, who helped and if they were anxious now. They rated each risk as a severe and/or frequent problem or only an occasional one. They were also asked if there were other risks; which were the most worrying; how the applicant would get help in an emergency and whether there were problems over this. Finally, all respondents were asked whether they considered that risk was one reason for the application and, if so, to rate the degree to which to which it had influenced their decision.

Six applicants became distressed during discussion of risk and so the subject was not pursued in full detail with them. In addition to this very distressed group, a further 105 of applicants were either too confused to reply or had difficulty in remembering precisely what their feelings about risk had been prior to their hospital admission.

The reactions of the closest caregivers to risks faced by applicants in their daily lives were coloured by the intimacy of their relationships and thus the dread of the applicants' injury or death. For this reason, the most intense anxieties about risk were expressed by relatives and by some of the neighbours who had known applicants for many years. Nearly all (87%) caregiving relatives or neighbours said some risk was a problem (including 57% who described this as severe). A similar proportion (72%) of these applicants also described problems from risk but they differed from their caregivers in that only 30% considered this severe.

Anxiety about risk was expressed by either applicant or caregiver as often in relation to applicants who lived with other people as to those who usually lived alone (Table 6.1). However, nine of the applicants who lived alone had a closest caregiver who was a "professional", and in general, relatives who visited to care for applicants living alone were the group who suffered most during the many hours they were away from them. Anxiety about elderly people who were living together could be almost as great, but at least there was a chance that one old person would be able to summon help if an accident happened to the other. Caregivers who had applicants living with them, especially those who were out at work during the day, also expressed anxiety about leaving them alone.

Table 6.1

Table 6.1

Applicants' and Informal Caregivers' Views about Risk,

Types of Risk Mentioned, and

Applicants' Usual Household Composition

Usual household composition

Types of risk mentioned by applicant and/or caregiver	Alone %	With others %	Total %	χ^2 (DF = 1)
	(21)	(26)	(47)	
Falls	95	72	82	2.60
Fire	35	24	29	0.23
Violence	10	32	22	1.97
Medical emergency	33	54	45	1.22

Note:

Please note that this and all subsequent tables in Chapter 6 are based on data from the Small Scale Study.

Not surprisingly, the importance attached to risks varied according to the applicants' reported mental state. Comparisons were made between applicants' reported confusion and whether or not risks were classified by applicants or their caregivers as either severe/frequent or occasional problems. Only 26% of confused applicants remembered and mentioned risk but 79% of their caregivers said risk was a problem. By contrast, applicants who were not reported to be confused were slightly more likely to mention risk (59%) than were their caregivers (42%).

The types of risk about which applicants were anxious did not always correspond with those which concerned their caregivers. An example of different definitions of risk was provided by a couple in their 90's who for fifty years had heated their bath water in a "copper" on the gas stove before carrying it across the room in a saucepan to a tin bath in front of the fire. They still did this although the wife was partially sighted and the husband was tottery after a stroke and had a tremor in his hand. Their daughter who visited them was so worried she said she sometimes cried on her way home. To the interviewer, the old couple were affectionately dismissive of their daughter's anxiety. "She's a good girl, she's always been worried about it but we're careful. We've always done it that way." Later they confided that they hardly ever had a bath these days anyway but a "good wash down".

However, this elderly pair were very frightened because the houses around them were being demolished, familiar neighbours had moved away and strange people slept at night in the ruins. The daughter knew of her parents' anxieties but did not apparently realise how frightened ("terrified" would not be too strong a word) they were during some nights.

Types of risk

Falls

On the 970 application forms of the large sample, one fifth of applicants were said either to have had falls (16%) or to be at risk of falling (4%). By contrast in interviews, in nearly four-fifths of the small sample, the risk of falls was mentioned by either applicant or caregiver, a figure in keeping with the fact that nationally, falls account for four-fifths of the deaths from accident amongst those aged 75 or older (Department of Trade and Industry, 1983).

Overall, three in five applicants said they were worried about falling and this included a third who described their anxiety as severe. Somewhat surprisingly, anxiety about the risk of falls was expressed by almost as many applicants who usually lived with other people (seventeen out of thirty) as by those living alone (twenty out of thirty).

Seven out of ten of the closest caregivers who were relatives or neighbours were also worried about the applicant falling and this anxiety was especially apparent amongst the fifteen relatives of applicants who lived alone (thirteen of whom were worried). However, three-fifths of the relatives who lived with applicants were also anxious about the risk of falls when the applicant was left alone.

Anxiety about risk of falling was associated with problems of balance. All except three applicants who had problems with balance were also described as at risk of falling. Over half the applicants at risk of falls had stairs to negotiate inside their accommodation.

Informal caregivers who were worried about this risk often described a nagging anxiety and a dread of visiting or returning home to the applicant even when they had just been out shopping.

> I feel frightened all the time I'm out about what I'll find when I get back, especially as he can't get up if he falls. I worry in case he falls on to the fire and then he can't get up. I tell him not to answer the door when I'm out but he does and lets people in, though he can't see them and has no idea who they are. [A daughter living with a partially sighted father.]

Medical emergency

Only seven applicants were anxious about suddenly becoming ill, but five of these relied for care entirely on professional help. The anxiety of these few applicants was intense. They included one old couple who gave the interviewer a detailed description of the many weeks they had both been ill during the previous winter and their struggles with self-care tasks during the hours their home help was not with them.

Two-fifths of the informal caregivers worried about medical emergencies and this anxiety was expressed by similar proportions of neighbours and relatives and as often by relatives who lived with applicants as by those who visited to care. The sudden illness of applicants could mean that the care regimes of informal carers were disrupted. As many had no "back-up" system of care, the illness of

65

applicants could precipitate a crisis of quite major proportions for informal caregivers and their families.

Fire

The rate of death nationally from burns and scalds is higher for those aged 85 or older than other age groups, most of these accidents happening at home (Cason, 1972). Despite these figures, only two applicants feared risk from fire, but nearly half the informal caregivers were worried about fire or scalding and there were many accounts of how severe their anxiety was. Three in five of the caregivers living with applicants worried about fire-risk; presumably if a fire occurred, there was danger not only to the applicant but also to their family and home. Half the caregivers who visited applicants also worried about fire and explosion.

A worried son told the interviewer that he had had his mother's gas cooker, gas fire and paraffin heater removed, and had provided her with an automatic electric kettle. Whereas he had removed the focus of his anxiety, the old lady was now without any means of cooking, had an electric kettle which she mistrusted and an electric fire which she considered was "colder" than her old paraffin heater.

Caregivers were particularly anxious about confused applicants. Numerous examples were given of minor fires caused by applicants forgetting that pans were on cooking stoves and leaving them to burn or forgetting to light the gas. One applicant, dissatisfied with the heat emitted by her electric fire, was found feeding paper on to the bars.

Caregivers were also especially concerned about the inability of immobile applicants to get out of their accommodation if a fire started. Of one applicant living alone in isolated rooms on the fifth floor his caregivers said:

> His flat's isolated - no one knows he's there. If he had an accident with the cooker it would be difficult for him to get out. He hasn't got a phone and all he could do is to shout out of the upstairs window and hope somebody looked up and heard him above the noise of the traffic.

Relatives and friends listed many fire-risk incidents and anxieties, including applicants leaving appliances on, being unable to smell gas, dropping lighted cigarettes or burning coals, scorching clothes and so on. Applicants were also anxious over burning themselves, especially if they felt unsteady on their feet, but as already pointed out only two thought this was sufficient reason for going into residential care. However, fear of accidents over cooking stoves were expressed both by applicants and their caregivers. In the assessment of interviewers, risk of fire was a factor in one in four of the sixty applications.

Violence

Nine applicants (15% of the sample) said they were worried about the risk of violence. Six of these nine usually lived with other people. The fears openly expressed were of such violence as being mugged in the street or harassed by local children. Only a few applicants admitted the risk of violence arising from hostile personal relationships.

Anxiety about the risk of violence was expressed by one in four caregivers and by six of the twenty-one caregivers who lived with applicants. Some of these caregivers were referring to the risk of violence from loss of control of their own feelings (Eastman, 1982) a subject which was not explored in detail in this study.

"Other" risks

A variety of other types of risk were described on 11% of the 970 application forms of the large sample. These included carelessness with medication, leaving food to rot, applicants locking themselves (or others) in or out, losing keys, causing their homes to be flooded, swallowing jewellery and tripping over pets. Various types of potentially serious accidents were described, such as shocks from pulling electric flexes from the walls. Severely confused applicants were unable to perceive danger and there were examples of them wandering up the middle of busy main roads and getting lost and frightened.

There was also an example of the hidden danger of gas leaks from old appliances. Aged 90, one applicant (and his general practitioner) assumed that two years of nausea, blackouts and weakness indicated physical deterioration and need for residential care. The ambulance man, who had often taken the old man to casualty when he fainted, suggested he have his gas fire tested. Incomplete combustion was found and repaired, the applicant's health restored and his application withdrawn.

Origins of applicants' anxieties

Interviews with applicants indicated that their degree of anxiety over risks (and so their willingness to accept them) was unrelated to the nature or severity of their physical disabilities. However, analysis of the content of the interviews suggested two (sometimes interactive) factors which influenced applicants' nervousness about dangers: the experience of a dangerous event/the transmission of anxiety from others. Interaction between these factors and the social isolation and low morale of some applicants changed the way in which they perceived disabilities which had often remained unchanged in severity or had deteriorated to only a minor degree. The experience of dangerous events and the ways in which the anxieties of other people were said to have affected applicants' self-confidence were therefore explored in greater detail.

Experience of dangerous events

A number of applicants had experienced dangerous events such as a fall, burglary or fire (Table 6.2). For some, such events had resulted in further traumas, such as a sudden admission to hospital. The most common fear of applicants was that of falls. As one put it:

> I'm feared to go out since me legs went wobbly. I never go in the bad weather now.

Nearly two-thirds (63%) of the applicants in the sample said they had had one or more falls during the five years immediately prior to their application. This was a higher proportion than reported in other studies (Exton-Smith, 1977) of old people falling in their own homes. Falls were described more often by applicants who usually lived alone (83% had had falls) than by those who usually lived with other people (43%). Accidental fires and personal violence were reported more

Table 6.2

Accidents and Usual Household Composition

Usual household composition

Types of accidents applicant has had	Alone %	With others %	Total %	χ^2 (DF = 1)
	(30)	(30)	(60)	
Falls	83	43	63	8.68**
Medical emergency	20	20	20	0.10
Fire	7	13	10	0.19
Violence	7	13	10	0.19

often by those who lived with others.

The repercussions of these accidents varied. Although applicants' fears of future danger often arose from previous experience, some applicants who had had several falls were not unduly anxious, usually because they felt they were able to summon help when they needed it. When describing their falls, applicants were less concerned about their injury and pain than about their fear and helplessness. A few who had fallen had sustained fractures but most described extensive bruising and shock. Several said that they had since become increasingly housebound or now were "nervous on the stairs" or "felt worried about being alone". Typically, applicants had not consulted their general practitioner about their falls for they (and their caregivers) assumed that dizziness or weak limbs were an inevitable consequence of their age.

Transmission of anxiety

The comments of applicants and caregivers indicated that the anxiety of others was an important factor in increasing applicants' anxiety about risks. "Concerned doubt" about applicants could undermine their self-confidence when they were at their lowest ebb and least able to cope - for example, just after they had had a fall or stroke or shortly after a bereavement.

> They don't seem to think I can do for myself now. I suppose they're right - though I was always all right before. [An applicant in hospital - very reluctant to enter residential care.]

There appeared little awareness amongst professional and informal caregivers of how much their ways of expressing anxiety could erode the applicant's confidence. In this sample there were three ways in which this happened, which we have called "shared shock", "absentees' anxiety" and "added urgency".

Shared shock

This arose from a caregiver's fright and distress about, for example, an accident to the old person. This was followed by panic action based on an assumption that applicants would be "better off" and "safer" in residential care.

For example, an applicant in her 90's lived alone, fell on the stairs and was on the floor for two hours before she was found and admitted to hospital, badly bruised. Within three weeks of her fall and hospital admission, her relatives persuaded her to make an application for Part III care. When feeling injured and shocked she acquiesced to this plan but on recovery regretted the decision. She told the interviewer that she stayed awake at night thinking about her home and wishing to return there. Her reactions were a mixture of panic, depression and anger and the ward staff bore the brunt of her fight for independence.

> I'm losing the use of my legs because they won't let me walk here. My bowels are going all wrong because they won't let me sit long enough on the lavatory to go properly.

This old lady was clearly challenging her need for residential care but, like others, she was unsure how to reverse this decision or what help might be offered her in her own home.

Absentees' anxiety

This was shown by relatives who although they did not live near to applicants could exert influence. "Absentee relatives" were often the next of kin and therefore the people contacted by hospitals when plans for the applicant's future care were being considered. These absentee relatives could not offer practical assistance on a regular basis but felt concern or responsibility. Sometimes their motives stemmed only from anxiety but sometimes they were influenced by family conflicts and other considerations.

For example, an applicant, in her 80's and living alone, had two daughters one of whom lived locally and the other in Canada. The locally based daughter had maintained the applicant "at risk" for several years but there had always been rivalry between the two sisters. When the sister from Canada came to visit she was shocked at the poor material conditions of the old lady's home and the muddle in which she apparently lived. Unlike the locally based sister, she was unprepared to tolerate the undoubted risk which her mother faced in her daily life.

> For two months she talked solidly to her about going into a home and how much better off she would be,

said the local sister. Just before her daughter's return to Canada the old lady applied for Part III care - almost as a parting gift. During the research interview, the applicant seemed tired, anxious and depressed - unsure about the wisdom of her application but lacking the spirit and confidence to continue on her own.

Added urgency

These causes of anxiety were given added urgency by the need in hospitals and "official" departments to get arrangements "tied up" and plans "moving". This sense of urgency arose from some doubt that an elderly person would be able to cope alone, from the need to get hospital beds cleared, and from administrative "efficiency".

For example, a man in his 70's had been admitted to a busy London teaching hospital where, unexpectedly, he had an eye removed, leaving him nearly blind. An application for Part III care had been made when he was still in a post-operative state as the prospect of leaving him to manage alone seemed to have aroused strong feelings in professional people. Two nieces who lived out of London were contacted as they were his next of kin and they had obtained the support of his general practitioner who agreed with the hospital that residential care was necessary. This man's application was never discussed with his many friends and neighbours who visited him daily.

The applicant chose to return to his own home to await a Part III place. The research interviewer described him as "in a ferment of anxiety" about the application. He wished to remain in his own home and his neighbours and friends also thought that this would be the wisest decision. However, he was reluctant to question the opinions of "important people" (his consultants and other medical staff). In his own flat he was able to do everything for himself (even hoovering, cooking and his laundry).

> I know this place like the back of my hand. I can find my way round in the dark.

Unfortunately for him, his application was handled by an inexperienced social worker who lacked the professional confidence, skill and status to combat the many forces which were operating and to ensure that this man's own wishes were given adequate attention.

Action based only on the anxiety of others could either result in a clear disregard of applicants' expressed wishes or spark a half formulated doubt in applicants' own minds. Typically, their recent experiences weakened their ability to state their wishes with conviction and eroded their self-confidence in their capacity to care for themselves. If their self doubt resulted in a reaction of anger and irritability, they could be labelled "difficult". If they reacted with depression, they could be ignored.

Background to risk

Getting help in an emergency

Applicants and caregivers were asked from whom the applicant would get help in an emergency and whether there were problems over this.

Over half the sixty applicants interviewed had no efficient way of summoning help. Asked what they would do if they fell, they said either that they would try to attract attention, or wait to be found or that they had no way of getting help. Over two-thirds of those who were anxious about the risk of falls had no way of summoning help (Table 6.3).

> I have to hope to crawl to a chair and wait until I feel better or someone comes.

Although half the sample usually lived with other people, calling a caregiver was mentioned as a way of getting help by only half of this group. Living with caregivers did not mean that somebody was always in the house and even if there were others at home, undetected accidents could still happen. One son recalled:

When I got up I found her on the floor by her bed. She must have been there all night [with a fractured collar bone.]

Table 6.3

Applicant's Way of Getting Help in an Emergency

and Applicant's Usual Household Composition

Usual household composition

Applicant's way of getting help:	Alone %	With others %	Total %
	(30)	(30)	(60)
Call relative	-	50	25
Call neighbour	7	7	7
Sheltered housing alarm	13	-	7
Use telephone	7	7	7
Wait to be found	33	13	23
Try to attract attention	13	17	15
No way of getting help/ don't know	27	7	17

However, to those living alone the risk of falling presented particular problems. Some of these were in cold accommodation and could have died if left on the floor undetected for a number of hours. Ways of getting help in an emergency were therefore of particular importance. Less than half of the applicants living alone who had previously fallen were on the telephone and so alarm systems which depended on a telephone link were not an option.

The applicants' expressed method of getting help was compared with the maximum number of contacts they or their caregivers reported they had each week. Over three-quarters of applicants who usually lived alone were visited at least daily and for these "waiting to be found" could mean a maximum period of twenty-four hours. The remainder, all except one of whom had previously had falls, could wait between three days and a week. Two applicants had no visitors and no way of summoning help and therefore their wait could be interminable.

Even being visited more than once daily was not necessarily a protection from considerable suffering. For example, an old lady fell whilst getting into bed shortly after her neighbour had visited her. She was not found until the next morning. Another applicant fell while getting out of bed at 4.00 a.m. to go the lavatory. When her neighbour called at 10.00 a.m., she had been on the floor for six hours (in a cold bedroom). Therefore, the need for a systematic way of summoning help in a crisis applied to those who were visited on a regular basis as well as to those who were seldom, if ever, visited.

Although several applicants who usually lived in local authority sheltered housing had fallen, interestingly, none expressed anxiety about the risk of falls in future. Alarm bells to summon wardens were reassuring and central heating in local authority sheltered housing flatlets probably made falling there a more comfortable experience than falling elsewhere. Even where wardens were not provided, residents "kept an eye out" for each other and this seemed to reassure informal caregivers as much as applicants.

Variations in viewpoints

Similar proportions of applicants (48%) and their informal or professional caregivers (53%) said that at least one type of risk (falls, medical emergency, fire or violence) was a problem. However, applicants' views about different types of risk did not always correspond with those of their informal caregivers, or the referring social workers. Applicants less often regarded risk as a reason for the application to enter residential care (Table 6.4).

Table 6.4

Respondents' Views of "Risk" as a Reason for Application

| | Respondent | | | |
Was risk a reason?	Applicant	Caregiver	Social worker	Interviewer
	%	%	%	%
	(60)	(56)	(60)	(60)
Yes	42	74	90	78
No	42	25	10	22
Applicant too confused to ask	17	1	-	-

Overall (excl. NR): $\chi^2 = 23.67$***, DF = 3.

Caregiver v. Social Worker v. Interviewer: $\chi^2 = 4.95$, DF = 2.

For nine out of ten of these applicants the referring social worker considered that the presence of risk was an important factor in their need for residential care. In three out of four cases the informal caregivers thought the same - although sometimes they were concerned about risks other than those identified by the social worker. By contrast, although most applicants identified events or tasks which made them nervous, only two-fifths considered these risks constituted a sufficient reason for applying for residential care. Thus, higher priority was given to risk by caregivers and social workers who were observing it than by applicants who experienced it.

Such variation constituted a conflict of feeling more than a question of fact. That risk existed was beyond dispute; the dilemma arose over questions such as whose view should prevail, and where was the borderline between over-protectiveness and neglect. Social workers, who most often considered the presence of risk indicated a need for residential care, carried professional responsibility for care of applicants and to some extent for their protection. Their actions could be open to public comment if, for example, the death occurred of an elderly person whom they knew to be living at risk. Therefore, professional courage, management approval and an adequate structure of surveillance and service provision might be prerequisites for social workers to encourage freedom of choice for applicants.

Sustaining applicants who chose to live at risk also meant that "the problem" was not being transferred elsewhere - namely to residential care. Like informal caregivers, social workers also might have to tolerate continuing anxiety and doubt about whether they were acting correctly. A frail, tottery old person in a hospital ward could seem so incapable of self care and look so vulnerable that social workers (and perhaps also doctors) might consider it would be unkind and unprofessional to fulfil the applicant's wish to return home. As one hospital social worker said:

> At least when I go home at night I know my patients are safely tucked up in bed, whereas area social workers never know what might be happening to their old people who live alone.

Conclusion

Numerous studies of the elderly have documented the risks they run from "instability" and "mental impairment". Our findings therefore should come as no surprise. In consequence of their frailty, applicants in our sample inevitably ran risks and many had previously fallen. Others (relatives and social workers) were naturally anxious, which meant that applicants' own views about the acceptability of these risks might be too easily ignored, or their confidence eroded by anxiety transmitted from others. Lack of facilities for summoning help in a crisis caused major anxiety to housebound applicants who lived alone, although as Tinker (1984) has pointed out the provision of, for example, body-carried alarms is best considered as part of a total package of care.

From the point of view of practitioners the findings underline the importance of detailed and objective assessment of the anxieties of applicants and their caregivers which appraises who is anxious about what and how realistically and, rather than transmitting anxiety, determines what, if anything, can be done about the problem.

Such assessments call for skill and care particularly when accidents such as falls have weakened the confidence of both applicants and caregivers. Social workers sometimes have to resist pressure to make decisions over permanent residential care. This arises especially when accidents or hospitalisation have made applicants sensitive to transmitted anxiety and concern from their informal caregivers and professionals.

Although irreversible decisions may not be wise at times of crisis, other types of action were clearly indicated. Applicants and caregivers described the repercussions of some sudden events such as falls or hospitalisation and, by doing so, demonstrated the care and treatment that might be required during the period of shock. Not only were applicants and caregivers responsive to anxiety at such times, they also seemed potentially responsive to review and discussion and possibly to the introduction of new packages of care. A range of provision appeared relevant in some situations. Effective measures might include an occupational therapist teaching some old people who had poor balance how best to rise unaided if they fell. Surveillance by neighbours might have been regularised, perhaps on a fee-paying basis. Safer heating and cooking appliances appeared essential as did telephones for those able to use them. Services needed to be quickly available to respond to medical emergencies.

The risk of violence from others is of a different order to risk arising from disability or an unsuitable environment. Some of the circumstances which contributed to personal hostility and conflict are described in Chapter 8 and emphasise the need for social workers and other professionals to be responsive to signs of undue stress in care networks.

7 Problems of caring: origins and development

Introduction

Relatives, friends or neighbours were involved in some aspect of the care of most applicants and in the large sample the problems of caregivers constituted a major group of reasons for application. Their problems were therefore another focus of the interviews with the small sample. In this chapter we concentrate on informal caregivers only (i.e. relatives, friends or neighbours).

Interviews with the closest caregiver provided insight into how the caregiving relationship had arisen, the experiences of caregivers and the reasons for their problems. In all these respects there was great variety. Some caregivers' problems were associated with the amount of personal care needed by applicants or with emotional stress arising from an applicant's confusion. Others were linked more closely to stresses on the caregiver unrelated to the old person.

Caregivers varied in their ability to tolerate stress, in their attitude to old age and in altruism. The applicants' responses to receiving care either reinforced the caregivers' feelings of self-worth or increased their exhaustion and guilt. The caregivers' wishes and ability to care were influenced by past relationships but could change over time in response to their own increasing age, declining health or even new opportunities or interests.

We find it useful to describe and analyse these variations under three main headings.

*   The <u>origins</u> <u>and</u> <u>development</u> of the caregiving relationships and hence the re-alignment that had been necessary in the relationships between applicants and caregivers to accommodate the applicants' disabilities.

*   The <u>current</u> <u>context</u> of caregiving, for example, whether the caregivers worked, whether the applicant gave some support to the caregivers and the relationships between the two of them.

* The particular dimensions which were problems to caregivers (for example, the stress of lifting or coping with difficult behaviour) and the degree to which these difficulties were alleviated by services.

The distinction between the origins, context and dimensions of caregiving seemed to be important. Attitudes to caregiving were likely to be influenced by whether it had been undertaken freely or in response to pressure or obligation. They were also influenced by caregivers' other responsibilities (for example, to children or work) and by particular caregiving problems. In some cases a spontaneous and affectionate relationship between applicant and caregiver could be (and some had been) scarred by the performance of caregiving tasks. Some applicants even described how they had acquiesced to a decision to enter residential care in order to preserve a good relationship with those most important to them, by getting caregiving tasks done elsewhere. Services may well have an important role to play in combating these problems.

In this chapter we consider the origins and development of caregiving. In the next we deal with the context and dimensions of caregiving. In each of these chapters we will need to take into account who the caregivers were (i.e. whether they were neighbours, spouses, sons, daughters, etc) and whether or not they lived with the applicants. We therefore begin with the basic data on the caregivers' relationship to the applicants and whether or not they lived with them.

Identity of the caregivers

Forty-nine of the sixty applicants in the sample had an informal caregiver and of these caregivers, forty-seven were interviewed about their caregiving roles (Table 7.1). This discrepancy arose because one neighbour was giving care to an elderly couple who were applying jointly, and in another case, a caregiving daughter (who had previously had her mother living with her) was not interviewed as her husband was very ill. The sample of applicants included three married couples who cared for each other and who were applying jointly. In all three of these "mutual care" situations, an external caregiver was identified (a daughter, a neighbour and a professional) and interviewed.

The closest informal caregivers in this sample fell into three groups.

* Seven caregivers were relatives of a similar age to applicants or only around ten years younger. Of these, three were spouses (who were not applicants) and four were siblings of applicants. Such caregiving meant that one old person was looking after another.

* Twenty-nine caregivers were relatives a generation younger than applicants. In most cases, these caregivers were their daughters (ten) or sons (eleven), but there were also eight caregivers in other relationships (such as nieces or nephews) who were fulfilling a filial role.

* Eleven caregivers (ten neighbours and one friend) were not related to applicants.

Table 7.1

Identity of Closest Caregiver and Applicants'

Usual Household Composition

	Usual household composition:		
	Alone	With others	Total
Closest informal caregiver	%	%	%
	(30)	(30)	(60)
Relation			
Same generation	-	23	12
Younger generation	37	63	50
Neighbour	33	7	20
Professional worker	27	7	17
No caregiver	3	-	2

Note:

Please note that this and all subsequent tables in Chapter 7 are based on data from the Small Scale Study.

The origins of the caregiving relationship

Caregivers were divided into three groups depending on whether they had "inherited", "invited" or "acquired" their caregiving responsibilities. A third implied that their caregiving role had been "inherited". Just over two-fifths felt they had originally "invited" their caregiving responsibilities (although this did not necessarily mean that they had fully anticipated how the situation might change and how difficult it might become for them). A further fifth had "acquired" the relationship almost accidentally.

The origins of the caregiving relationship varied according to who the caregiver was. All except one of the spouses or siblings implied that their caregiving role had been inherited. By contrast, all neighbours except one (who happened to be very angry with the applicant at the time of the interview) implied that they had entered into caregiving responsibilities voluntarily.

Younger caregivers were more evenly divided over how they had come to care. Two-fifths of the sons, daughters, nieces or nephews had invited a caregiving responsibility but three-fifths considered they had inherited it. There were some differences between sons and daughters in this respect. Half of the daughters had chosen to care and had "invited" responsibilities but two-thirds of the sons felt obliged to care because of inherited responsibilities. This particularly applied to only sons.

The origins of caregiving were naturally related to whether or not applicants and caregivers were living together. Most caregivers who visited applicants living alone implied that they chose to care. By contrast, this opinion was held by only one third of caregivers who had applicants living as part of their household.

However it had arisen, caregiving was likely to have developed in the context of a relationship between applicant and caregiver which was formed initially on a very different basis. Once applicants had given up their own home and moved in with relatives, the situation was difficult to reverse.

"Invited" caregiving

The predominant reason for applicants' original decision to move in with their sons, daughters or other younger relatives was their own bereavement. Typically, a lady of 94 at application had been bereaved sixteen years earlier - at around the time her grand-daughter married leaving a spare room in her daughter's house. Her son-in-law suggested that she move in with them. In some situations there had been financial advantage to caregivers when these joint arrangements were first made. Four applicants had originally sold their houses and paid the money to their relatives to buy a larger house or to have adaptations done. With two exceptions, such adaptations or purchases did not include a downstairs lavatory.

Strikingly, only two applicants had been invited to live with sons or daughters because they were physically ill. In each case this move had been suggested by a general practitioner and the applicants had lived in their new households for two years before the arrangement had broken down. In one case the old person had become confused as well as physically ill.

In the other, a childless couple had invited the wife's mother and the husband's father to live with them in the hope that they "would be company for each other". This younger couple had an annexe built on to their house but overlooked the fact that the wife had never felt close to her father-in-law and the two old people themselves (although they had known each other on a friendly basis for some years) did not particularly wish to live in such close proximity. Over time, the husband's father recovered from his stroke whereas the wife's mother became demented and had to be admitted as a long-stay patient to a psychiatric hospital. The wife then had the unnerving experience of increasingly resenting her father-in-law's recovery the more demented her mother became. Although alert and mobile, the old man became passive and depressed and eventually acquiesced to residential care because "his daughter-in-law was having a nervous breakdown". Having sold his home he had nowhere else to go.

The assumption that they would be "company for each other" was also made by elderly people who had invited relationships of mutual care. Two old sisters were both bereaved and felt lonely and depressed when living alone, so sharing a home seemed a good idea. They mistakenly thought that their mutual need would negate their life-long relationship problems.

After five years the relationship had become so hostile that when the older sister was admitted to hospital, the younger one refused to have her back home thus precipitating a Part III application. As the younger sister told the interviewer:

> We never really got on even as children - we seemed to be totally incompatible.

Neighbours also did not always have affectionate relationships with the applicants for whom they cared even though they had "invited" caregiving. One neighbour, for example, had lived next door to an applicant for thirty years but described her as "most ungrateful and bossy". Nevertheless, her contact was on a daily, and sometimes several times daily, basis.

Other neighbours had known applicants for only a very brief period and in most cases they had been asked to "keep an eye" either by a general practitioner or by a relative. As one neighbour said of an applicant:

> I'd lived opposite her for six years but we'd never met - although I knew an elderly person lived there. I only got to know her six weeks ago when another neighbour asked me to phone the doctor because she was ill.

"Inherited" caregiving

The sense of inherited responsibility often felt by only sons could produce some bizarre situations. One applicant, aged 94, lived alone and was cared for by his retired son who visited him daily. This son was himself disabled (with a brain tumour) and lived with his own daughter and her family who were looking after him on a caregiving basis.

Other caregivers had made personal sacrifices in previous years to fulfil their family responsibilities. One son said:

> I promised my father on his death bed that I would look after my mother.

Accordingly, this son gave up his career in the RAF (which he loved) and went to work in a bank (which he hated) so that he and his wife could buy a house in order to have his mother to live with them. Fifteen years later, this son still regretted this decision and felt that he and his wife had "missed out on all their young married life". Apart from the first year of their marriage, they had always had his mother living with them.

Past good deeds had resulted in complex reactions of affection and duty which lasted over the years. One applicant, when in her 20's, had given up her job and her boyfriend in order to assume care for her niece and three nephews when her sister died. The nephews had eventually married and left home but the niece remained with her and they had lived together for over sixty years. At application, the applicant was blind, immobile, housebound and almost 90. The niece (herself aged 66) said of her aunt:

> It's almost as though she takes me for granted - it's almost as though she expects me to look after her. After all, why should I?

Long-standing caregiving relationships could also be regarded as

79

inherited. Two applicants were described by their families as mentally handicapped. One, a man, had lived with his brother and sister-in-law for thirty years since his parents died. Now in their 70's themselves, this brother and sister-in-law wished the applicant to be admitted to residential care - as an insurance against deserting him through their own deaths. Neither of these "mentally handicapped" applicants had had IQ or functional ability professionally assessed. Both were mobile and independent in self care and might well have been able to look after themselves in a protected environment.

Although some applicants and their closest caregivers did not like each other very much and had never done so, this had not precluded caregiving over an extended period, seemingly based on feelings of obligation and duty rather than affection. This could be an uncomfortable experience for applicants as one expressed vividly:

> Being old and having to rely on folk shouldn't be horrid - but it is.

"Acquired" caregiving

"Acquired" caregiving was seen as neither invited nor inherited but accidental and unplanned. Accommodation problems had started some caregiving arrangements. A single, elderly man (the applicant) had to move from his lodgings and had nowhere to go. His sister (who lived with her son and 5-year-old grand-daughter) took him in as a temporary measure.

> After all, I couldn't see him walking the streets, could I?

This meant the sister sharing a bedroom with her grand-daughter. Sixteen years later her brother was still a member of the household and the grand-daughter who was 21 years old was still sharing her bedroom.

Other caregiving arrangements had arisen in an even more unplanned way. An applicant who had come for a three-week holiday to her daughter was taken ill and admitted to the geriatric hospital where she remained for eight months. Disabled and frail on her hospital discharge she had to be re-admitted to her daughter's address and three years later the daughter and her family were responsible for the care of an increasingly disabled and dependent old lady.

Some caregivers had invited one caregiving arrangement but had acquired another. A grandson set up home with his girlfriend and obtained the tenancy of the ground-floor flat in the same house for his grandfather. Initially, this seemed an ideal arrangement, for the grandson was willing to "keep an eye" on the old man and his woman friend offered to cook weekend meals for him. However, they did not anticipate the repercussions of uprooting him from his former contacts. Dealing with incontinence, an increasing number of falls and an old man constantly knocking on their door because he was lonely, proved an intolerable strain on their own relationship.

Factors precipitating change in caregivers' situations

In the situations we have been describing, caregivers were having to re-align their routines and responsibilities in the face of new problems. The relationship between caregivers and applicants, in most cases, had a long history. The particular problems faced by caregivers had a much shorter one.

Most applicants who had given up their own home to move in with sons, daughters or other relatives had been there for several years (mean time in residence 15.7 years) and very few for less than five years. However, when caregivers who had applicants living with them were asked how long they had experienced problems in caring, most cited a relatively brief period (mean time care problems experienced 3.6 years). Relatives who visited applicants living alone to give care had experienced caring problems, on average, for 4.1 years.

Caregiving neighbours had known applicants for either a very long or a very brief period, about half for between twenty to fifty years and the rest for less than four years. All lived in close proximity - either next door, opposite or in the same house. Caregiving neighbours and friends described acute caring difficulty on average for 2.2 years prior to application.

As described in Chapter 4 and illustrated in this chapter, the most obvious change over time had been the increasing physical frailty, illness and sometimes mental confusion of the applicants themselves. For many, this had been punctuated or accelerated by bereavement and becoming housebound. However, deteriorating health was by no means the only (or possibly the most important) factor which had led caregivers to feel that continuation of their responsibilities was no longer possible. Changes in the family roles and responsibilities of applicants and caregivers were also important as "precipitating events" which eventually increased the burden and brought matters to a head.

Changes in role

When they first came to live in the household of sons or daughters, most applicants had been in their 60's or 70's and able to participate in the work of the household. Grandchildren had in many cases been babies and frequently applicants had shared a bedroom with a young child in the family and had provided a resident babysitting service to enable daughters and daughters-in-law to go out to work.

The situation at application was very different. Applicants who had become housebound, frail and perhaps incontinent were unable to actively participate in family life, so that families curtailed leisure activities (such as holidays) because they did not like leaving the old person at home alone. The baby who had shared a bedroom was now an adolescent who wished for a room of her own and was embarrassed to bring her friends home to meet an incontinent or confused granny. Children could no longer sit on adult laps in a car. One family with children aged 11 and 13 and a car for four said family outings which included granny were now impossible.

Changes also occurred in the marital roles of elderly applicants when elderly spouses became caregivers. Reactions varied. Some husbands or wives provided devoted care, often to the detriment of their own health, and the intimate and sometimes unpleasant physical tasks necessary were performed as part of a caring relationship which had existed throughout the marriage. Other marriages, however, could not sustain such changes in marital roles.

Caregivers who had an applicant living with them had also sometimes experienced difficulties in their marriage as a result of incorporating another person into their household. For example, a caregiving son had taken his father into his home two years prior to the application. The daughter-in-law described tearfully to the interviewer some of the unanticipated problems she had experienced. Throughout her thirty years of marriage (during. which she was childless) she and her husband had never shared their home with another person. Their personal and social lives had always been difficult as her husband worked night shifts. Now, instead of having time for her when he came home from work, the husband was busy taking his father a cup of tea in bed and helping him to dress. Mealtimes were shared and in the evenings the son took his father to the pub for a drink which again meant that the daughter-in-law no longer had her husband to herself. The inter-dependence of husbands and wives in most caregiving situations inevitably meant that stress on one had repercussions on the other.

Changes in the caregiving role often occurred at "watersheds" in the lives of caregivers and their families. Foremost amongst these watersheds was the retirement of the husband of the family. Caregivers became more aware of the social restrictions of caring because of the re-alignment of their marriage. Applicants who lived with caregiving sons and daughters had usually done so for some years. At application, these sons and daughters were, on average, ten years younger than the applicants had been when they first came to stay. This may have contributed to the sense of urgency which some caregivers expressed about the need to enjoy the remaining active years of their lives together without the burden of an elderly parent.

Death or serious illness of the spouse of a caregiver also precipitated applications for residential care. In several cases, retirements had coincided with the husband becoming ill. Such changes in physical health as well as economic activity highlighted the long-standing and important roles of sons and sons-in-law. In four cases, heart attacks in husbands who had previously helped their wives to lift applicants brought sudden realisation to caregiving families of their own mortality and caused wives to re-order their priorities:

My husband's always supported me - now I must support him.

Certainly, the physical burdens of having two sick or disabled people in one family were considerable. Less serious physical stress, such as menopausal symptoms of women caregivers, also caused some to feel that "life was passing them by", which accentuated their resentment of their responsibilities.

The birth of a new generation also led to a re-alignment of family energies and interest. When the first great-grandchildren were born, caregiving daughters gained a new interest in life. Some were looking forward to having more time with their grandchildren once the applicant had been admitted to residential care. Other "watersheds" included the marriage of grandchildren. In two cases, caregiving daughters indicated that the marriage of their last children at home had influenced their wish to free themselves of other responsibilities such as care of the applicant.

Precipitating events

In general, caregiving tasks had crept up on caregivers. Over a relatively brief period of time they had come to do more for applicants without always being conscious of the extent to which the applicants' dependency was increasing. Then, precipitating events either accelerated this process of dependency or crystallised the caregivers' awareness of how much applicants were relying upon them.

When caregivers and applicants were asked what had started the acute problems which contributed to a request for residential care, two main types of difficulty were reported. The first of these was illness or accident - in either applicants or caregivers. The second concerned loss, usually from bereavement, but also of other types. For example, an only daughter moved to the south coast with her family and her departure was described as a devastating loss of support by an old couple who were only just managing to care for each other.

A common precipitating event was the applicant's admission to hospital. A break from their responsibilities made some caregivers realise how stressed and exhausted they were and enabled them to feel the full force of relief from caring. "If they let him come home I couldn't bear it - I'd just run away," said a daughter with five young children. The strength of this relief was evidence of the degree of stress previously experienced by many caregivers but it meant that hospitalisation could be the prelude to further disruption in the lives of applicants.

Of the thirty applicants in the sample who were in hospital at application, twenty-three had closest informal caregivers who were interviewed. Of these twenty-three caregivers, thirteen (twelve relatives and one neighbour) had said to the applicant after the hospital admission that they could no longer continue to give care. In ten of these cases, applicants usually lived with their caregivers and therefore had no home of their own and little alternative to Part III.

Relatives of a further eleven applicants in hospital (some of whom were not the closest caregivers) did not explicitly refuse to continue to care after discharge but exerted other pressures, such as giving up applicants' tenancies, disposing of their home or "giving them a good talking to" about the wisdom of residential care. In two of these cases there was also additional pressure from doctors towards a decision for residential care. Most of these applicants usually lived alone.

Eight in ten of those who were in hospital at application faced a situation either where their closest caregivers explicitly stated that they could no longer give care, or other relatives had taken action which made it difficult or impossible for them to return home. Admissions to hospital provided the crisis which enabled caregivers to relinquish their day-to-day caregiving activities.

Conclusion

The importance of family and friends in maintaining very old people in their own homes has been well documented. Twenty years ago Townsend (1962) identified the breakdown of caring relationships as one of the main causes for admission to residential care and our own findings add further to this view.

Eight out of ten of the applicants who were interviewed received care from relatives (36 applicants), neighbours (11 applicants) or a friend (one applicant). Most (29) of these caregivers were relatives of a younger generation, usually sons or daughters. The caregivers differed in the way they had come to take on the caregiving role but the great majority of them had not made a deliberate decision to undertake the old person's care. Instead, the increasing frailty of the applicant had forced a re-alignment of responsibilities and roles within an existing relationship. Precipitating events (particularly hospital admission) could thus result in a situation where the applicant had very little choice but to enter Part III.

From a practical point of view this analysis further confirms the importance of carers for social services departments and underlines the need to take into account the stages through which a caregiving relationship may pass. Bereaved or very frail old people need to pause and consider alternatives before they sell their homes and move in with children or siblings with whom they may not have got on. There is a need to know more about how practical help can be offered as caregiving relationships become re-aligned or are affected by a crisis such as the hospitalisation of the old person, or the illness of the caregiver's spouse. In offering this help it may be important to recognise that the interests of members of a family other than the main caregiver may also be involved. Sometimes it may be important to question an assumption that because an old person can no longer be looked after by their family, he or she has no alternative but to enter a Home.

8 Problems of caring: context and dimensions

Introduction

As we have seen, the four main groups of informal caregivers consisted of spouses, daughters, sons and neighbours. Other carers (for example, nieces, nephews and siblings) were few and their situation approximated to that of one of the main groups. For example, the difficulties of an elderly caregiving sister were in many ways similar to those of an elderly caregiving wife.

In some respects, the situations of the four groups were very different. Neighbours generally cared because they wanted to, their health was mainly good and their contact with the applicant was intermittent. The care given by spouses was coloured by a lifetime of mutual care, conflict and obligation, their health was often poor and their contact with the applicant was more or less continuous.

In this chapter we examine these "contextual features" of caregiving, looking at the age, sex, marital status and living groups of carers, the types of help and support they received from their families and statutory services, and some repercussions of caregiving on their relationship with the applicant. We then turn to the tasks which caregivers performed and the problems they found in performing them.

Age and health of caregivers

The ages of caregivers varied with their relationship to the applicant. All except three caregiving sons, daughters, nieces and nephews were under retirement age. Caregiving neighbours were on average older, their ages ranging between 50 and 70 years. Caregiving spouses and siblings were all over 70 years old and most were 80 years or older.

Nearly two-thirds of caregivers who had applicants living with them said that their own general health was either bad or "so-so" compared with one fifth of those who gave care on a visiting basis (Table 8.1).

Caregivers were then asked whether their physical health and strength were factors which made it difficult for them to go on helping. Two-fifths of the caregivers said that the repercussions of caring on their own health and strength definitely was one reason for the application and this included three-quarters of those who had applicants living with them.

Table 8.1

Informal Caregiver's View of Own Health

and Whether Caregiver Visited or Lived with Applicant

| | Caregiver: | | |
	Visited applicant	Lived with applicant	Total
Caregiver's health	%	%	%
	(26)	(21)	(47)
Very good	15	5	11
Fairly good	39	33	36
"So-so"	19	29	23
Bad	4	33	17
Can't say	23	-	13

Note:

Please note that this and all subsequent tables in Chapter 8 are based on data from the Small Scale Study.

Overall: $\chi^2 = 12.53^*$, DF = 4.

Trend (excl. can't say): $Z = 2.57^{**}$.

Some caregivers had suffered ill health as a direct consequence of caring. A man in his 60's, deeply religious, became the sole caregiver when both his wife and 94-year-old mother-in-law had strokes. For over three years, he had cared alone for both doubly incontinent women, helping them in and out of bed, to dress and undress, on and off the lavatory several times during the night, as well as doing the cooking, shopping and housework.

The general practitioner suggested residential or hospital care for the two women when the caregiving son-in-law consulted him about his own health problems. His symptoms included such a seriously ulcerated mouth that it hurt him to speak, frequent fainting attacks and a stiff, painful right arm thought to be due to lifting the two women so frequently. Loss of memory and an inability to think were attributed by the general practitioner to nervous exhaustion and lack of sleep.

Sometimes, the illness of one family member had a knock-on effect upon the health of others. A son-in-law had to retire suddenly due to a serious heart condition and became uncharacteristically irritable. Subsequently, his mother-in-law (the applicant) lost her appetite, became depressed and developed mild pneumonia. The caregiving daughter had more to do and began to find supporting her mother up and down stairs without her husband's help increasingly exhausting. In addition, it was discovered that she had high blood pressure. The applicant's concern at the deteriorating health of the daughter and son-in-law, of whom she was very fond, led to the old lady herself suggesting that she go into a Home. The caregiving daughter confessed that she was relieved at this suggestion although she would never have introduced the subject herself.

The applicant just described was exceptional since the effects of caring on health were, like risk, an issue on which carers and applicants typically had differing perceptions. Only four of the forty-seven applicants whose informal caregivers were interviewed thought that frailty or poor health in their caregivers was associated with the application, a much lower proportion than that among caregivers. In only one case did the views of applicant and caregiver concur. Indeed, many applicants seemed genuinely unaware of the physical stress upon their caregivers and the realisation which often came with the suggestion of a Part III application was a great shock to them. This lack of awareness arose from several causes. Some applicants were undoubtedly self-centred and pre-occupied with their own illnesses and problems. They were used to their caregivers being younger and fitter than themselves and, from their own greater age, were unaware that age was also taking its toll of their sons and daughters. A further reason was the stoicism of many caregivers, who persevered with their responsibilities for so long and under such stress that at application it was difficult to see whether the caregiver or applicant was in the worse physical or emotional condition.

Stress was often manifested by caregivers in undramatic forms such as back pain, inability to sleep or headaches. Some had talked to their spouse about their personal difficulties, but others had not. In some research interviews there was an outpouring of feeling which indicated the degree to which caregivers needed to share their experiences of exhaustion and their fears of the strength of their own hostility towards applicants of whom they were also fond. Skill and experience were needed to recognise the relationship between types of stress expressed in so many different ways.

Sex of caregivers

Although, as found in other studies (EOC, 1982; Nissel and Bonnerjea, 1982), women caregivers predominated in the sample as a whole, this was because all the caregiving neighbours were women. Amongst the caregiving relatives there were similar numbers of men and women (nineteen and seventeen respectively).

Since the majority of applicants were women, a number of male carers were caring for women. Including neighbours, two-thirds of the caregivers were of the same sex as the applicant, but amongst the caregiving relatives four times as many men were caring for women as women caring for men. This increases amongst the younger generation caregivers to 11:1 (Table 8.2).

Table 8.2

Sex and Generation of Caregiving Relatives and

Sex of Applicant

	Generation of caregiver compared with applicant:			
	Same	Younger	Total	
Sex of caregiver and applicant	N	N	N	%
			(36)+	
Men caring for men	1	5	6	17
Men caring for women	2	11	13	36
Women caring for women	2	12	14	39
Women caring for men	2	1	3	8

+ Excludes one male friend and ten female neighbours
   all, except one, caring for applicants of the same
   sex. One neighbour cared for a male applicant.

Overall: $\chi^2 = 4.68$, DF = 3.

Difficulty related to sexual difference was described by a son who said of his mother:

> I couldn't do anything personal for her - like a strip wash. It's funny, because I did everything for my father when he was ill and I didn't mind. I would just feel embarrassed with her because she's my mother.

Applicants did not usually comment spontaneously on such matters and only one applicant referred to the sex of her helper, when she described how her son-in-law regularly lifted her into the bath. She added with emphasis:

> Of course, he can't see anything because my daughter always holds the towel in front of me.

With these exceptions, there seemed to be little or no difference between the tasks done by men and women "closest" caregivers. However, some differences might be masked by the respective roles of sons-in-law and daughters-in-law. For example, if a male caregiver was supplying an applicant with food it had usually been cooked by his wife and he would more often take dirty laundry home for his wife to wash than do it himself. For their part, caregiving daughters appeared to rely heavily upon their husbands for help with lifting applicants and supporting them up and down stairs.

As found in other studies (EOC, 1981), men and women caregivers differed in whether or not they were prepared to have applicants living as part of their household. Where daughters were the closest caregivers, all except one had the applicants living with them. In this sample, however, sons were more often reluctant to suggest this step, although they knew that this was what the applicant wanted. Difficulties over sons sharing their households with applicants were influenced by the fact that seven out of ten of them were only children, whereas all the caregiving daughters had had siblings. Some female applicants had strongly resisted the marriage of their only sons and there was a long-standing resentment between them and their daughters-in-law. As one daughter-in-law said:

I couldn't have her living with us - she would cause too much trouble.

Family situation and support to caregiver

With two exceptions (a single niece and a divorced son aged 30), all caregiving sons, daughters, nieces and nephews were married and had their spouses living with them. Four daughters and three sons also had school-age or young adult children still at home and most of these families had the applicant living with them also. The attitudes and caregiving roles of spouses of younger caregivers were therefore crucial in the network of care. This was reflected by most caregiving sons choosing to be interviewed with their wives present.

In relation to practical tasks, one in three caregivers had sole responsibility for the applicants for whom they cared and did not admit to receiving any practical help with caregiving tasks. A further quarter of the caregivers were helped by one other person (usually their spouse). In seven cases the applicant's carer was a spouse or sibling but in some ways their care was mutual. Their survival in the community depended on their ability to complement each other's efforts.

The likelihood of being a sole caregiver varied by kinship ties. Four of the seven elderly siblings and spouses of applicants were sole caregivers but only one in three neighbours were coping unaided. Half of the daughters but only one in four caregiving sons were sole caregivers. When asked to whom they turned for emotional support, two-thirds of the caregivers said they depended upon others in their family and particularly upon their spouse when they felt tired or depressed or needed to talk things over. Nearly two-fifths of the caregivers were sustained by two or more other people.

However, although others in the household were willing to assist the closest caregiver emotionally or sometimes with practical caregiving tasks, they were less prepared, or able, to assume total responsibility to enable the closest caregiver to have a complete respite. Caregivers were asked, "What happens when you are not able to help in the way you usually do - are ill or away?" They were also asked whether in the previous year anybody had "taken over" for 24 hours to give them a break. One in five caregivers said they had nobody to take over their responsibilities completely to allow them a "break" even for 24 hours. Nearly one third of the caregivers who had applicants living with them were in this position but a further third in this group had used services such as short-stay residential care to enable them to have a break from caring. No caregiver who visited to care had obtained respite through services, but some had relied on other relatives or friends to take over.

Paid employment

The type of problem experienced by caregivers was also influenced by whether or not the caregiver was at work. Of the daughters and daughters-in-law under retirement age, nearly two-thirds were in paid employment (all except one, full-time). Of those not employed, two had school-age children and one daughter had (reluctantly) given up work to care for her mother. Two daughters not in paid employment said that they were looking forward to finding work once the applicant was admitted to a Home.

The full-time paid employment of most women caregivers meant that applicants who lived with them were likely to be left alone for several hours on weekdays. Few applicants who lived with their caregivers had home helps or meals on wheels and there seemed to be little contact with the neighbours. Indeed, in some respects, applicants who lived with caregivers appeared more isolated than applicants who actually lived alone but had domiciliary services calling in.

Deterioration in an applicant's physical or mental state, particularly loss of balance or a tendency to fall, caused anxieties to caregivers when they were out at work. "Flashpoints" of care were related to the routines required by work. Applicants who did not turn their televisions off until late, who wandered during the night, or who woke up their caregivers (for example, for help to go to the lavatory) caused problems which were often voiced in "employment" terms.

> She doesn't seem to realise I have to be up at five in the morning [from a son on shift work.]

Diminished ability to make a midday cup of tea in safety or find and eat the snack that was left out also created problems, as did minor degrees of confusion and lapses of memory which meant applicants left the stove on or caused other risks of fire. Caregivers often told applicants not to answer the door to strangers when they were alone. One severely confused applicant was locked in the house when her caregivers were out - a practice found amongst other applicants in the large sample.

Despite the problems of employed caregivers, the most tense caregiving situations were described by caregivers who did not go out to work. As one "housebound" daughter said:

> I feel trapped - I feel I must get out or I shall just run away.

Another said (stretching her arms wide):

> I feel my nerves are just stretched like that.

Of this caregiving daughter the interviewer wrote:

> She looked strained and near to breaking point. I felt it was unfair to encourage her to open the floodgates with somebody she was not likely to see again."

In general, it did not appear that applicants who lived with caregivers in paid work were any more or less disabled than those whose caregivers were not in employment.

Relationships between applicants and caregivers and their families

The interviews with applicants and caregivers were conducted at a time of crisis (immediately after the application for Part III care had been submitted) when feelings were running high. It was impossible to know whether such intense feeling had existed in the relationship prior to the application.

Caregivers were, however, asked about their other responsibilities, and about the reaction of others in the household to the help given to the applicant.

A quarter of the caregivers who had applicants living with them complained of stress within their families which they attributed to the demands of caring. This was proportionately twice as many as caregivers who gave care on a visiting basis. Similarly, more (62%) of the visiting caregivers said their own families understood their situation, whereas, such understanding from families only applied to one in three cases where applicants were also part of the household (Table 8.3).

Table 8.3

Attitude of Informal Caregiver's Family

towards Caregiver's Responsibilities

	Caregiver:		
	Visited applicant	Lived with applicant	Total
Family's attitude	%	%	%
	(26)	(21)	(47)
Understands	62	33	49
Resigned	8	19	13
Distressed/resentful	12	24	17
Can't say/Not applicable	19	24	21

Overall: $\chi^2 = 4.20$, DF = 3.

Trend (excl. Can't say): Z = 1.80.

Caregivers and applicants were asked about their "usual" feelings towards each other. Their replies were classified as "positive" (i.e. affectionate, appreciative), "ordinary" (i.e. "usual" relationship, "it varies", ambivalent) or "negative" (complaining, critical, demanding).

Over half the caregivers said applicants' attitudes to them were affectionate and positive. Few caregivers experienced applicants' attitudes as negative and most of those who did had the applicant living with them (Table 8.4).

Table 8.4

Informal Caregiver's View of Applicant's Feelings towards

Caregiver and Whether Caregiver Visited or

Lived with Applicant

	Caregiver:		
	Visited applicant	Lived with applicant	Total
Caregiver's view of applicant's feelings	%	%	%
	(26)	(21)	(47)
Positive	62	38	51
"Ordinary"	31	19	26
Negative	8	24	15
Can't say	-	19	9

Overall: $\chi^2 = 8.85^*$, DF = 3.

Trend (excl. Can't say): Z = 1.52.

Table 8.5

Informal Caregiver's Feelings towards Applicant

and Whether Caregiver Visited or Lived with Applicant

	Caregiver		
	Visited applicant	Lived with applicant	Total
Caregiver's feelings towards applicant	%	%	%
	(26)	(21)	(47)
Positive	46	24	36
"Ordinary"	31	43	36
Negative	15	24	19
Can't say	8	10	9

Overall: $\chi^2 = 2.55$, DF = 3.

Trend (excl. Can't say): Z = 1.43.

92

The caregivers' own feelings towards the applicants were more muted. Only one third of the caregivers said they usually felt positively towards the applicants and positive feelings were expressed by fewer caregivers who had applicants living in their households (Table 8.5).

Caregivers and applicants were also asked if the relationship between them had changed in recent years, and if so when, how and why. Two-fifths of the caregivers said that the relationship had remained unchanged, but one third considered that it had changed for the worse. Again, there was an association with the living situation of the elderly person. As can be seen from Table 8.6 changes for the worse were noted by half those who were living with the applicant.

Table 8.6:

Informal Caregiver's View of Changes in Relationship

between Applicant and Caregiver and Whether Caregiver

Visited or Lived with Applicant

| | Caregiver: | | |
Relationship changed	Visited applicant %	Lived with applicant %	Total %
	(26)	(21)	(47)
For better	12	-	6
Not changed	46	38	43
For worse	19	52	34
Nature of change unspecified/other	23	10	17

Overall: $\chi^2 = 7.60$,   DF = 3.

Trend (excl. Unspecified): $Z = 2.53^{**}$.

Family relationships of caregivers

Three of the younger caregivers had explicit marital or sexual problems and the applicants felt the repercussions of these. One son was unable to continue the care of his mother because he wished to re-establish his broken marriage.   A grandson had deserted his wife, leaving his grandfather (the applicant) in her care.   This meant that the old man received all the pent-up resentment arising from the broken marriage. The deserted wife never spoke to him, gave up cooking and caring for him and behaved to him as though he were the husband who had deserted her.

In general, caregivers who had had applicants living with them for many years felt that they had missed much in their married life and that they wished to do different things with their time.

> My husband would like me to go out with him more. We can't spend Christmas with the children now because the noise is too much for her.

Other conflicts arose from the normal clashes of family life such as those between adolescents and adults. These impinged upon the applicants, who seemed, in some cases, to have entered into a competitive relationship with the teenagers in the household. Against a background of tension, disagreements about which television channel should be on, whether loud pop music was to be played on the record player in preference to music on the radio and resentment about applicants sharing the family sitting room in the evenings could all become magnified into a family quarrel. It seemed that daughters and daughters-in-law were often required to mediate in such situations.

Other quarrels seemed to have earlier origins. Over half the caregiving sons in the sample had been only children and for them particularly, earlier difficult relationships accentuated current caregiving problems.

One son and his wife had visited his mother twice weekly for years and deviation from this routine (for example, to go on holiday) precipitated a crisis and a deterioration in the applicant's health. The son dreaded visiting his mother as he felt that he was still treated like a naughty child. His mother told other people what a good son he was but to his face she told him he was "the biggest sod living". They had a row every time he went to see her. The daughter-in-law suggested that her mother-in-law might not be able to show her feelings. The son agreed that he had never had a cuddle from his mother when he was a child, he never remembered getting into bed with his parents and he felt that any sign of tenderness or touch was unknown in his early family relationships. This meant that the tenderness of touch which the old lady might now require in her physical care was taboo.

In this sample, relationships within extended family groups appeared very important in determining whether "closest" caregivers experienced a supportive network around them. We have called relatives who could have given care but did not "contracted out" caregivers. This situation arose sometimes from their own withdrawal from the responsibility and sometimes from hostilities within the extended family.

Resentment was expressed by "closest" caregivers over siblings or other close relatives who, in their view, did not take their full share of responsibility. Characteristically, applicants did not share this bitterness but spoke with affection about the other siblings. This meant that quarrels between their children not only restricted the network of care available to applicants but meant that the affection the applicants felt for one had to be concealed from another.

A caregiving daughter said her brother (who lived nearby) had had her mother to stay for two weeks two years earlier to enable her to have a holiday. Since then:

> He's never invited her even for a day - I always have to ask him whenever I want to go on holiday.

Another daughter had two sisters and maintained that neither of them cared for their mother.

> They've just left me to cope. I feel angry because of the lack of

support from the rest of the family.

However, the old lady herself told the interviewer (in confidence) how fond she was of one of her other daughters because "she makes me laugh." Like other applicants who were in the middle of such conflicts, this old lady felt grieved and cut off from other relatives of whom she was (secretly) very fond.

The helplessness of applicants in this dilemma was evident. If they did not align themselves with the household in which they lived, they risked the hostility between siblings being transferred to them.

Caregiving neighbours

Ten of the closest caregivers in the sample were neighbours and one a friend of the applicant. Unlike relatives, only one neighbour wished to discontinue her caregiving role and most did not feel that caring problems were a reason for the application. However, most caregiving neighbours said that their roles and responsibilities were unrecognised both by relatives of the applicant and by most of the social workers who had visited. Neighbours (like home helps) were very sensitive to any suggestion of dishonesty either from relatives or from social workers. To some extent, this sensitivity was justified, for in this sample there was evidence that both relatives and referring social workers tended to mistrust the motives of neighbours.

In this group of neighbours at least, recognition of their role was more important than payment. The caregivers were asked if applicants paid them out-of-pocket expenses (such as fares to visit them in hospital) but none of the neighbours or friends said they wanted (or would accept) payment for what they did. However, they did wish to be consulted about plans for the future care of the applicant and resented being ignored.

The fact that most neighbours were not in close contact with applicants' relatives resulted in criticism and stress. Some neighbours described feeling either angry or sad when they thought applicants were neglected by their relatives. For example, a neighbour shared the hurt experienced by one applicant who, without explanation, was not invited to spend Christmas with her niece's family. The neighbour suspected that the applicant's increased confusion and incontinence was a reason for this break with tradition. Another neighbour criticised an applicant's son for not visiting his mother and seeming not to share her grief when his father died. She described how this old lady still tried "to buy her son's affection" (with money and gifts) and she felt angry when she witnessed the applicant's distress at his continued neglect.

Four of the ten neighbours said there had been unhelpful intervention by "contracted out" relatives. Pension books had been removed from two applicants by relatives who lived out of London and one applicant was given £25 a month to buy food and personal necessities. In another two cases, "contracted out" relatives disposed of furniture and possessions when applicants were admitted to hospital and caregiving neighbours were helpless in this situation. It was especially difficult for those neighbours who had known applicants for twenty or more years.

Although three neighbours were caring for applicants who were very dependent, this was on a short-term basis only. In general, neighbours did not have the unremitting responsibility which was carried by relatives. They did not consider themselves bound by ties of duty but felt free to increase or decrease the amount of care they gave as they wished. The neighbours' control over the burdens of caregiving may have given them a more objective approach to the application. In this sample, neighbours were the only caregivers who, to the interviewers, acted as advocates for the old people. Several presented clearly and insistently their version of the wishes of the applicants for whom they cared. These opinions closely coincided with those expressed by the applicants themselves.

The importance to neighbours of the recognition of their caregiving role was illustrated by the only one who was unprepared (before the research interview) to continue. Her anger had been aroused because, on admission to hospital, the applicant's relatives had removed the house keys from her and had been "mentioning" several items of clothing which they could not find. Furthermore, the applicant herself had become friendly with a visitor of another patient on the ward and (breaking the habit of over ten years) had started giving her dirty washing to this "new friend" rather than to her old neighbour. In the research interview, the neighbour ventilated her feeling that the applicant was "a most selfish and ungrateful woman" and that she wished to have no more to do with her. As the applicant's ability to return to her own home was totally dependent upon this neighbour's care, the old lady was much worried by this quarrel. However, the request for a research interview with this neighbour and thus the recognition of her status as the "closest" caregiver changed the course of events (although this was not intended). After a brief period in a residential home, where she was unhappy, this applicant received a visit from her neighbour, patched up her quarrel with her and returned to her own home.

Problems of caregiving

Caregivers were questioned about the aspects of care which they found most difficult. A detailed checklist included types of personal care required and their effect on household routines, social restrictions on caregiver, the stress arising from the applicant's behaviour (for example, night disturbances, recalcitrance, clinging), physical stress (for example, tiredness), and personal stress (for example, "gets on my nerves"/"not able to relax"). Other aspects of difficulty mentioned by individual caregivers were also explored and classified.

Nearly half the informal caregivers said they experienced problems with the personal care of applicants and one third with the physical stresses of caring. Once again, the effects of the applicants' living situation was apparent. Problems with physical stress, personal care and managing the applicants' behaviour were reported by a higher proportion of caregivers who lived with applicants than by those who visited.

The tasks which caregivers found physically stressful were those which involved lifting and supporting applicants. Problems most frequently mentioned included helping them in and out of bed and in and out of chairs, to wash or dress and, above all, to go up and down stairs. Helping applicants to have a bath was seldom a problem, partly because some preferred "a wash down". Also, the man of the household (often the son-in-law) would help to lift an applicant into the bath. Three caregivers complained of the physical stress of pushing manual wheelchairs.

Most caregivers cooked for other household members and applicants together so meals were not a problem. Although some applicants were incontinent, the volume of washing which caregivers were required to do was also not regarded as a problem of major proportions.

One in six applicants in the sample were heavily dependent in that they required constant assistance with their self-care tasks. None had electrically operated wheelchairs, hoists or stairlifts and some had not been assessed for grab rails or raised toilet seats.

Behavioural problems

The behaviour of applicants was aggravating to one third of their caregivers. Over twice as many of the confused as of the alert applicants exhibited behaviour which aggravated their caregivers, such as restless wandering at night, repetitive questioning, frequently "losing" things like false teeth or spectacles, or hiding caregivers' possessions "for safety". Three times as many applicants who lived with their caregivers as applicants living alone were said to have aggravating behaviour. The types of behaviour which caregivers who lived with applicants found most aggravating were those which disrupted family life. Night disturbance (by both confused and alert applicants) was both aggravating and stressful to the entire household. Responding to applicants who were both confused and hard of hearing and asked repetitive questions could also be especially exhausting.

However, the strongest feelings were expressed about the lavatory - the only room in the house shared equally by all the family. One son said:

> She always leaves the toilet filthy with mess all round the seat. I rush up there when I come home from work to clear it up in the hope that my wife won't find it first.

Another said:

> She doesn't wash her hands after she goes to the lavatory so she soils everything she touches.

A daughter said:

> The only thing that gets my husband down is when he comes home from work and sits in a chair and finds it's wet because she's been sitting there and had an accident.

Other types of "messiness" also aggravated caregivers - especially daughters-in-law.

> She drops everything on the floor - clothes, books and papers. It's not my nature to leave the room in a mess. I feel I have to clear it up before I can get into bed.

Another daughter-in-law complained about her father-in-law who had had a stroke. She said:

> He's a messy eater. He dribbles. His hand shakes when he tries to put the spoon to his mouth.

This old man said he felt unwanted in his son's home. He knew that the effects of his stroke and his eating habits aggravated his daughter-in-law but this tension only made his tremor worse.

97

Interviewers explored such restrictions on social life as changes in leisure activity, freedom to go out, infringement of privacy, and taking up time. The content of the replies was analysed to determine which restrictions had apparently stemmed from changes in the amount of care required by applicants and which arose from other factors.

Over half the caregivers reported restrictions on their social lives which they attributed to their care of the applicant. Restrictions which arose from the condition of applicants were more often reported by caregivers of confused than of physically disabled applicants. Interestingly, social restrictions were reported more often by caregivers of applicants who were in hospital at the time their application was made (74%) than by caregivers of those who were in the community (38%). It seemed that when applicants went into hospital, their caregivers experienced relief and realised the extent of restriction there had been on their social lives.

Social restrictions also arose from embarrassment about "what other people think" of the applicant's behaviour. Some caregivers, themselves bewildered by the onset of incontinence or confusion in their elderly parents, appeared unsure how unpleasant smells or loss of memory would be interpreted by their friends. Several said that their friends had stopped coming. Such a degree of tension and depression made some caregivers resist the social contacts that were available to them, almost as if they were needing to "be miserable" with somebody rather than "sociable".

Half the sample of applicants required help only with particular tasks at specific times but they were usually also housebound. With these applicants, the social restrictions on their caregivers arose from the need to give regular and reliable care rather than from the amount of help which was needed. These caregivers felt restricted because they were unable to enjoy their free time away as they were anxious about risks when applicants were left alone. Caregivers suffered from both apprehension about the vulnerability of confused applicants and a generalised feeling of guilt because they were able to enjoy themselves while the applicant was so lonely and depressed.

A minority of applicants were so dependent that their caregivers tended to become "housebound". Twenty-four-hour care was required and the caregivers' social lives became seriously restricted, causing one daughter to say:

> I feel like a prisoner.

However, four caregivers of these very dependent applicants said they experienced no undue social restrictions or other caregiving problems because they had good relationships with other members of the wider family group so that a routine of "shared care" was possible.

Stress and depression

As we have seen, the strains of caregiving were often heavy and pervasive. As a measure of the cumulative effect upon the application, we asked caregivers whether their anxiety and depression had been a factor in deciding to make it. Twelve caregivers thought their own anxiety or depression definitely was a factor in the application and a further twelve thought it probably was. All except four of these depressed or anxious caregivers had the applicant living with them. In keeping with our earlier findings, 90% of caregivers living with applicants saw their own mental health as contributing to the need for residential care compared with 15% of visiting relatives or neighbours.

In some cases there seemed to be a vicious circle, since depressed applicants both exacerbated and reflected depression in their caregivers. A daughter said:

> She gets up complaining of feeling unwell and then sits around being miserable. I've got to the pitch when I can only feel negative.

Another daughter said:

> I feel like crying when I see mum depressed. I'd feel better if I could have the odd weekend away and people to talk things over with.

Remarks such as "little things get on my nerves" and "something has to go" were made in most of these interviews. A minority of caregivers openly resented the amount of emotional energy and time which they had devoted to their task. One son said:

> Bluntly speaking, we just want to get rid of her.

With respect to three applicants who lived with their caregivers, there were indications that the degree of tension within the household had reached such a pitch that in the interviewer's opinion there was some risk of physical violence towards the old person.

Some caregivers had tried to escape from their worries. One daughter who had her mother living with her said that she bought the old lady three and a half bottles of whisky a week as she thought that this helped to make her less miserable.

This daughter had asked her brother to approach the social worker to say that she wished her mother to go into a residential home:

> After all there's nothing else he does for her.

The brother had told the social worker that his sister was an alcoholic and was turning his mother into one. The daughter had met the social worker on two occasions but was unlikely to meet her again as the contact had focused on her mother's prospective admission to residential care.

Conclusion

The example we have just given of excessive drinking is atypical but makes a more general and important point. The legislation covering Part III and the services for potential applicants focus on the needs of individual old people for physical care and attention. What is at issue in applications, however, is not only the individual's capacities but also family dramas of love, hate, guilt, depression and obligation; not only the difficulties of caregivers in providing care but also the actions they take which by design or accident make it difficult for the old person to remain at home.

As we have seen, the tasks undertaken by caregivers and the problems they faced varied according to their relationship with the elderly person, their age and health, whether they worked, the attitudes and supportiveness of their families and whether or not they shared a home with the applicant. Neighbours rarely undertook the heavy or personal tasks which fell to children but the contribution they did make was not always sufficiently recognised by relatives or professionals, who often failed to consult them about future plans and major decisions. Daughters were often looking after applicants in their own homes, daughters-in-law were not.

Sadly, relationships between caregiver and applicant were much more likely to have deteriorated than improved as a result of caregiving. Half the caregivers living with applicants said that relationships between them had changed for the worse. Interviews revealed the knock-on effect of ill health and stress from one family member to another, the effect of past conflicts in relationships on the ability to tolerate current problems and the importance of the wider family network. There were also indications that applicants living with others could be lonely and unstimulated.

These findings emphasise the need for social workers to focus on the applicant's situation and not just on an individual in it.

The implications for practice in assessment, methods of work and types of resources include:

Assessment

The need:

* to assess caring in the context of households and wider family networks.

* to take account of the nature of previous relationships between the old person and the caregivers so that past resentments can be acknowledged and put into perspective.

* to investigate the differences there may be when men are carers and to identify their implications for service provision.

Methods of work

The need:

* to develop ways of working with "contracted out" caregivers within wider family networks so that contracts of shared care can be evolved despite family quarrels.

* to develop a wider perspective of who caregivers are, so that help from neighbours is acknowledged and supported.

Types of resources

The need:

* to relieve the stresses of providing physical and personal care, for example, through home helps, aids or adaptations such as the installation of downstairs lavatories.

* to ease social restrictions on caregivers by providing breaks, for example, through sitters, day care, relief breaks in institutions or family care schemes.

* to counter the effects of the behavioural problems of some applicants (especially the confused), again perhaps by providing breaks.

Whatever the resources available or the method used, the case for supporting caregivers is partly humanitarian - for the burden they bear is heavy - and partly prudential, for without their collaboration the maintenance of many old people at home would be difficult, if not impossible.

9 Accommodation

Introduction

On his bereavement, one old man had come to the study authority to be near his only son. All he could afford to rent was a small upstairs bedsitting room which was damp, and heated only by an electric fire. He got into arrears with his electricity bill and was referred to the social services department who negotiated on his behalf but did not tackle his basic housing problem. The old man's health deteriorated and he and his son went to "the Town Hall" to ask about rehousing. The son said:

> We got passed backwards and forwards by the receptionist between the housing and social services departments. It seemed that nobody could decide who we should go to. In the end they said nobody could help us as dad hadn't been in the borough long enough. I don't know how old people on their own would manage with all those departments.

The old man was subsequently offered meals on wheels but discontinued them at the end of a week. As he said:

> They didn't come until 12.00 and so I had to stay in [in the cold]. I'd rather go to the cafe [where it was warmer].

His room was so cold in the winter that he could not sleep, so he took to wandering around the streets at night to keep warm. Eventually, he was picked up by the police, his plight recognised and he was admitted to residential care on an emergency basis. Therefore, what had started as a housing problem became, over three years, a situation calling for long-term residential care.

This old man's dilemma provides a graphic illustration of a national problem. The elderly are well known to have, on average, less satisfactory housing than the general run of the population and it is hardly surprising that in the large sample "unsuitable" accommodation provided our third main group of reasons for application. The small sample enabled us to look in detail at the interaction between basic care, risk, morale and accommodation. In this chapter we discuss the results under two main headings: "homelessness" (lack of tenure), and "unsuitable accommodation". We then discuss, more speculatively, changes that might be made in order to overcome these problems.

Homelessness

In the large sample, applicants were much less likely than other elderly people to own their homes. A similar contrast appeared in the small sample between applicants and the caregivers with whom they lived. Among applicants who still had tenure, only four out of thirty-nine were owner occupiers. By contrast, half the caregivers who had applicants living with them were living in owner occupied property (Table 9.1).

Table 9.1

Applicants' Homelessness and Tenure of Accommodation

		Tenure		
	Owner occupied	Rented LA	Private	Total
Applicants' accommodation was	%	%	%	%
	(14)	(21)	(25)	(60)
Own home	(4)	86	68	65
Other's home	(10)	14	32	35

Note:

Please note that this and all subsequent tables in Chapter 9 are based on data from the Small Scale Study.

Applicants were regarded as "homeless" when they were living as part of somebody else's household, because another person had power to evict them or to refuse them re-entry if they were in hospital. One third of the larger sample of 970 applicants neither owned nor rented a home of their own and this "homelessness" was a major factor which restricted their choice of future residence. Although long-term hospital patients were excluded from the small sample, such homelessness at application occurred in a similar proportion.

In addition to applicants who had been "homeless" for some time, some applicants had relinquished their home as the application was proceeding (and were thus "homeless" by the time of interview). This was against the policy of the social services department who advised all applicants to retain their homes for three months after admission to Part III.

However, if relatives started to dispose of an applicant's home, there was apparently little the social worker or, more importantly, the applicant could do to prevent this, especially if applicants were in hospital and the consultant supported this step.

The eventual "homelessness" of these hospital applicants arose from a combination of their own frailty, pressure from relatives, and the need to clear hospital beds which meant that decisions over care had to be taken quickly. Without question, when in their own homes most of these applicants had been at risk and some had neglected themselves. For example, a lady of 75 lived in a privately rented downstairs flat with an outside WC. She had diabetes, a prolapse, was incontinent and when she fell had to wait for people in the flat upstairs to find her. She was admitted to the general hospital where "they told me I shouldn't return to my flat". Her brother was sorting and disposing of her belongings (without her permission). Staff at the geriatric hospital (to which she was transferred to await a Part III bed) were annoyed that a decision for residential care had been taken without a prior attempt at rehabilitation.

Another applicant, also in an acute hospital bed after a stroke, was feeling even more distressed and helpless. She had lived in an upstairs sheltered housing flat. She said she had falls but "looked after herself all right and was no trouble to the warden". Since her stroke she could not get downstairs when the lift broke down. There was pressure to free her bed in hospital and also a nephew who was willing to dispose of her furniture but could not undertake further care. She had nobody to advocate her wish to return home and a personality which avoided conflict: "I hope I don't live long enough to be a burden."

Unexpected recovery of hospitalised applicants could also result in distress, when they realised their previous "roots" had been lost. Three applicants "recovered" after they had been admitted to the psychiatric hospital. Two were epileptic and had been heavy drinkers and the third was an aggressive, self-neglecting widower who, on admission, was malnourished and confused. All three had previously lived in sheltered flats rented from the local authority, all became fit and lucid after some months in hospital and all said that they had not agreed to their relatives giving up their tenancies or disposing of their possessions. None of these three had closer blood relatives than nieces or nephews, or friends willing to assist with their care, and none had been particularly well-liked by their sheltered housing wardens when they were living in their own homes.

Unsuitable or detrimental accommodation

Townsend (1962) argued that whereas homelessness was a factor in applications, unsatisfactory housing was not. The basis of his argument was that lack of a home was associated with a low level of disability among recent residents and hence probably an independent cause of admission but that there was no similar association between poor housing and low disability. Contrary to Townsend's argument, the application forms studied in the large sample did emphasise poor housing in some cases. Comments about accommodation on these forms were classified according to whether it was described as suitable for the applicant, unsuitable in relation to their current disabilities or was clearly detrimental to their physical health. On the basis of their application forms, one third of the large sample were rated as living in unsuitable or detrimental accommodation.

In interviews, applicants and their caregivers were also asked to rate the applicant's accommodation as suitable, fairly suitable, unsuitable or detrimental - taking into account such factors as proximity to shops, relatives and friends and security from vandals. They were also asked whether there were problems with stairs or with warmth and whether accommodation problems had anything to do with the decision to apply for a place in a Home. Applicants in hospital were asked if their accommodation would be suitable were they to return home. Two-fifths of applicants said that their accommodation was unsuitable as did 45% of their caregivers and 51% of the referring social workers. Where applicants were living with their caregivers, their accommodation problems (if present) were of a different order from those of applicants who were living in their own homes where they had to pay for the cost of heat and light. In general, the living standards and environment of all "closest" caregivers was far higher than that of applicants and in several cases this contrast in living standards evoked spontaneous comment from the interviewers.

The interviews suggested that poor accommodation was particularly difficult for those who were frail. Nearly all (90%) of the applicants who said that unsuitable accommodation was a factor in their decision to apply for residential care also cited problems with their basic care as another reason. The association between unsuitable accommodation and lack of basic care arose partly because housing that might have been adequate for the fit was not so for the frail (Table 9.2).

Table 9.2

Applicant's View of Basic Problems and Unsuitable

Accommodation as Reasons for Application

	"Has unsuitable accommodation to do with decision to apply?"			
Have basic care difficulties to do with decision to apply?	Definitely/ probably	No	Can't say	Total
	%	%	%	%
	(21)	(30)	(9)	(60)
Definitely/probably	90	37	(2)	53
No	10	53	-	30
Can't say/NR	-	10	(7)	17

For example, a couple had lived happily in a flat above a bank in a shopping centre for nearly forty years. When younger they had appreciated the views and privacy. Now aged 86, widowed, disabled, partially sighted and housebound, the old man was isolated and nervous. Draughts from ill-fitting windows, doors and skirting boards had probably always been there but were now more apparent to him. At night, the deserted main road and the vandals who played on his external iron staircase increased his depression and anxiety.

The most common reasons for unsuitability were inaccessible WCs, damp, cold rooms and vandalised environments. Most applicants had difficulty in climbing stairs and around half had some problems with walking. Yet, 57% of applicants had internal stairs (usually to upstairs lavatories) and a further 7% had stairs or steps to negotiate before reaching their front door. One in five applicants said that stairs to lavatories increased their self-care problems. Difficulties over stairs were especially important to relatives who had applicants living with them, for most resided in houses and few had lavatories both up and downstairs. Even one step down to a lavatory could present problems.

Inaccessible WCs sometimes resulted in an old person being confined to a bedroom on the floor on which the lavatory was situated, which meant they could be alone for long periods when others in the household were downstairs. Modern designs such as the fashion of one large "through" lounge made it difficult to provide downstairs bedrooms. A niece (who had lived all her life with an elderly aunt) put a bed in her "through" lounge but could not tolerate the idea of a commode there too. For her, this was one of the "last straws".

Stairs were also hazardous for those living alone or with other elderly people. A bronchitic old man dreaded having to climb the stairs to empty the commode. Some managed to get upstairs on their hands and knees but had alarming ways of coming down again (often backwards). Even flats (including those rented from the local authority) could contain steps, often in passageways which were dark and draughty - a bad place to have a fall and lie on the ground.

Some applicants lived in housing conditions which constituted a threat to their health or safety. These homes would have been unsatisfactory for anyone. Usually such accommodation was rented privately. Over one fifth of applicants lived in accommodation which was cold and damp and it was this group whose accommodation was most often classified as detrimental. "Cold" did not mean "a bit chilly" but, as an interviewer wrote about one man who lived alone in a three-bedroom house:

> His house was freezing. I shivered, and I had a warm coat on. It was quite a nice day outside too.

In this sample, problems of cold were often exacerbated by structural defects. Rotting floorboards, dangerous electric wiring, corroded plumbing, ill-fitting windows and uninsulated roofs were not unusual features of "detrimental" housing conditions in both the small and large samples.

One son described the living conditions of his mother and aunt. He said that the flat was damp and unheated. The beds and clothes in the wardrobe were wet and cold and there was damp and mildew everywhere. The banisters were in a rotting and dangerous condition and the cooker was thick with grease. Mould had grown in cupboards and on cooking utensils.

Some applicants who lived in such conditions were said to be especially apprehensive over high fuel bills and this increased the problem. A home help said:

> He will only have one bar of his electric fire on" [the only heat in a bedsitting room].

A preference for open fires meant that even if coal was placed by the fire the old person still had to bend to put it on. There were a few in the large sample who had fallen on to or near a fire whilst bending forward.

Attempts to keep warm and to avoid climbing stairs resulted in degradation and humiliating conditions for some. An elderly couple who lived and slept in chairs in their living room kept the gas fire on night and day. Their commode was placed cosily by the fire and used by both of them and they took it in turns to empty it once weekly. Their neighbour said:

> I emptied it once, but never again. It made me heave and put me off my food for the rest of the day.

The disgust of others at their environment increased the isolation of this couple as few visited them willingly. Yet they were actually keeping themselves safer and warmer than other applicants who were struggling upstairs to the lavatory and sleeping in bitterly cold bedrooms.

Finally, some accommodation problems were linked to the external environment. A few applicants had experienced radical changes in the community in which they had lived for much of their adult lives and were distressed when familiar streets were demolished or redeveloped. Fear of deserted houses and of the transient people who slept in them was exacerbated by no longer having familiar neighbours nearby. Such "death" of formerly well-kept localities distressed some old people who felt that their environmental "roots" were being destroyed.

Other environmental problems arose from distance to shops or public transport, or living on hills. Local authority flats with such disadvantages could be unsuitable for the elderly. Despite her arthritis, one applicant had been rehoused (in her 70's) in a first floor flatlet, in a house half way up a hill and nearly one mile's walking distance from the nearest bus or post office. The interviewer wrote:

> Surely it could have been predicted that this lady would be getting older and this accommodation would become even more unsuitable in future than it was at the time of her rehousing.

Applicants who managed to walk outside described having nowhere to sit in the open air in safety. Several feared being knocked over by dogs or children, taunted by teenagers, or robbed. Whether such anxieties arose from actual conditions in the estates or from media publicity about attacks on the elderly is not known. The need for safe sitting areas for the elderly, especially on large housing estates, seemed as acute as the need for adequate play areas for the young. One large housing estate had a "pop-in" centre for the elderly adjacent to the shopping parade and for several applicants this was their main source of social contact. It was much missed by those who became too physically frail to make the journey.

Implications for service delivery

In the final section of this chapter we speculate on the ways in which improvements might have been achieved. Unsuitable housing seemed as important as physical disability in many decisions to apply for residential care. Theoretically, unsuitable housing was easier to "cure" than, for example, arthritis. In the opinion of the interviewers, seventeen applicants in the sample (28%) might have been enabled to remain longer in the community had it been possible to improve their present accommodation or offer them sheltered housing quickly.

However, social workers appeared to despair about resolving these housing problems. Some were anxious about the risks faced by old people in dilapidated housing; others gave an impression that it was quicker and simpler to get them admitted to residential care than to grapple with the problem of trying to obtain more suitable accommodation. This could mean that even the actions which were possible (like putting a name on a housing list) were sometimes not done.

Actions to remedy this situation could be divided into measures which might have prevented these housing problems arising and actions which could be taken once they had. In our view both types of action had to be adapted to different sections of the housing market.

Privately rented housing

Half the accommodation rented privately was suitable in the opinion of applicants in the small sample, but some of the rest was in a very dilapidated condition. Nearly all (88%) applicants in privately rented accommodation either had stairs inside or steps to their front doors and four had outside WCs only. Applicants in unsuitable privately rented property faced the problem of persuading private landlords to apply for improvement grants. Elderly tenants who had rented their present accommodation for many years (sometimes around half a century) were, almost certainly, paying a low rent on a "protected" basis. From the viewpoint of landlords, this possibly made extensive repairs or renovations an uneconomic proposition.

In the long term, it would possibly cost the local authority less to make one room warm, dry and safe than to maintain an old person in residential care. In most cases, it would certainly be more humane. More general measures would need to include giving priority for sheltered or good standard local authority housing to elderly tenants of unsatisfactory privately rented accommodation.

Owner occupied housing

Four applicants lived in their own owner occupied houses in dilapidated conditions similar to those in privately rented accommodation. Although they may have been eligible for practical and financial help to improve their homes, this small group of owner occupiers needed help and advice to make use of these resources. In practice, it could not be assumed that these very old and frail people knew the most appropriate, modern methods for heating the rooms they occupied, solving problems of damp or draughts, installing downstairs lavatories or making their cooking implements safe and convenient to use.

Local authority rented housing

Fourteen out of twenty-one applicants in local authority accommodation considered themselves to be suitably housed. The problems of the remainder arose from two main causes:

The character of the estates. There were complaints of vandalism, and isolation arising partly from the distance from shops, lack of public transport and hills.

<u>The character of the homes</u>. None of the applicants were in local authority properties which were centrally heated and the absence of heat in bedrooms was potentially serious for some who had problems with balance, especially when getting in and out of bed. Although two-thirds lived in flats, ten of these twenty-one applicants either had stairs inside their accommodation or steps to their front door. A small number of flats were said to be too large to keep clean.

In remedying these problems thought needs to be given to:

* Foresight in rehousing old people in their 60's and 70's. A hill which may be manageable when one is 60 may look like a mountain to an 80 year old.

* The possibility of rehousing some elderly people in smaller accommodation or even in shared tenancies. Widowers who lacked skills in housekeeping and budgeting or others who disliked living alone might have benefited from such group living.

* Some forms of modern convector heating might have provided a level background heat throughout a flat, but possibly the only way of ensuring that this was switched on would be for the heating cost to be added to the rent and reclaimed through supplementary benefit.

* Measures to improve the sociability of estates - for example, applicants living in housing estates often described their isolation and said they did not know other tenants despite their long residence. "Mobile" pop-in centres in converted caravans or coaches might be provided at central points on estates on one or two days each week. Such a local resource might be used to provide a variety of services as well as enable social contact and a preventive surveillance.

Conclusion

It is recognised that on a national level, a higher proportion of elderly than younger people live in poor housing conditions. Hunt (1978) pointed out: "The groups whose standard of accommodation, both internal and external, leave most to be desired are those with heads aged 85 and over and private tenants". In 1971, nearly one quarter of the over 80's lacked an inside WC, nearly three-fifths had no telephone and over four-fifths had no central heating. Two-fifths lived in accommodation built before 1919 (OPCS, 1971 Census, comparable data were not collected in 1981). The potentially serious repercussions and the prevalence of cold environments have also been discussed in other studies (Wicks, 1978). The range of housing options available to elderly people has been documented comprehensively (Bacon, 1980; Tinker, 1977) and something is known about the acceptability of these to the old people themselves (Butler et al., 1983). There is growing awareness that some very old people prefer to stay where they are but need special provision to enable them to do so.

In this study, one third of the large sample and a half of the small sample were living in accommodation which was unsuitable to their needs. This included 10% who lived in conditions which were so damp, cold or dilapidated that they endangered health or safety. "Unsuitable" housing exacerbated applicants' self-care difficulties and was often related to the need for lavatories downstairs as well as upstairs. Some applicants had, on retirement, moved into accommodation which would inevitably become unsuitable as they became increasingly disabled.

Some "homeless" applicants had given up their homes of their own free will (for example, to move in with relatives). Others said that they had had their tenancies terminated or their homes and possessions sold without their considered and explicit agreement. If this was so, such practices, especially if applied to applicants who are not severely confused, infringe their civil liberties.

Policies designed to overcome these problems would have to pursue two rather different aims. First, they would have to ensure that old people did not become unnecessarily homeless, for example, because tenancies were given up too quickly on their admission to hospital. Ways would also have to be found of preventing old people from entering Part III simply because they did not have anywhere to go, when they could cope in sheltered housing given adequate support on moving in. Second, they would have to tackle the problems of unsatisfactory housing. This would mean ensuring that as far as possible old people did not move in their 60's or 70's to housing that would later be unsatisfactory for them. Very frail old people who were in unsatisfactory housing would need to be given the opportunity either of rehousing or of having their housing adapted. In some cases this would mean ensuring that the old people were able to live in one room which was reasonably warm, dry and free from smell and which provided them with a comfortable place to sleep.

10 Social workers

Introduction

In this chapter we turn from the views of applicants and their informal carers to consider the perspectives of the social workers who referred them. Like the applicants and their caregivers, the social workers often faced dilemmas of divided responsibilities, had limitations on their choice of action and were caught up in conflicts which they had varying degrees of power to control.

We have reason to believe that the thirty-five social workers who were interviewed were reasonably representative of others in the authority who had assessed people for residential care (see Appendix 1). In this chapter we examine:

* The characteristics of the social workers.

* The contact they had with applicants.

* The pressures upon the social workers in different settings over Part III applications.

* Their views of training.

* The relationship between social worker characteristics and the applicants' attitude towards the prospect of Part III care.

The characteristics of the social workers

Thirty-five social workers between them referred the sixty applicants in the sample. The social workers differed in four characteristics which seemed likely to be relevant to their skill and confidence in dealing with Part III applications:

* Their professional qualification (CQSW or equivalent; other relevant; none).

* The length of their experience in social work.

* The numbers of Part III applications they had previously completed.

* Whether they had particular interest in old people and worked as "specialists" with them (i.e. more than three-quarters of their caseload was usually composed of elderly clients).

Table 10.1

Numbers of Social Workers, Their Qualifications,

Experience and Setting

Setting and years in social work

Type of social work qualification	Community Years		Hospital Years		Total
	0-4	**5+**	**0-4**	**5+**	
	N	N	N	N	N
	(8)	(12)	(3)	(12)	(35)
Professional	1	7	1	4	13
Relevant	-	2	1	6	9
None	7	3	1	2	13

Note:

Please note that this and all subsequent tables in Chapter 10 are based on data from the Small Scale Study.

Community v. Hospital (Combining 0-4 and 5+ years):

$$\chi^2 = 6.66^*, \quad DF = 2.$$

Thirteen of the thirty-five workers were fully qualified, and thirteen unqualified (Table 10.1). A further nine had a "relevant" qualification such as occupational therapy or a certificate in social science. In this sample most (ten) of the thirteen unqualified social workers worked in area offices and seven were social work assistants, trainees or students on placement. Apart from these seven, the thirty-five social workers overall were an experienced group. Two-thirds of them had five or more years experience of social work and two-thirds had completed more than ten applications for Part III care.

Fifteen social workers had a special interest in the elderly and worked primarily with them. Seven of these worked in the geriatric or psychogeriatric (Table 10.2) hospitals and were also qualified. Only one of the twenty area social workers who completed applications in the sample was both qualified and worked as a specialist with the elderly.

Table 10.2

Number of Social Workers, If Qualified/ Specialist Interest

in Elderly and Setting

	Setting		
	Community	Hospital	Total
If qualified/specialist interest in elderly	N	N	N
	(20)	(15)	(35)
Qualified			
Has specialist interest	1	7	8
Has no specialist interest	7	7	14
Not qualified			
Has specialist interest	7	-	7
Has no specialist interest	5	1	6

In this sample of applicants the consequences of these variations between referring social workers meant that applicants in hospital were likely to have been assessed by a social worker who was both qualified and specialist in work with the elderly. Applicants applying from private households were more likely to have met social workers who were either interested in the elderly but not qualified in social work, or qualified social workers who did not have a specialist interest in working with old people.

Contact between social workers, applicants and caregivers

It was difficult to establish precisely how many contacts there had been between social workers and applicants to discuss the prospect of residential care. In part this was because applicants in hospital may also have seen social workers on consultant ward rounds or met them during a previous admission. Some applicants in hospital had difficulty in distinguishing social workers from other staff:

You see there are so many people in white coats, you never know who they are.

In addition, some applicants in private households were known to have

113

had contact with a social worker in the past about matters other than residential care. What was certain, however, was that prolonged or considered discussion about admission to Part III had not impinged on some applicants. Twenty-three of the sixty applicants could not recall meeting a social worker to discuss their application. Four of these said definitely that they had never met one, twelve others could not remember having done so and seven were too confused to reply. Only half the applicants in the sample said they had met the social worker more than once to discuss their application. This finding is strikingly similar to that of Shaw and Walton (1979) who reported that 55% of recently admitted residents in their sample could not remember the social worker's visit to discuss their application.

More caregiving relatives said they had met the social worker (14% had had no contact and 11% telephone contact only) than had caregiving neighbours (one in three had had no contact). Some social workers appeared reluctant to discuss the applicant's situation with a neighbour but these reservations about confidentiality were not reflected in the attitudes of applicants, who readily identified their closest caregivers and gave permission for the interviewer to meet them. Hospital social workers were particularly likely to give priority to contact with the next of kin since the identity of the next of kin was one of the first items of information sought upon a hospital admission. However, relatives who were the next of kin were not necessarily those who gave applicants the most care on a daily basis, or the people with whom applicants would choose to discuss important decisions.

Pressures on social workers over applications

The pressures on social workers over Part III applications varied in their detail between hospitals and area offices, but there were four issues common to all settings. Pressures arose from:

* Professional ideals.

* The low status of the elderly and work priorities.

* Poor communication.

* Unclear delineation of powers.

We describe some of these common issues before turning to the particular problems of social workers in hospitals and area offices.

Professional ideals

During interviews, most social workers revealed an idealistic yet practical attitude towards the issues surrounding Part III applications and were concerned that their practice fell short of their ideals. Although they did not describe this stress as a "pressure", it was clear that for many social workers the discrepancy between what they would like to do and what was possible resulted in guilt and anxiety. Several described how they would like to spend more time over applications. One gave a typical view of what would be better practice:

> There should be more time before and after an application for the decision to be made and for preparation for admission. I would like

to introduce them to one or two Homes to meet the residents and staff and absorb some of the atmosphere before they finally decide on admission.

Others discussed the importance of an application to the applicant:

The elderly don't get the priority they deserve. When placing an old person in a Home you could be talking of practically ten years of their lives.

The need to retain awareness of the gap between professional ideals and what was practicable in current circumstances, and yet to accept a compromise was a theme which ran throughout much of the discussion with social workers on other matters.

Status of work with the elderly and work priorities

The relatively low status of work with the elderly arose sometimes from stereotypes of old people and their problems and sometimes from the need to give higher priority to work with other client groups such as children and families. A few social workers expressed a personal lack of interest which arose from stereotypes:

I can't help it, but elderly people depress me as does the thought of an old people's Home.

Others felt that work with the elderly lacked challenge and variety.

Part III applications do not seem to require social work skill. You get a bit blase as often there is no alternative to Part III. Other exciting methods, for example group work, don't seem relevant to the elderly.

Both these social workers were qualified, and their respective training courses had not imbued them with enthusiasm for work with old people.
Such lack of interest in the elderly was perceived by social workers as being shared by other professionals. An area office social worker commented:

General practitioners appear uninterested in many elderly people and often refer them for residential care inappropriately. Also, they make referrals without the client's knowledge. GPs "pass the buck".

The low status of work with the elderly became translated into the lower priority given by some social workers in relation to the heavy demands of other clients:

Social workers find Part III applications a nuisance to fill in. Generally speaking, the elderly get put at the bottom of the pile. They are not a priority, not a particularly attractive group to work with or maybe it is just the way it is put across, and therefore one doesn't see what the potential might be.

It could also be the basis for a disregard of an old person's wishes:

115

A lot of social workers are just trying to offload clients as soon as possible - as are a lot of relatives.

A hospital social worker made a similar comment about doctors in her setting:

If the elderly person refuses an offer (of a bed in a Home) they are under pressure from the hospital to move on. So they have no real choice or freedom. The doctors are not really aware of what Part III is. Everyone is looking for somewhere for people to go - they don't want them.

Poor communication

Difficulties of ensuring good co-operation between professionals in social services and other departments were mentioned by social workers in all settings.

Some difficulty in communication could arise between different sections of the same department. For example, problems of sharing information were experienced by social workers and home help organisers, who did not submit Part III applications themselves although they often had extensive knowledge of applicants and worked alongside social workers in area offices.

On some occasions also, decisions about Part III care were taken by hospital staff without reference to area social workers who knew the applicants involved. On others, social workers in all settings took decisions over applications without reference to the informal caregivers (such as neighbours) who had had the closest personal contact with applicants.

Difficulties over role definition occurred frequently. For example, in assessment for Part III, occupational therapists and social workers often worked as substitutes for each other, but did not have distinct complementary roles. The assessment of applicants required a co-ordination of skills which were not usually all possessed by the same professional. There was a debate about the desirable role each profession should fulfil with elderly applicants, and the practice of regarding occupational therapists and social workers as interchangeable did not mean that they necessarily took on all aspects of each other's roles. Thus, while some occupational therapists might provide information about alternatives to Part III care and explore inter-personal problems in the same way as social workers, others would not. As one social worker put it:

In cases where there is amputation or physical handicap there is a need to help an elderly person accept the disability. The occupational therapists who assess the disability do not necessarily see it as their responsibility to consider its emotional consequences or to refer to others who might.

Similarly, applicants assessed by social workers might not receive an adequate functional assessment. A social worker based in a general hospital felt she was required to give opinions which should have been based on the expertise of occupational therapists or physiotherapists.

Unclear powers

In all settings there were disagreements over who should make decisions

116

about residential care. Hospital doctors, because they had power to discharge patients, considered that they should have influence over the allocation of Part III places. Social workers and residential care workers sometimes disagreed about who had the right to decide matters of eligibility and priority and who had powers of veto. Social workers considered that as they were required to do a careful assessment of the applicant, their opinions should be taken seriously and their recommendation accepted by the residential care section. However, managers in the residential services section pointed out that they alone had intimate knowledge of Part III Homes in the authority, the staff in them and the current dependency of the residents. As they had executive responsibility for residential resources, they thought they should decide matters of eligibility, priority and placement.

The experience of such conflicts in particular settings

The pressures on hospital social workers stemmed from relationships with their colleagues and their concern at the effect of hospitalisation upon patients. They differed somewhat between the geriatric, psychiatric and general hospital.

In the geriatric hospital, social workers, doctors and other medical staff had chosen to work in this setting and worked as a team. They shared an interest in the elderly, were knowledgeable about their problems and there was much informal as well as formal contact among these. Social workers had interconnecting offices and their general office contained a sink and a kettle. Tea or coffee could be made by social workers, doctors and other visitors and much discussion about patients happened in this relaxed atmosphere. In addition, all hospital staff shared one hospital canteen for meals which facilitated discussion between different types and levels of staff. It was also the practice for social workers to accompany consultants on domiciliary visits prior to a planned hospital admission as well as on their ward rounds. This contact meant social workers and consultants shared their concerns about the medical and social needs of current in-patients as well as those awaiting admission. The need "to clear a hospital bed" therefore referred to the competing priorities of patients known to the geriatric hospital social workers. Informal discussion had also stimulated ideas and simplified their implementation on a trial basis. In the geriatric hospital, social workers had introduced innovations such as bereavement groups for relatives of patients who had died and reminiscence groups to stimulate patients in long-stay wards who had become apathetic.

Nevertheless, social workers in the geriatric hospital claimed that problems arose because others perceived their hospital as a "warehouse". It was not unusual for a decision to apply for Part III care to be made whilst a patient was in the general hospital and for the patient to be transferred to the geriatric hospital to await a Part III place. As staff in the geriatric hospital had rehabilitation as an important professional aim, they considered applications for Part III care made before patients had been transferred militated against an elderly person's self confidence and a possible programme of rehabilitation to their home address.

Informal professional relationships and teamwork between social workers and medical staff were more apparent in the geriatric hospital than in general hospitals where the pressure on beds was even more urgent and social workers had less experience of Part III assessments. Social workers in general hospitals often said that they felt anxious when doing Part III applications. They often had to work at speed, with little or no prior knowledge of the applicants, no time to visit them at their homes and still less time to understand the applicants' wishes or the relatives' problems.

The burden of being trusted by dependent elderly people who were hospital patients caused some social workers to feel distressed and guilty. In psychiatric and acute wards especially, social workers said that an application for Part III was often a compromise and an attempt to resolve the conflicting interests of the professionals involved:

> The doctors are aiming to get the person out. The social workers are fighting for more appropriate alternatives.

Others felt that acute hospitals were not really geared to proper assessment of the elderly:

> The emphasis is on their discharge to almost anywhere.

Providing alternatives to Part III might require prolonged social work intervention which, in hospital conditions, the social worker was unable to give.

However good their professional relationships, hospital social workers knew that consultants had the right to discharge patients without discussion. They described ward rounds in which they felt consultants were breathing down their necks to find a solution for an elderly person's care that would vacate the hospital bed. There were several examples of how difficult it was for elderly people in hospital to express views which were contrary to opinions held by the medical staff.

> In hospital it is sometimes assumed that if a patient does not object he must agree.

These problems appeared to be compounded by the reaction of the elderly people to hospitalisation. Increasing apathy and lack of self determination was said to be accompanied by an increase in the overt trust which they placed in the hospital social worker and others in the medical team.

> There is emphasis on conformity in a hospital ward, the world outside quickly becomes unreal and there is need for an elderly patient to trust those around him. Elderly people in hospital are required to believe that other professionals are acting with their best interests at heart although they themselves may not be fully convinced of the wisdom of such a far reaching decision.

These and other pressures meant that it was tempting for hospital social workers to compromise in order to maintain good working relationships rather than become an unpopular advocate for their patients.

There were usually only one or two "specialist" workers with the elderly in each area office but these experienced professional dilemmas similar to those of hospital social workers. Indeed, conflicts over applications were described even more frequently by social workers in area offices than by those based in hospitals.

The elderly clients of area social workers often lived alone, were very frail and lacked the ability to look after themselves adequately. The "risks" they ran were a constant source of anxiety to their relatives, neighbours and general practitioners. As a result, pressure was put on the social workers to complete an application form (with or without the applicant's agreement), to expedite an admission, or to "do" something about an applicant's risk or self-neglect. Social workers reported that general practitioners, if pressure on social workers to "expedite" admissions failed, could use their powers to tap into their alternative residential resource - a hospital bed - or could exert pressure on applicants to enter a private Home.

In reality, the most social workers (in any setting) could do to expedite an applicant's admission to residential care was to communicate this pressure to staff in the residential services section. This passing on of pressure was reminiscent of the ways anxiety about risk could be transmitted to old people during times of stress. During a process in which pressures were passed from one profession or section to another there was a danger that the wishes and interests of the old people became obscured by the general anxiety, conflict and misunderstanding which existed between the professionals and informal caregivers around them.

Social workers' views on training

Training was a subject on which two-thirds of the social workers interviewed expressed views. Most commented on courses already experienced, but half the unqualified workers described training they would like to receive.

Some qualified social workers considered that there had been gaps in the content of their courses.

> Nobody gets training on practical things. For example, financial affairs and welfare rights benefits, the elderly confused in the community and the needs of patients and families where there is terminal illness.

Others expressed the view that social workers should have more medical knowledge.

> Training courses include little teaching about the processes of normal ageing - including the medical aspects of ageing. More information on the health of the elderly would enable a social worker to detect danger signs of infection, conditions such as hypothermia or dehydration or psychological problems which appeared to be "odd behaviour". Lack of knowledge and understanding of causes could contribute to mistaken decisions being made.

Social workers acknowledged the crowded content of syllabuses and the fact that decisions about priorities were often necessary:

> In training courses the elderly do not get priority because there is so much emphasis on child care needs. Training for work with the elderly needs a more inspiring and inspired approach with greater emphasis on the use of different social work methods and their relevance to the varying problems of elderly people.

Some considered that there was much that could be done on an in-service basis:

There is much information about resources within the borough which people who work with elderly clients lack. For example, all who work with Part III applications should be familiar with all, and not just some, of the Part III Homes in the authority.

Other suggestions included the need for more information about recent developments in the authority, in-service training courses which included health and social services personnel and more joint training for residential and field work staff which used role play and group methods. It was suggested that other groups which included relatives and residents might stimulate more active participation within residential Homes.

Relationship between characteristics of social workers and quality of application

We wished to know whether social workers who were qualified, experienced and specialised in work with the elderly would tend to make "better" Part III applications than other social workers. By "better", we meant that the client would be positive about entering Part III and that the application should not be, in the opinion of the interviewers, "preventable".

Pursuing these ideas we found that applicants were more likely to feel positively about the prospect of entering Part III if they had social workers who scored highly on four characteristics. These were that the social worker:

* Was qualified.

* Was interested and specialised in work with the elderly.

* Was experienced in social work (five or more years employed).

* Had done more than ten Part III applications.

Applicants were also more likely to have positive attitudes if the social worker scored highly on a "social work practice" score. This was based on the interviewer's evaluation that:

* The applicant was in a characteristic state at application (for example, was not applying in a state of upheaval after a recent crisis).

* The applicant had been given adequate information on:

  - regime in Part III Homes

  - application procedures

  - alternatives to Part III care

* The social worker had met the closest informal caregiver on at least one occasion.

Findings on preventability were also more favourable to the "good" social workers. Social workers who scored highly on the four characteristics selected were also significantly less likely to submit applications (in the sample) which were rated by the interviewers as "preventable".

Conclusion

Studies conducted in the 1970s (Goldberg and Warburton, 1979; Neill et al., 1973, 1976) showed that unqualified social workers were more often interested in work with the elderly and had more of this group on their caseloads. These findings reflected an unfortunate state of affairs since Goldberg (1970) found that in certain respects trained social workers achieved better outcomes with the elderly than untrained ones and were more likely to see a need for both practical and "casework" help. Trained and interested social workers may be more likely than unqualified social work assistants to have more power to take decisions themselves and be able to allocate resources, thus avoiding needless referral to others or delay in service provision. They may also be more likely to have the status and confidence to liaise with other professionals.

These findings were reflected in our sample where most applications had been completed by social workers who were either unqualified or who were qualified but not particularly interested in work with the elderly. Despite this, there was a relationship between the aggregated scores based on the qualification, experience and skill of social workers and the attitudes of applicants towards their Part III application.

Irrespective of their work setting, social workers in this study considered that work with the elderly was given low status compared to work with other client groups, that there were conflicts and misunderstandings between social workers and other professionals (especially doctors), that there was lack of communication within their own department about Part III applications and lack of clarity about who had the power to take decisions related to Part III care. Most social workers interviewed suggested improvements in social work training. Several who had completed training courses were critical of the content and methods of teaching relating to this client group.

Thus the challenge for those training social workers remains, as in the 1970s, how to raise the status of social work with the elderly, how to increase the proportion of time on social work courses devoted to the elderly, and how to ensure that at least some of this training is done on an inter-disciplinary basis.

11 Perceptions of services

Introduction

Many of the problems which influenced decisions to apply for Part III care seemed amenable to provision from health, housing and social services. How far had applicants received adequate information about alternative packages of care? How far had services already provided to them proved adequate and acceptable? In this chapter we describe the services applicants had received and the views they expressed about them. We then examine applicants' and caregivers' knowledge of services and some possible reasons why such services were not provided more comprehensively or at an earlier stage.

Information about alternative packages of care

One quarter (23%) of the applicants, 22% of their caregivers and 15% of the social workers considered the applicants had not received adequate information about alternatives to residential care. Interviewers, however, considered that over half (57%) of the applicants had not received adequate information about these alternatives.

As discussed in the previous chapter, there was limited contact between some applicants and their social workers. Further problems about providing adequate information to applicants seemed to arise from three main causes:

* The stereotyping of solutions based on age.

* The attitude of defeat in some social workers about the possibility of obtaining alternative resources.

* The attitude of some applicants and their caregivers about the virtue of managing without help.

As few applicants apparently had regular contact with their general practitioners and only a quarter had prolonged contact with a social worker, the only sources of information for most were people they saw regularly such as home helps. Therefore the provision of a service such as home help was important not only in terms of the practical assistance it gave but also because it could, in theory, provide the gateway to other services.

Services received

According to their application forms more than four-fifths of applicants in the small sample had received some type of service before they sought residential care or were admitted to hospital (Table 11.1). As we found in the large sample, service provision was biased toward those who lived alone. Home help and/or meals on wheels had been provided to 77% of those who lived alone, but to only 23% of those who lived with others. A district nurse had been visiting around one in three applicants and this was the only service deployed slightly more often to those living with others than to those living alone.

Apart from district nurses, home helps and meals, applicants in the small sample had had a range of other services and for 22% this had been their only contact with statutory provision. Three applicants had been attending a day centre on five days each week and had also been helped by a community psychiatric nurse, but in most cases these miscellaneous services were episodic and limited in function. Domiciliary chiropody was the only service provided to two applicants and three others were visited by a rehabilitation officer. Yet others went to a lunch club or "pop-in" centre when they could manage to get there.

Typically, applicants expressed appreciation for what they had, but this varied from the affection which some felt for their home help or district nurse to a reluctance to appear ungrateful about their meals on wheels. Relatives and neighbours were more open in their comments but seldom questioned whether the tasks which services set themselves were appropriate. Some wanted more of the same but although they described difficulties currently unmet, they appeared to regard the scope of services as immutable. There was little expectation that services could be flexible and modified to fit individual circumstances.

Home helps

Home help was by far the most frequently provided service. Three in four of the elderly people living alone had home helps and no applicant criticised them. Indeed, some applicants depended heavily upon a home help and in some cases had had the same person calling for several years. The affection with which such home helps were described was reminiscent of a relationship with a daughter:

She's a real friend to me. Marvellous. She'd do anything for me.

In such circumstances a change of home help could be upsetting, especially when it happened without warning.

In most cases relatives spoke approvingly of this service and wished that more home help time could be provided, not because more domestic help was needed but because increased hours meant that somebody would be visiting more frequently or for longer.

Table 11.1

Main Services Received at Application

	Residence at application					
Services received	Hospital		Community		Total	
	Alone	Others	Alone	Others		
	N	N	N	N	N	%
Home help only	5	2	2	-	9	15
Meals on wheels only	-	-	1	-	1	(2)
District nurse only*	-	5	-	1	6	10
Home help + meals on wheels	5	1	3	-	9	15
Home help + district nurse	-	1	2	2	5	8
Meals on wheels + district nurse	-	-	-	-	-	-
All 3 above (at least)	3	-	2	1	6	10
Other only	2	3	2	6	13	22
None at all	-	3	3	5	11	18
	15	15	15	15	60	100

Note:

Please note that this and all subsequent tables in Chapter 11 are based on data from the Small Scale Study.

* Excludes community psychiatric nurse.

Neighbours were more forthright and critical in their view of home helps. One neighbour said:

I'm not sure what she does. I think it would be better if she did less talking and more of the washing and shopping.

Three neighbours criticised home helps because they "stopped coming without an explanation". One said:

The home help always seems to be on holiday and when she's away no replacement is sent.

In general, neighbours felt that the more they themselves did, the fewer services were provided, particularly from the home help section.

Only one in four applicants who lived with other people had a home help and most of these lived with an elderly spouse or sibling. The impression gained from interviews was that providing services within households composed of old people could be a complex and difficult task and that particular skill and tact was often required from a home help. The delicate balance between mutual care and shared deprivation needed to be understood against a background of the domestic routine, roles and standards which may have evolved during fifty or more years of marriage. The lives of elderly couples and siblings in the sample were characterised by bickering and mutual complaint. In such situations, helpers had to remain impartial, perceiving the mutual devotion and inter-dependence which such conflict could mask.

In three cases there had been some conflict over eligibility for the home help service. For example, a home help had been provided to an elderly brother and sister during the sister's long terminal illness. On her death the home help was discontinued because the brother was mobile and alert and apparently capable of caring for himself. However, he had never lived alone, did not know how to cook, wash his clothes or manage his money and withdrawal of the home help at the time of his bereavement was an important factor in the process which eventually led to his own application for residential care.

From the viewpoint of home helps, the difficulty of maintaining old people in the community arose partly from the unpleasant tasks they might be required to perform and partly from the concern and anxiety they felt (and often described) when the elderly people became incontinent or increasingly neglected themselves and deteriorated physically. More sensitive difficulties arose when old people became forgetful, mislaid their possessions and accused home helps of stealing their belongings.

In a few cases, home helps were nervous of so called "dirty old men". Some home helps became scared of the continuing sexual activity of these men but the man's longing to touch and be touched was apparently seldom discussed to see how their loneliness might be alleviated. There were few male home helps employed in the authority and the sexual needs of the elderly were seldom mentioned.

Meals on wheels

All except three applicants receiving meals on wheels lived alone and comments about this service were sparse and sometimes guarded. Most said they appreciated the meals because they were usually the only cooked food available each day. "They're all right", "I eat them", "I wouldn't bother otherwise" were typical responses from applicants. When prompted, some commented:

> They do their best but they have to come early because there's so many to get round.

> They taste like cardboard.

> The roast potatoes are hard.

It was perhaps inevitable that a diet which had to satisfy many requirements should apparently not be wholly satisfactory to most, especially as food eaten alone did not fulfil social needs.

District nursing

Specific questions were not asked about experiences of the nursing service. However, it was interesting that applicants and their caregivers more often reported receiving information from nurses than from doctors or home helps. For example, the four applicants who received an attendance allowance had heard about this from their district nurse. Only one applicant in the sample had been visited daily by a nurse; in most cases contact was for a weekly wash down and for general surveillance. The one exception was a lady with severe arthritis who was helped to get up and dress and was again visited at night and assisted into bed. Where comments were made, they were appreciative of help from the nursing service.

> She comes every week to give me an all over wash. I like to be clean.

Day care

Three applicants had been attending a psychiatric day centre and were in touch with a community psychiatric nurse. These applicants were too confused to express articulate views about the day centre but the caregivers with whom they lived had experienced it as a lifeline. For two elderly spouses who cared for their severely confused partners, the day centre and the community psychiatric nurse had been the key services which had enabled them to continue caring.

> I feel she's safe and they're looking after her. I couldn't get by without it.

Nevertheless, in both cases the great age and increasing frailty of the caring spouse meant that the stress of evenings, weekends and interrupted nights eventually proved intolerable. There was apparently no night sitter service or weekend respite care which, together with day care, might have eased this increasing burden.

The types of day/social centres most enjoyed by applicants were lunch clubs and a "pop-in" centre on one of the larger housing estates. Lunch clubs were enjoyed, it seemed, as much for the companionship as for the food. The food served at the lunch club was praised but, in fact, it came from the same source as meals on wheels. Neither the lunch clubs nor the "pop-in" centre were served by official transport, so that when applicants became unable to travel their attendance had lapsed.

Four applicants had tried day care without success and one had applied for it but had been refused. The four applicants who had discontinued day care had been on one occasion only. Apparently, there had been no follow up from the day care or social services when they refused to go again. One hard of hearing applicant had arrived back home in tears because, she said, she had been with a group of people all day but had not been able to hear a word they said. Another (aged 94) said:

> They're all too old there. I don't want to mix with a lot of old people like that.

Another reason for failure was that the day care day (8.30 a.m. to

4.30 p.m.) was too long and it was difficult to get the applicant ready in the morning in time for the transport to pick her up. Given the value of this service it seemed a pity that more effort was not made to get attendance at day care established or to see whether afternoon and early evening care might have been more acceptable.

Knowledge of services and attitudes towards them

One reason for the surprisingly low take-up of services among applicants could have been that neither they nor their caregivers knew what services might be available (Kirkman, 1984). Applicants and their caregivers were therefore asked whether they knew about five services: home help, meals on wheels, day care, sheltered housing and short-stay in Part III Homes. However, in what was a long and sometimes tiring interview for these elderly applicants this was a question which was omitted in around a third of the sample. It was found that when applicants were asked about their knowledge of services, their replies almost always matched those of their caregiver, especially if this was a relative or friend. It is therefore reasonable to assume that the knowledge possessed by caregivers represented the degree of information available to applicants.

All relatives and neighbours knew about the home help service and most applicants living alone had this. Although only one in four applicants who lived with others had a home help, most relatives who had applicants living with them did not feel that their situation would be helped by such provision. "I prefer to do my own housework" was a typical response. One caregiver herself had a home help for a brief period after being in hospital for surgery. She said:

I was pleased when it stopped. Although she was very nice, it felt like an intrusion. I prefer to run my own home.

All caregiving relatives and neighbours also knew about meals on wheels but as with the home help service, relatives who had applicants living with them did not feel that the provision of meals would assist them, although several applicants were being left alone during the day. Sometimes this rejection of the meals service without trial was attributed to the applicant:

She wouldn't like the taste.

She prefers the food I cook for her.

Neighbours were more approving than relatives of the meals on wheels service but felt that one reason why applicants were sometimes resistant was because they were reluctant to pay for it. One neighbour thought that free meals should be provided to old people who were living alone and who had a history of neglecting themselves.

All except four caregiving relatives knew of the day care service, but this was only known to three caregiving neighbours or friends. However, few relatives knew that transport to day care was available and when they learnt this in the interview several felt that day care in the past would have been very helpful, especially if applicants could have been helped to have a bath at the centre.

Around two-thirds of the caregiving relatives and half the neighbours knew about sheltered housing schemes but they had not considered this step at an earlier stage when it might have been appropriate. Several relatives regretted this, for in retrospect they considered that it might have been a better solution to the applicants' problems. One applicant had been offered a sheltered housing flat some years previously, but had refused it because it was up a steep hill.

Less than half the caregiving relatives and only one neighbour knew about Part III short-stay respite care. Several said that this would have been helpful in the past, especially if it had been available at weekends or for care on special family occasions.

As well as questions on these five services, respondents were also asked whether extra money might have alleviated problems or averted the need for residential care. Few applicants (12%) or their caregivers (4%) considered that extra money would have affected the need for residential care. However, social workers thought that it might have done so for 15% and interviewers for 10%. When asked to consider the possibilities of extra money more carefully, caregivers also began to realise that they might have "bought" themselves assistance to provide respites from caring. Some applicants who were housebound thought that being able to afford a taxi might have enabled them to maintain contact with clubs or old friends and relatives.

There was much ignorance about the attendance allowance. Only eight applicants and/or their caregivers knew of it, although many more could well have been eligible for it. The four applicants who received an attendance allowance had only been doing so since the application had stimulated discussion of their situation.

Reasons for lack of comprehensive service provision

Ignorance on the part of potential recipients was not the only or indeed most powerful reason for lack of comprehensive service provision. For some applicants there had been a gradual deterioration prior to application during which services had not been alerted or preventive action taken. An interviewer described a typical example:

It was a gradual process following widowhood - living alone and not enough to do, he developed a strict routine to keep himself going. He had a home help for four years but, despite this, increasing depression and poor health confined him more to his house and he began to lose self-esteem and to neglect himself. Two years ago he turned up at the area office presenting problems over his pension. Most recently, he fell outside during a fit of giddiness and lost confidence about going out. In the two months prior to application, he had increased feelings of depression, feared the winter in a cold house, feared committing suicide and so he went to social services for help to go into a Home.

Clearly, it is asking much of hard-pressed area social workers to expect them to differentiate between the numerous welfare rights enquiries from elderly people which are simply enquiries and those which mask deeper problems. Nevertheless, this man was in touch with a home help who might have alerted others so that a better medical, functional and social assessment could have been given. There was no evidence of lack of concern amongst the professionals who knew this man but, nevertheless, general practitioner, home help, area social services staff and housing welfare officer had, between them, taken little or no action to investigate his intractable and increasing depression, his

128

increasing social isolation, his cold house or his giddy fits. When he was offered a sheltered housing flat he was allowed to refuse it without further discussion or being taken to see the accommodation which was on offer.

Like this man, most applicants had been in touch with services (albeit episodically) over a number of years. Before a more adequate package of services could be provided problems had to be recognised. Opportunity for more comprehensive assessment had commonly arisen at earlier stages of difficulty, but concentration by professionals on presenting social problems or medical symptoms meant that wider difficulties in applicants' situations were not detected.

A related problem was that of timing. Sometimes, problems had persisted for many years but were only picked up at the point of application. Information about separate incidents was not linked nor was there discussion of recurring problems either within or between services. Interviewers were asked to comment on the possibility of earlier detection and service provision:

> In view of these two old ladies' severe arthritis and appalling housing conditions, why were they not referred to social services earlier? Surely their general practitioner had some idea of the situation?

One client (aged 62) admitted to Part III as an emergency when her mother died, had been on the register of the mentally handicapped for years. The interviewer wrote:

> This lady lived in poor conditions with very elderly caregivers. Preparation for her care after their death could have been made. In the event, this client, who has lived all her life with her family in the same house, was moved to an old people's Home without a prior visit and with little consultation.

Another applicant had had several falls and each time had been taken to the same casualty department.

> Why isn't there a proper pick up at casualty? Is there a social worker attached? If so, are they called on and if not, why not? A follow up at an earlier stage might have prevented much of this.

In a number of cases, points of crisis had been identified within a process of gradual deterioration and more decisive action might have been effective at these crucial times. Rehabilitation after hospital stays seemed particularly important as social workers and other professionals could collaborate in forward planning and put together an imaginative and flexible package of care.

A number of applicants had received unchanged and minimal packages of services despite gradually increasing physical disability. An old lady living alone had been maintained by her home help and illustrated how receipt of one service might conceal the need for others:

> In recent years there was a gradual deterioration in her eyesight and arthritis in her legs - coupled with the disadvantages of her accommodation. This has had a cumulative effect of wearing her down, making life a struggle, and risky. Family and home help network coped well until recently, but the prospect of the coming winter and the apparent risk of falls led to application procedures

being started. By this stage, this applicant was thoroughly worn out and ready to accept what she seemed to see as "a living death" - in Part III. She wanted to get out of the house where living had become so much effort. There had been an apparent lack of any real help following gradual onset of almost total blindness. She had lost confidence about going out. Intensive and ongoing support over the last few years including mobility training, being taught how to manage everyday tasks in safety, contact with others in a similar position might have avoided her becoming so exhausted and at the end of her own resources.

Packages of services

This applicant illustrates, as do others, the types of packages of services which seemed necessary if some applicants were to be helped to remain in the community. After discussions with applicants, caregivers and social workers the interviewers listed the services which had been mentioned.

As can be seen in Table 11.2, 173 services were suggested in respect of the sixty applicants in the sample. Nearly a quarter of these suggestions concerned domiciliary social services, a similar number reflected the need for improved accommodation and almost as many illustrated the shortfall in these applicants' social networks and quality of life. There was also a need for more district nursing and help from general practitioners.

The packages of services suggested as potentially effective fell into four broad groups.

First, there was a group of applicants who were living alone in a private household when they applied. In over half of these it seemed the need for residential care might have been prevented. In general terms, the packages of services such applicants required needed to encompass:

* Problems with their environment by providing, for example, aids, adaptations or sheltered housing. Some applicants may have been suitable for schemes available to younger age groups such as boarding out, small group homes or fostering, but these were not considered.

* Problems with their self care and safety through more targeted and sometimes more intensive domiciliary health and social services. This group did not always need a great deal more done for them but some needed help at different times or with specific tasks (such as, taking their medication). This group included some mobile but bereaved men, some of whom needed education and encouragement in domestic duties rather than to have these tasks removed.

* Problems with their morale and quality of life. This group often lacked outside stimulus and something to struggle to live for, which might be gained through clubs, volunteers or paid good neighbours.

Secondly, there were a group of applicants living with other people at application. For two in five of these it seemed that residential care was preventable and, in a similar number, it might have been. The packages of services needed to encompass:

* Understanding and practical help with the specific problems of

caring at the times these occurred.

* Adaptations to accommodation.

* Measures to counteract the repercussions of emotional stress on the closest caregiver and others in the household through, for example, short-stay care, sitters or domiciliary care attendants.

* Recognition of the old person's possible need for outside stimulus and independent activity.

Thirdly, there were a group of applicants who usually lived alone but who were currently in hospital. In most of these cases it was impossible to say whether residential care could have been prevented. In this small sample of old people, one crucial difference between those in hospital and those not, seemed to be the degree to which self-confidence and spirit to fight for independence had diminished in hospitalised applicants.

However, the packages of services which might have been effective needed to encompass:

* Interim care between hospital and living alone, such as frequent and intensive district nursing, home help or day care or fostering out for a period of rehabilitation or convalescence.

* Problems with self care, safety, accommodation and morale, similar to those listed for applicants who were actually living alone when they applied.

The fourth group were also applicants in hospital but these usually lived with others. This group included elderly couples who had a long history of deterioration and hospital admissions and old people whose hospitalisation had precipitated a refusal by relatives or friends to continue to care. For these reasons it seemed that preventive measures might have been difficult.

The packages of services which might have proved effective for a small number in this group were often complex and some needed to encompass:

* The need for applicants who had lived with relatives to re-establish themselves in homes of their own through, for example, sheltered housing, or shared tenancies or for increased independence through family placement or boarding out schemes.

* The need to identify and respect the amount of care relatives were prepared or able to give and meet the gaps through, for example, day care and home helps.

When continuity of care had been broken by hospitalisation, some caring relatives appeared to realise the pent-up exhaustion and stress they had endured. Not uncommonly, they had tried to obtain help in the past but had felt let down and exploited. Such previous experiences made some unprepared to take the assurance of services in future in good faith.

Overall, it was clear that the assessment, negotiation and design of effective packages of services and organising a sensitive system for

Table 11.2

Residential Care Considered "Preventable" and Services Mentioned

in Interviewers' Suggested "Packages of Care" (Multiple Coding)

Needs mentioned	Preventable				
	Yes	Can't say	No	All in sample	% of service items suggested (N=173)
	N	N	N	N	%
	23	21	16	60	
Domiciliary social services					
Mobile warden	2	-	-	2)	
Home help	15	7	-	22)	27
Meals on wheels	10	5	1	16)	
Social worker	3	4	-	7)	
Domiciliary health services					
District nurse	2	9	2	13)	
Health visitor	2	2	1	5)	
Community psychiatric nurse	-	-	2	2)	18
General practitioner	5	5	-	10)	
Chiropody	-	1	-	1)	
Accommodation					
Sheltered housing	15	7	4	26)	
Hostel/fostering/ boarding out	1	5	-	6)	21
Repairs/alternations	2	-	-	2)	
Heating improvements	3	-	-	3)	
Aids/Adaptations/Finance					
General provision of	6	5	-	11)	
Telephone	2	-	-	2)	11
Body carried alarm	1	-	-	1)	
Finance/help to budget	4	-	1	5)	
Social network					
Day care	5	9	2	16)	
Lunch/social clubs	1	1	1	3)	20
Paid sitters/neighbours	2	3	1	6)	
Volunteers	3	4	3	10)	
Multi-professional rehabilitation programme	1	2	1	4)	2

their review was a skilled and time-consuming task. Even if applicants and caregivers had accurate information about services, it seemed that they seldom knew where and how to effectively present their request so that the cause of their difficulty rather than only the symptoms of their distress would be touched.

Conclusion

Applicants were not in general receiving intensive packages of services, although they and their caregivers were usually appreciative of the services they received. In part, the lack of service provision was related to applicants' and caregivers' views of whether services were appropriate to difficulties over transport, or to lack of knowledge by applicants and caregivers over what was available. A more general problem stemmed from the lack of links between services, so that problems were handled piecemeal and episodically, and opportunities for earlier assessment and intervention were missed.

These findings are not exceptional. As we have mentioned earlier, surveys suggest that the level of services received by vulnerable individuals is often low, even when they are in touch with services (Levin et al., 1983; Plank, 1977). The Avon study (1980) found that a surprisingly high proportion of applicants were not in touch with services and that in the opinion of social workers a third or more applicants could have been kept out of residential care. Plank's (1977) review of waiting lists was even more optimistic about the possibilities for prevention.

If such possibilities are to be grasped before application, the implications are clear - use has to be made of the services which are in touch with the majority of applicants, notably the home help service, and of the crisis points, notably hospital, at which help might be offered. Such a strategy, however, has costs. Some potential applicants can no doubt be identified and their application prevented. Others, however, will be identified who would have died before application or struggled on in great difficulty. We ourselves have no doubt that earlier intervention is required but its difficulties in terms of cost, developing the skills required for screening and the need for targeting of services should not be underestimated.

12 Decisions and choices

Introduction

The frail, vulnerable applicants described in previous chapters were choosing the environment in which they would live probably until their final illness or death. Ideally, such far reaching decisions arise from a process of exploring and evaluating different courses of action without undue pressure of time.

In this chapter we consider three groups of factors which reflected the quality of these decisions:

*   The applicants' consent and attitudes.

*   The information available about Part III and the process of application.

*   The context of the decision (for example, whether the applicant was in hospital).

The applicants' consent and attitudes

As a prelude to further discussion the interviewers had to establish that the old people in the sample knew that they had applied for a place in a residential Home. The tenor of their replies gave clear indications of their attitudes towards this decision at the time of the interview, which usually happened a few days after the application had been completed.

When asked if they had definitely decided to apply, fifty-two applicants were able to reply. Seven were too confused and one thought she was applying for sheltered housing. Two-thirds of the fifty-two applicants said that they themselves had made the decision to apply and intended to accept a place when it was offered. Thirteen elderly people knew the application had been made but were still in conflict about it.

Six of these said that they had no intention of accepting a place when it was offered and seven doubted if they would. Surprisingly, four applicants said they knew nothing of an application being made on their behalf.

Table 12.1

Applicant's Attitude to Part III

and Usual Household Composition

	Usual household composition		
	Alone	**With others**	**Total**
Attitude to Part III	%	%	%
	(27)	(25)	(52)+
Not going	5	5	10
Undecided	6	1	7
Going	16	19	35
Resigned	7	14	21
Willing	9	5	14

+ Excludes one applicant admitted to sheltered housing between application and interview and seven confused applicants.

Note:

Please note that this and all subsequent tables in Chapter 12 are based on data from the Small Scale Study.

Overall (combining Resigned and Willing): $\chi^2 = 3.76$, DF = 2.

Resigned v. Willing: $\chi^2 = 2.12$, DF = 1.

Applicants who had agreed

The thirty-five applicants who intended to accept a place expressed varying degrees of enthusiasm about the prospect of residential care. Fourteen said that they were looking forward to it. These included one third of those who usually lived alone (Table 12.1), most of whom had been considering this step for some time. There were three ways of becoming "willing", two of which involved a wish to escape from situations which had become untenable. First, some applicants living alone could no longer tolerate struggles with self care, their loneliness, being housebound, sometimes poor accommodation, and apprehension about further deterioration in the future.

> The doctor said arthritis is my trouble. He said I could end up in
> a wheelchair. This knee plays me up. The winters get me down.
> It's lonely. I feel trapped. I'd rather go into a Home for
> company. I'd be settled then. It'd be difficult to have a
> wheelchair in the flat.

Secondly, some applicants wished to escape from hostile relationships
with people with whom they lived. Thirdly, although some applicants in
hospital disliked a ward regime, they liked the care which was provided.
This especially applied to some hospitalised widowers who were lonely
and domestically inept.

Twenty-one applicants were unenthusiastic about the prospect of
residential care but resigned to its necessity. Two-thirds of these
usually lived with other people and, in most cases, "resignation"
implied depression or anger because a caregiving network had broken
down. Furthermore, most were powerless because they were living in
somebody else's household and did not have a home of their own.

One old lady, whose grand-daughter (with whom she lived) was selling
her house, said:

> There was a row at the outset. I felt I was being pushed out. I
> cried about it. I'd rather stay where I am but it isn't possible.
> I've no choice have I - so I'd like to be settled.

In a few cases the applicant's decision to enter residential care was
a sign of affection to a loved but exhausted caregiving relative. As
one old lady said of her daughter:

> She's been a good girl to me - but I'm getting too much for her
> now.

Applicants who had not agreed

Ten applicants had not agreed to the application. Four said they had no
knowledge of it and a further six that although they knew about it, it
had been made without their agreement.

Some conflicts of interest were openly acknowledged. One man, at his
son's instigation, had been moved unwillingly into his daughter's home.
The daughter, burdened by her life-long dislike of her father, the care
of her own young children and the effects of a recent hysterectomy, had
reached a point of physical collapse and emotional exhaustion. The
father refused to agree to enter residential care from hospital and
demanded to be sent "home" to his daughter's household. In such
circumstances, whose choice and well-being should prevail?

In two cases a fitter spouse was excluding their partner from their
shared home because they were unable to give them the care they now
required. Neither of these more disabled spouses had agreed to an
enforced move into residential care but they could not see what
alternative they had. The practical and legal issues raised by such
situations, although obvious, are difficult to resolve.

Applicants in doubt

Seven applicants were undecided and reluctant about the prospect of
residential care. Most lived alone but were either in hospital at the

time of application or had lost their normal way of coping through a recent crisis such as a fall, surgery or a bereavement. This had often been followed by further shocks such as sudden hospital admission or suggestions of long-term residential care whilst they were still feeling upset and unsettled. At such times applicants were especially susceptible to the doubts of others about their capacity to care for themselves.

> My son feels I should go into a Home. I've no idea what's happening and where my future is. I'd rather go home than into "care". I'd no idea of it until I came into hospital. That person in the bed over there says it's very nice and all that but I don't want to sell my house. I'd miss my home and my memories. Really and truly, I don't like sharing. I've lived on my own for a long time.

Residential care was suggested to one applicant who was recovering from a fracture sustained during a road accident. Another was physically weak after being in hospital with cystitis. This lady had been discharged home "to convalesce" although she lived alone, was barely strong enough to get out of bed and had no pre-arranged domiciliary services. Without her caring neighbour, it is difficult to see how she could have managed.

It was small wonder that very old people in such situations felt unsure of their future ability to care for themselves. Initially, they had agreed to suggestions of residential care but by the time of interview were in a state of doubt and regret which one interviewer described as a "ferment of anxiety".

The information available

In order to make an informed decision, applicants needed to know what a Part III Home was like. They also needed to discuss whether the medical and functional problems which had influenced their decision were remediable or likely to increase, and what alternatives were available to enable them to stay in their own homes. How far did they have this knowledge?

Information about the Home and the process of application

Townsend (1962) first drew attention to the importance of prospective residents visiting a Home before admission. Only a minority of applicants in our sample (28%) said they had, although nearly half (48%) of their caregivers had visited one (Table 12.2). This meant that in over one third (38%) of the sample neither the applicant nor their closest caregiver had personal knowledge of a Part III Home.

A minority (17%) had previously experienced short-stay care in a Part III Home. These applicants were able to make a considered choice based on experience. One applicant had liked "the company", another "the simple life" and yet another "freedom from worry". All were expecting the same conditions they had known as short-stay residents to prevail when they became permanently resident. Some might be disappointed. For example, one applicant frequently referred to the room she had to herself and the comforting glow of the street light outside its window. She did not realise that in this particular Home single rooms (which faced the road) were usually reserved for short-stay residents.

Among other applicants, there were a number of misconceptions about Part III Homes. One gave a clear description of life in a workhouse:

I expect I shall have to work there but I don't mind as long I'm not pushed around. You get pushed around by everybody.

Table 12.2

Visited LA Home Prior to Admission and Applicants'

Residence at Application

Visits made by applicant and caregiver	Residence at application		
	Private household	Hospital	Total
	%	%	%
	(30)	(30)	(60)
Both have visited	23	7	15
Applicant has, caregiver has not	13	13	13
Caregiver has, applicant has not	47	20	33
Neither have visited	17	60	38

Overall: $\chi^2 = 13.33^{**}$, DF = 3.

Either v. Neither: $\chi^2 = 10.15^{**}$, DF = 1.

Another applicant, currently in the geriatric hospital, thought that she was already in an old people's home. As the geriatric hospital was in the same building which had previously been the workhouse for the borough, this was a reasonable conclusion.

One applicant clearly expected Part III care to resemble a holiday camp. He was planning to start fishing again:

I hope there's some water near there.

Two applicants were planning to take most of their furniture with them and were anticipating that the Home would provide opportunity for independent living.

When asked what they expected to like about life in a Home, applicants gave priority to the company of other residents, the security of being looked after and having somebody nearby at a time of crisis. Hope for companionship included "the chance to have stimulating conversation", and the need to feel useful "being able to help around the Home" and "helping with little jobs like knitting or sewing".

Features they expected to dislike included loss of independence and freedom and, most of all, having less informal and regular contact with their family and grandchildren. Many applicants were apprehensive about their own ability to get on with others. Although most said that they would not mind sharing a bedroom, they feared they might be unacceptable to other residents in the room. Such lack of confidence was most obvious amongst those applicants who had been living alone or who had been otherwise isolated from social contacts in recent years. Family conflict had damaged the morale of some applicants. Several also dreaded other residents being confused and unable to hold a sensible conversation.

Applicants were asked if they felt they knew enough about how long they would have to wait for a vacancy, the possible need to share a bedroom, arrangements for visits and how much spending money they would have each week. Their caregivers were asked parallel questions. Of these four items of information, knowledge of the need to share a bedroom was most often considered adequate and knowledge of the amount of weekly spending money least often.

Half the applicants and a similar proportion of caregivers knew that the applicants might have to share a bedroom, but 15% did not know of this possibility. One third of both applicants and caregivers thought they had sufficient information about waiting times for a vacancy but one third of applicants would have liked more. Although one in three applicants knew about visiting arrangements in Part III Homes, one fifth felt they lacked knowledge. The questions they asked interviewers reflected their expectation that the regime would be strict and authoritarian: "Will they allow me out to go to see my daughter?". Half the caregivers said they had enough information about visiting. Only a few (15%) said they knew enough about how much spending money they would have each week and over two-fifths (43%) said they wished they knew more about this. One in three caregivers said they had enough information about residents' spending money but one fifth felt they did not. Applicants often expressed considerable anxiety that they would not have enough money for their personal needs to feel independent of their relatives and to have some power to call a taxi and leave the Home if they wished.

Information about medical problems

Issues of medical and functional assessment were explored with applicants and caregivers in relation to the specific problems of individual applicants. Applicants, caregivers and social workers were then asked whether, overall, they thought medical and social assessment prior to application had been adequate. In the light of the three interviews they had conducted, interviewers were also asked for their evaluation of these assessments. Care has to be taken over the status of these judgements since the interviewers were not doctors, physiotherapists or occupational therapists and did not know what assessments had in fact been made. In practice, however, it was clear which medical or functional problems had apparently not been assessed especially as the interviewers' information was obtained from three different sources. In such cases, it seemed reasonable to think that the assessment process had been inadequate.

Replies to these questions revealed a low expectation amongst applicants and caregivers. Many were unaware of what was available and applicants in particular were reluctant to criticise and appear "ungrateful". Rather than criticise, they preferred to disassociate themselves from this painful retrospective appraisal. They said,

"They're very busy people" or "I suppose they know what they're doing." This view of the infallibility of professional helpers by old people is supported by other studies.

Social workers thought that the medical assessments on 77% of applicants had been adequate - a view held by 49% of caregivers and 42% of applicants. Understandably, most hospital social workers considered their clients had been assessed adequately by their medical colleagues. The opinions of social workers were based on resources which were actually available, those of interviewers' on what would have been done in an ideal situation. For a third (31%) of applicants, it seemed to the interviewers that medical assessment had been inadequate. Sometimes this was because applicants had been reluctant to trouble their general practitioners or to complain to them about physical ailments. However, repeat prescriptions, with a personal contact every eighteen months or so, seemed to be the most common pattern of contact between applicants and their general practitioners. This was sometimes praised by applicants:

> He's very good - he always sends me a prescription whenever I write for one.

Medication which was seldom reviewed and provided on request worried caregivers who were anxious about the carelessness of applicants and the risk of overdose.

It will be recalled that two-fifths of the applicants we interviewed said they experienced physical pain. As well as pain, other matters had also often not been discussed with a doctor, such as incontinence, sudden onsets of weariness, dizziness, disturbance of sleep patterns, or lack of concentration or depression. These and other symptoms which distressed applicants often seemed to have been regarded by professionals as the inevitable consequences of old age. It appeared that applicants or caregivers had seldom been told the results of any tests which had been done. Anti-depressants, prescribed following strokes or bereavements, were often not discontinued or linked to other types of help. No social worker or caregiver described incontinence as a situation which required a diagnosis or might be alleviated.

Routine psychiatric assessments were done before applicants were put on the waiting list for admission to a Home for the elderly mentally infirm but few others were referred for a psychiatric opinion. Social workers almost always considered that applicants had had an adequate psychiatric assessment or did not need one. However, for 30% of applicants, interviewers considered that psychiatric assessment had been inadequate. The applicants concerned were typically those who appeared unduly passive or depressed, or who had attempted suicide or said they had thought of doing so. Some, but not all, were still reacting to bereavement. In a few cases in the large sample and one in the small, there were signs of mental ill health of a different order. One applicant was very proud of her slim figure and smart appearance but her caregiver reported that this old lady regularly caused herself to vomit after meals so that she should not put on weight. This behaviour had proved intolerable to those with whom she lived and in recent years she had moved between the homes of several relatives. However, her symptoms had not been discussed with either a doctor or the social worker.

Information about functional problems

In relation to functional assessments, most applicants and caregivers had little knowledge of the range of aids and adaptations and the types of functional assessment which were available and so were unable to say whether the assessment had been adequate or not. Although social workers thought that the functional assessment had been adequate for two-thirds of applicants, interviewers felt that for half it left much to be desired. Much has already been said about applicants' problems with stiffness, balance, mobility and vision and about the specific difficulties with basic care tasks which they described. Assessment and provision of aids and adaptations had more often been for restricted mobility than for other types of disability.

In some cases, an assessment had been done but there was an apparent need for ongoing training and support. For example, although some deaf applicants said that their hearing aids worked well, others said that they were useless. It was difficult to know whether the uselessness of these aids arose from lack of perseverance, lack of knowledge of how to use them, or ineffectiveness of the aids themselves.

Applicants with partial sight (but not the blind) appeared also to have often lacked recent assessment and the provision of aids which would have assisted them in their daily lives. Deteriorating vision also impoverished the leisure activities of some applicants. A housebound lady had been an avid reader but now said she could not see the print clearly enough. She had not had her sight tested or her glasses checked for several years nor had she been provided with large print books.

Two applicants in the sample had basic and obvious functional problems which had been neither assessed nor helped. A housebound man had had several falls and was said (by his grandson) to have very long thick toenails. His grandson had tried unsuccessfully to cut them with wire clippers. A chiropodist had never been consulted. Another applicant said that he could not chew his food properly. The interviewer reported that his false teeth were so loose that they kept falling out during the interview. It is not known whether a visit to the dentist and the provision of a new set of false teeth had ever been suggested to him.

The context of the decision

In this section we consider four possible sources of pressure on the applicant - hospitalisation, lack of rehabilitation, the emotional context of the decision, and the procedures that had taken place after the application had been made.

Hospitalisation

Applicants in hospital and their caregivers were asked whether being in hospital had affected the decision to apply. Interviewers were also asked to comment on the degree to which hospitalisation seemed to have restricted the applicants' freedom of choice (Table 12.3).

Over half the applicants in hospital felt that hospitalisation had limited their freedom of choice. The hospital regime had seemed to demoralise and disorientate them and most had an unquestioning awe of medical decisions and power.

Some applicants implied that being admitted to hospital was in itself a rejection and sometimes a punishment. One old lady said of her son and his family:

> They seemed to think I was being difficult.

Table 12.3

Respondents' Views of Whether Applicant's Residence

in Hospital (at Application) Had Affected Choice

	Respondent			
	Applicant	Caregiver	Social worker	Interviewer
Being in hospital affected choice:	%	%	%	%
	(30)	(29)	(30)	(30)
Yes	57	72	33	60
No	20	10	60	40
Can't say/NR	23	17	7	-

Overall (excl. Can't Say): $\chi^2 = 16.39^{***}$, DF = 3.

Caregiver v. Social Worker v. Interviewer: $\chi^2 = 14.41^{***}$, DF = 2.

She did not know how she came to be in hospital but supposed somebody had thought she needed it. Also, she could not remember making an application for Part III care but thought she was visited by the head of a residential Home:

> Goodness knows what she talked about. I'd like to go back to my own home but they don't think I should be on my own.

She supposed she would have to go into a Home but she was unsure when or where. She seemed passive and depressed and when the interviewer commented on this she replied it was the worry of the thought of giving up her home.

Passivity and a feeling of powerlessness were apparent in other hospitalised applicants. Of one old lady the interviewer said:

> It is difficult to describe adequately the tenor of the interview. She was feeling pretty upset and several times broke down. She was very alert and this made her complete lack of knowledge of what was happening or would happen to her the more upsetting. She adopted a passive attitude to the application but this was not out of indifference. It seemed that the social worker and the medical staff were quite unaware of this lady's current agony of mind.

This applicant said she did not know an application form had been completed - this had been done by somebody else, she didn't really know who. She could remember being told that she might not hear anything for a long time. Prior to her hospital admission she had had no thought of applying for residential care, but now she felt she would have to do as the hospital decided and as the doctor recommended.

Some applicants presented a different side of their personality when in hospital and, in their own ways, tried to exert their authority. A 92-year-old lady applied for residential care from her own home where she felt safe and in control of the situation. She was described by the area office social worker as:

> Small, frail, rather bent but with a bright and alert look about her. She has a fear of being treated either as a child or like a prisoner. She likes company and has a good sense of humour which would be a sad thing to lose. She should be encouraged to stay as independent as possible.

However, she had a fall shortly afterwards and was admitted to hospital where she said she felt reduced to the level of "a child". She reacted not with passivity but with fear and hostility. She fought the hospital regime, and criticised the other patients and the nurses. During the interview she launched into a tirade during which she called her family "useless", said they were taking her house away from her and selling it, that nobody had asked her permission about anything and that she had managed all right before she had fallen and come into hospital. Admission to a Part III Home had become one of the matters on which she felt her freedom of choice had been taken away and her attitude to it changed completely. The interviewer said:

> She seemed a very different person to the one described by the social worker. I did not get a glimmer of the sense of humour the social worker had hoped she would retain.

Other applicants awaiting residential care in hospital referred more often to their wish to get out of hospital than to their wish to go into a Home. Most hoped that life in residential care would bring freedom from the "tedious" and "odd" ward routine and from "having to sit with a lot of noisy old women all together in the day room".

In contrast to the majority, two male applicants liked being in hospital and did not wish to return to their own homes. One, after bereavement, had neglected himself, had drunk heavily and was admitted to hospital with malnutrition, hypothermia and bruises from several falls. Whilst in hospital his general health improved, his cockney humour returned, he was a favourite with the nurses and thoroughly enjoyed an institutional life. He said:

> I feel I've taken on a new lease of life.

Paradoxically, it is probable that this applicant did not actually "need" Part III care because he was mobile, fit and alert.

The importance of having an advocate to help old people in hospital express their wishes cannot be over-emphasised. Advocates in this sample were more likely to be neighbours (who did not feel under stress) than relatives (who felt burdened). However, neighbours were seldom consulted and some relatives feared that giving support to the expressed wish of the old person might encourage discharge and lead to a trap of increasing dependence which they could not sustain.

Lack of rehabilitation

The effects of hospitalisation were often exacerbated by the lack of rehabilitation which might have been available to younger people. There appeared to be four main causes for this:

* A tendency among medical personnel to regard the repercussions of disabling incidents such as falls, strokes or surgery as inevitable.

  For example, a man who had lost three-quarters of his vision during surgery had had his name put on a Part III waiting list during his hospital stay but had not received any mobility training. The reason given for this omission was that "he lacked sufficient intelligence and motivation for this". His reactions to the shock of sudden loss of much of his vision had apparently not been recognised.

* The lack of continuity between services administered by hospitals and those administered by community-based health services. This particularly applied to para-medical services such as physiotherapy which, for several applicants in the sample, had been discontinued on their discharge home.

* Lack of skilled personnel in the community - especially physiotherapists and occupational therapists.

* Vacillation by professionals who were committed to enabling old people to remain in their own homes but anxious about the financial implications. Grants for equipment or services over and above normal provision sometimes required approval by committees. Such procedures relied on the presentation of a "good" case and took time. Doubtful about the value of spending money on equipment to see whether an old person could continue at home, they often provided the minimum available rather than the maximum possible by way of aids and adaptations.

  For example, an applicant who suffered serious fractures during a road accident was advised to apply for residential care whilst in hospital and was discharged home to await admission without domiciliary services or a home visit from an occupational therapist. It took days for domiciliary services to arrive and weeks for essential aids and adaptations to be provided. Therefore, instead of returning home to an independent existence which had been made as easy for her as possible, it was almost as if there was some process in operation which required this elderly applicant to find life too difficult in her own home.

The emotional context of the decision

Applicants and their caregivers were asked about the pressure they had experienced during the decision-making process. We also investigated whether an acceptable time had been allowed for making the decision, whether it had involved conflict, and whether applicants and caregivers had been in a "normal" state when making it.

To explore the amount of "pressure" involved in the decision, applicants and their caregivers were asked if there had been personal pressure on the applicant. More applicants than caregivers said they felt there had been pressure on them. Seventeen applicants (29% of the sample) said they had felt under pressure and thirteen of these rated this pressure as severe. Nine caregivers considered the applicants had been under pressure when making the decision and six considered this pressure severe. The types of personal pressure experienced by applicants ranged from caregivers telling them that they could not continue to care, to heavy persuasion and assurance that they would be "better off" and "safer" in a Home.

Most applicants and their caregivers did not complain about pressure of time during the decision-making process. Only one in six applicants and a similar number of caregivers thought that the time available was either too long or too short. However, for three out of four applicants, social workers thought that the waiting period between the applicant taking a decision to apply and being offered a place was too long. This view was as often expressed about applicants in private households as about those in hospital which meant that it was not only influenced by the need to clear acute hospital beds.

The experience of conflict and disagreement over such an important decision could be very distressing. One in five applicants said to interviewers that there had been conflict and a similar number of the forty-seven caregiving relatives and neighbours also reported this, (Table 12.4).

Table 12.4

Respondents' Views about Whether They Had Experienced

Conflict over the Application

	Respondent			
	Applicant	Caregiver	Social worker	Interviewer (evaluation)
Respondent experienced conflict	%	%	%	%
	(60)	(56)	(60)	(60)
Yes	19	38	33	35
No	53	47	67	65
Can't say	29	15	-	-

Overall (excl. Can't Say): $\chi^2 = 3.69$, DF = 3.

Finally, interviewers were asked whether it seemed that applicants and their caregivers had been in a "characteristic" state when the decision to apply for Part III care was made. In two out of five cases they thought that both were in their normal frame of mind, but in another two out of five interviewers reported evidence that either the applicant, their caregiver or both were not in their "characteristic" state. In one in five cases, interviewers were unable to express an opinion.

Applicants were not in a "characteristic" state for various reasons -

145

"in a state of shock because her home is being sold", "has only just come out of hospital", "shocked after bereavement". Such severe shocks and emotional upsets could throw other events and feelings out of perspective, but they could be expected to lose at least their sharp edge of distress given time and appropriate help. The ability to weigh up the pros and cons of various courses of action and to consider the implications of life in an institution could have been enhanced by waiting until an individual's "normal" state was at least partially restored.

The distress of some caregivers resulted primarily from personal crises such as the illness of a spouse and not from care of the applicant. However, most of the caregivers considered not to be in a "characteristic" state were distressed about the applicant, "in a highly nervous and depressed state due to mother's illness", "great tension", "disturbed and agitated".

Three-fifths (57%) of the sample of applicants had therefore made their decision in an emotional context in which they experienced pressures of various sorts, or were in conflict with others over their application, or were assessed by interviewers as not being in a "characteristic" state.

Procedures: the time of transition

Requests for particular Homes or Homes in named districts of the borough could result in a longer than average waiting period. Despite this, two-thirds of the sample made such requests, usually for a locality near to the caregiver's home and convenient for visiting. Some applicants wished to remain in the area which they knew, or to return to Homes in which they had been short-stay residents.

Interviews with applicants revealed that many were acutely anxious during the period between submitting an application for Part III care and admission to a Home. It was a time during which either nothing happened or much precipitate action was taken such as the disposal of homes or possessions. Some social workers maintained contact during the waiting period, but because they did not know how long it would be, any interim help tried during this time might be discontinued at very short notice.

Furthermore, social workers found that requests for admission to be delayed so that the effectiveness of interim help could be tested were not always honoured, especially if the applicant happened to be alert, able to manage stairs and male (a group for whom vacancies arose most quickly). For example, a bereaved and mobile man who was applying because his caregivers were under stress was responding well to the interim solution of regular day care attendance. Had the referring social worker's wish that his admission be delayed for three months been granted, his rehabilitation into sheltered housing might have been possible. However, within a month of his application he was offered a place. His caregivers urged him to accept this because they feared that a further vacancy would not arise soon and they would have to continue to share their home in an atmosphere of conflict.

Conclusion

Constraints on choice described by applicants in our sample arose from their hospitalisation, lack of rehabilitation, the emotional context of the application, events in the transition period, and their lack of advocates. The absence of a programme of rehabilitation, either for applicants who had been ill in their own homes or those who had been admitted to hospital, meant that some decisions about long-term residential care were made at a time of maximum disability rather than at a point of optimum recovery. An attitude of inevitability by medical personnel towards the repercussions of disability in the old, the lack of continuity between services administered by hospitals and community, and difficulty and delay in providing expensive resources in an applicant's own home, made long-term residential care appear the easiest available option. In two-fifths of the sample, the far-reaching decision for permanent residential care was made when one or more important people in the situation were in a state of upheaval and not feeling "their normal selves".

Comparison of our findings with other studies shows close similarities. Ovenstone and Bean (1981), Lowther and McCleod (1974) and Wilkin et al. (1978) reported that medical, social and psychiatric assessments on recently admitted residents to Part III revealed a high level of undetected pathology. Ovenstone and Bean found that four-fifths of residents admitted from private households had undiagnosed medical conditions.

Similarities were found between the attitudes of our applicants and those reported by Shaw and Walton (1979) and Bowling and Salvage (1984). A quarter (27%) of our applicants felt positively about the prospect of residential care and 30% of Shaw and Walton's sample were said to be feeling "at ease" about it. One third (32%) of our sample either were doubtful or did not intend to accept a place compared with 28% of applicants in Bowling's sample who expressed such views.

In a study of residents, Wade et al. (1983) reported that only 54% of residents considered they had been sufficiently consulted about entering residential care. Overall, these studies show that a considerable number of old people are applying for residential care when they do not wholly wish to take this step.

Implications for practice include the need to ensure that applicants:

* Have access to a comprehensive medical, functional, social and, if necessary, psychiatric assessment.

* Are told the prognosis of their disability if they wish to know.

* Have adequate information about Part III (for example about room sharing, charges, regime and rights of tenure).

* Have visited one, or preferably more, Homes in the authority.

* Make a decision when they are in a normal state and not reeling from a crisis such as hospitalisation or bereavement.

Implications for resources include the need for awareness that:

* More thorough assessment inevitably consumes extra professional time and skill.

* The speedy provision of services and equipment implies the need for field or key workers to have power to deploy resources.

* Absolute freedom of choice may imply an unrealistic degree of spare capacity in Homes and sheltered housing units. The degree to which

resources are likely to be available needs to be realistically discussed with applicants, and among managers and professionals.

* Above all perhaps it is important that those assessing applicants for residential care should identify and discuss the feasibility of all the possible options including that of independant living.

13 Outcome

Introduction

As we have seen, applicants were often in a position where the wishes and anxieties of others were likely to override their own. Some were in hospital beds where they were unable to remain, and were being discouraged from returning home. Some were living with relations who were reluctant to continue caring for them. Others had had their self-confidence undermined by carers' concerns about risk or their morale eroded by struggles with self care in poor accommodation.

In this chapter we consider how far these contextual reasons for application influenced their outome (i.e. whether the applicants entered or remained in Part III, entered or remained in hospital or some other institution, or returned to or remained in the community). More generally we examine the factors associated with the applicants' movements - how long they waited to enter Part III, whether they moved during the year following application and whether and when they died. As will be seen, the results suggest that it was the applicants' social situations as much as their reported state of health and disabilities which determined outcome. The extent to which applicants remained in a private household or returned to live there appeared to depend as much on where they had been when they made their application for Part III as upon their degree of disability.

We base our conclusions on an analysis of all 1053 applications received between 1 June 1978 and 31 May 1981. These were followed up for a minimum of three months until 31 August 1981 (Table 13.1). Information on outcome and on the dates and types of movement such as admission to Part III care, hospitals, private or voluntary Homes or a return to a private household was obtained from various sources including the records kept by home help organisers, hospital admissions officers, hospital social workers, district nurses, voluntary Homes and others. We found that the outcome of most (96%) applications with respect to Part III had been decided within six months as required by the authority. For this reason, most analysis is based on applications which had at least a six-month follow up.

Table 13.1

Length of Follow Up, Permanent Admission to Part III and Survival

Length of follow up (months between application and 31.8.81)			Admission to Part III ever+		Survival at follow up	
			Yes	No	Alive	Dead
Less than 6	(86)	%	8	42	90	10
6, less than 12	(204)	%	67	33	79	21
12 or more	(763)	%	69	31	61	39
Total	(1053)	%	67	33	67	33

+   Admission by 31.8.81 and as a result of a single application i.e. prior to any subsequent re-application.

Admissions to Part III

As can be seen from Table 13.1, of all the applicants with at least a six-month follow up, 68% resulted in permanent admission to Part III. This includes many of the 4% who waited more than six months for a decision, as shown in Table 13.2. Most of these admissions were to "ordinary" Part III homes but 8% of the sample entered one of the two homes for the elderly mentally infirm.

Applicants who were admitted were similar to those not admitted in age and sex. As described in Chapter 3, few married people applied for residential care and those who did so were less likely to be admitted than applicants who were single or widowed.

The degrees and types of help needed by applicants with self-care tasks distinguished between those admitted and the rest. In this respect it was striking that the most severely disabled were less likely to be admitted, especially if they required extensive help with personal care. Thus applicants who entered Part III were less likely to require help with dressing themselves or using the lavatory and were also less likely to be incontinent or severely confused. Those who had considerable difficulty with washing themselves or getting in and out of bed were also less likely to be admitted. The effect of disability on admission was cumulative. The more self-care difficulties applicants had the less likely they were to be admitted especially if these difficulties were severe, included incontinence or problems in using the lavatory and, above all, were related to severe confusion. Such types and degrees of dependence may have made the homes reluctant to accept an applicant.

Table 13.2

Outcome within Six Months of Application

Outcome of application	N	%
	(967) +	
Admission to Part III on permanent basis		
Stay of at least 3 months	516	54
Discharge within 3 months of admission because applicant:	102	11
Discharged to hospital	35	4
Died	21	2
Changed mind - went home	16	2
Changed mind - went to private/ voluntary OPH	2	-
Other	29	3
No permanent admission to Part III because applicant:	302	31
Admitted on temporary basis only	15	2
Changed mind - went/stayed at home	74	8
Changed mind - went/stayed in private/ voluntary OPH	17	2
Admitted/stayed in hospital - application withdrawn	76	8
Considered unsuitable by SSD/other	91	9
Died	29	3
Applicant still waiting for decision re Part III after 6 months	42 + +	4

+   Applications with at least six months follow up between date of application and 31.8.81. Includes five cases known to be admitted but dates not known.

+ +   Thirty-seven cases resulted in permanent admission after six months.

The effect of disabilities on the likelihood of admission to Part III was particularly marked in the case of applicants in hospital. Hospitalised applicants with a high number of self-care difficulties were significantly less likely to be admitted, possibly because it was considered that they were already receiving care. As noted in Chapter 3 applicants in the community were more likely to be recorded as having a high number of self-care difficulties. These difficulties however did not seem to act as a barrier to admission. The inherent difficulties of integrating elderly people who require a high degree of help into a residential home are obvious. On the other hand care staff are employed in residential homes to help with personal care tasks. Certainly the findings raise the question of whether the homes find it difficult to care for the very old people whom it is hardest to maintain in the community.

Apart from the small group of severely disabled people who tended to be excluded from Part III, there were at the other extreme a small group of relatively fit applicants who were admitted. Nearly one in six of those admitted had no recorded problems with their mobility and were not confused.

There were also indications that certain types of behaviour may be related to the likelihood of admission, possibly because they may be especially difficult to accommodate in residential care. A "negative characteristic" scale was developed from information about whether applicants were said to be incontinent, aggressive, to wander off or drink heavily and it was found that the likelihood of admission decreased with the number of "negative characteristics" recorded on application forms.

There was a variety of other influences on admission apart from self-care abilities and anti-social behaviour. Applicants who expressed an explicit wish to enter residential care were more likely to be admitted than those who had a negative attitude towards the prospect. The two fifths of applicants who were described as very socially isolated were more likely than others to be offered a Part III place, as were those who had been bereaved in the five years prior to their application. Applicants who did not have a home of their own and applied from the community were more likely to be admitted to Part III than other community applicants, although the difference did not quite reach significance.

There were also differences between those admitted and those not in terms of their previous experience of residential care. Applicants who had had a previous short stay in a Part III home were more likely to be admitted on a permanent basis than those who had no prior experience of what life in a residential home was like.

Perhaps the most interesting difference between those admitted and those not was in the speed of their death. Far fewer of the applicants who were admitted to Part III died in the first year. Of those admitted 6% died within six months of their application and 10% of the survivors died within the next six months. The comparable figures for those not admitted were 21% and 16%.

The reasons for this difference in mortality can only be matters of conjecture. The difference did not appear to be explained by the characteristics of those admitted and remained considerable when we took account of factors which predicted death (age, gender, number of self-care difficulties and hospitalisation). It could be that the application forms lacked information on life-threatening illness. It may be that despite the disinclination of most applicants to enter residential care the "failure" of an application for whatever reason in some way reduced the will to live - especially if the struggle to continue outside residential care was not alleviated by heavier provision of services and other forms of help or if it meant long-term hospitalisation. It may also be that the physical care and warmth provided to residents in Part III homes extended their lives. Finally, early death may have made some applicants unavailable for admission, while suspicions of a relatively short prognosis may have made admission for others appear inappropriate.

Waiting times

Overall, one third of applications which resulted in admission to Part III involved waiting periods of a month, a further 43% of between one to three months, and 22% of three months or longer. How far were these variations explained by the characteristics of applicants, how far by contextual factors, and how far by system characteristics such as the number of places available for different kinds of applicants?

Table 13.3

Waiting Time and Residence at Application

Residence at application	Mean waiting time (weeks)	
	N	Mean
Total	602+	9.1
Private household		
Own	184	8.0
Relations	93	10.0
Hospital		
General	76	7.2
Geriatric	180	10.0
Psychiatric	48	11.2
Private/voluntary home	13	8.9
Other institution	8	5.8

+ 967 applications with six-month follow up excluding:

Fifty cases "in Part III at application".
Eleven cases where dates were unclear and
304 of remaining cases resulting in no permanent admission.

The importance of the context of the application was illustrated by the variations in waiting time according to the type of hospital from which admissions were being received. Most applications from acute

153

hospital resulted in admissions to Part III and 84% of these were within three months. The pressure for acute hospital beds contributed to this speed. By contrast, admissions from the psychiatric hospital waited longer than those from any other source, and 10% waited longer than the agreed six months. Particularly lengthy delays occurred for severely confused applicants who were physically mobile. These applicants were considered difficult to accommodate in an "ordinary" Part III Home and were therefore put on the waiting list for the two Homes for the elderly mentally infirm. They were roughly twice as likely as others to have waited for three months or more before entering a Home (Table 13.3).

Applicants who chose or needed a particular Home (such as a purpose built Home with a lift, a Home for the elderly mentally infirm, or a Home in a particular locality) inevitably had to wait longer than applicants prepared to accept the first vacancy to come up. Nearly half (48%) of applications without an expressed choice or need for a particular Home or district resulted in admission within one month compared with 27% with an expressed choice.

Waiting times were also related to social workers' perceptions of "urgency". On application forms social workers were required to record whether they regarded the application as "urgent". The priority given to applications by referring social workers varied according to the setting in which they worked. Thus, hospital social workers did not categorise applications as "urgent" or "not urgent", indicating instead that the priority was "to clear a hospital bed". However, apart from the priority accorded to acute hospital beds and the longer wait for patients from psychiatric hospitals, hospital patients did not differ from others in the average length of time they waited. Applications deemed "urgent" by the social workers in settings other than hospitals received some priority. Nearly half (47%) of "urgent" applications resulted in admission within a month. The degree of urgency attached by referring social workers to applications was strongly associated with the likelihood of admission to Part III care.

Non admissions

One striking finding on the 967 applications with a six-month follow up was that even at this late stage an application did not automatically result in a Part III admission. Only half (54%) the applications resulted in the applicant entering a Part III Home and staying for longer than three months. A further one in nine resulted in the applicant entering Part III but leaving or dying within three months; death, admission to hospital and the applicant changing their mind about residential care accounted for most of these stays of three months or less in Part III. However, roughly a third of the applications did not result in a Part III admission at all, a finding replicated in another study of the allocation of residential Home places in a London borough (Mitchell and Earwicker, 1982).

As can be seen from Table 13.2, there were various reasons for the fact that one third of the applications did not result in a Part III admission.

In a third of these applications (10% of the total sample) the applicants changed their minds. In most cases this was because they decided to stay in their own homes, but some opted to go into a voluntary or private Home.

Table 13.4

Outcome at Six Months and Applicants'

Residence at Application

	Residence at application				
	Private household	Hospital	LA OPH	Other institution	Total
Outcome	%	%	%	%	%
	(432)	(444)	(50)	(41)	(967)
Permanent admission ever +	66	69	92	59	68
No permanent admission ever	34	31	8	41	32
Hospital/other institution	7	20	6	32	14
Private household	22	3	2	2	12
Death	5	8	-	7	6

+ Permanent admission by 31.8.81 and as a result of a single application, i.e. prior to any subsequent reapplication.

Permanent admission ever v. No permanent admission:

Overall: $\chi^2 = 16.46^{***}$, DF = 3.

Private Household v. Hospital: $\chi^2 = 1.16$, DF = 1.

Private Household v. Hospital at application (amongst no permanent admission ever):

Overall: $\chi^2 = 96.80^{***}$, DF = 2.

Alive v. Dead: $\chi^2 = 3.91^{*}$, DF = 1.

Hospital v. Private Household outcome: $\chi^2 = 90.60^{***}$, DF = 1.

In just under a third of these applications (9% of the total sample) the applicants were explicitly refused Part III admission as "unsuitable" (others may have been less explicitly discouraged or joined the group discussed later who move frequently between institutions). These explicit refusals were because applicants were thought to be:

* <u>Too fit.</u> For example, a mobile alert applicant wanted admission to join close friends already resident.

*   <u>Too frail.</u> For example, a 94-year-old applicant who was unable to rise from a chair unaided, was often incontinent of urine and sometimes of faeces.

*   <u>Too difficult.</u> Unacceptable behaviour included undue aggression (considered potentially dangerous to other frail residents) and anti-social habits such as smearing faeces (difficult to accommodate in shared bedrooms). The principal officer ensured that this category was kept to an absolute minimum.

The only other sizeable group of applicants who did not enter Part III consisted of those who remained in hospital and a few who were admitted to hospital.

Applicants who applied from hospital and remained in hospital far outnumbered hospital applicants who returned to their homes. This association between location at application and outcome was apparent wherever the applications were made. Clients who applied from private households in the community were more likely than others to remain in the community; clients who applied from geriatric hospital, psychiatric hospital or voluntary Home were more likely than others to be found six months later in the type of institution from which they applied.

It was particularly striking that virtually the only applicants likely to remain in the community were those who applied from it (Table 13.4). Only fifteen applications, (3%) made whilst applicants were in hospital or other institution or after they had already been admitted to Part III care on a short-stay or emergency basis resulted in a return to a private household in the community at the end of six months. By contrast, 22% of applications made by old people living in private households resulted in the applicants still living in the community six months later.

The difference in outcome between applications which originated in institutions and those made from the community remained even when allowance had been made for numerous background variables. For example, an application relating to an old person who usually lived with younger caregivers was six times more likely to result in residence in an institution (either Part III or hospital) if the applicant was already in an institution when the application was made. Similarly, only 5% of applications relating to people who usually lived alone, but who were in hospital at application, resulted in a return to the community during the following six months. However, 25% of those who lived alone and who applied whilst in their private household resulted in a community outcome six months afterwards.

These findings suggest that some factors commonly seen as implying "need" (i.e. the physical and mental state of the old person) may be less important in determining the outcome of an application than what we called in Chapter 3 "contextual factors". Not surprisingly, therefore, other contextual factors such as whether the applicants had tenure or ownership of a home of their own, and the problems and views of those involved with the application were also related to outcome.

Allowing for the influence of location at application on outcome, community outcomes (i.e. residence in a private household) were significantly more likely if the applicants were under 80 years old. However, such outcomes were not strongly associated with applicants' disabilities (difficulty in climbing stairs, number of self-care difficulties) or with the presence of mental confusion. There were stronger associations between types of outcome and the applicants'

156

attitude towards the prospect of Part III care, whether or not they were "homeless", the nature of their caregivers' problems and the social worker's assessment of the urgency of the need for residential care.

Thus, among applications from private households in the community, community outcomes were found among:

* 42% of those where the social workers considered the application "not urgent" compared with 14% of applications considered "urgent" by social workers.

* 33% of those where the applicant was rated as reluctant or negative about the application compared with 19% of those where the applicant wished for Part III care or was willing to accept it.

* 30% of those where there were apparently no problems being experienced by applicants' caregivers compared with 20% where caregivers' problems were mentioned as one reason for the application.

* 25% of those where applicants had homes of their own in which they could remain compared with 15% of those where applicants were "homeless" (i.e. where they neither owned nor rented their own homes).

The overall impression from these results was that very disabled applicants could remain in the community but that this was more likely if they were determined to do so, were not under pressure from caregivers, were not vulnerable through lack of tenancy or ownership of a home of their own, had not been judged by social workers as in urgent need of Part III; and above all if they were not in hospital at the time of application. In determining whether or not an applicant received long-term institutional care, what mattered was not how disabled the old people were but the social context within which they applied. (For further details see Appendix 3.)

Hospital outcomes

Of the Part III applications made while the applicants were in hospital, 17% were made by applicants who were in hospital six months afterwards. Only 5% of those made from private households resulted in the applicants being in hospital six months later. As already discussed, the applicants who applied from hospital and remained there were in some ways more disabled and more "difficult" than those who were admitted to Part III. This suggests that the applicants involved in these applications included those whose degree of physical or mental impairment made the Home reluctant to accept them. If they had problems with both confusion and mobility they were likely to be in the geriatric hospital at follow up but if they suffered from severe confusion alone, they were likely to be in the psychiatric hospital.

Interviews with principal caregivers about applicants' conditions on the date of follow up, together with many informal discussions with hospital personnel throughout the years of the study, gave additional insight into the precursors involved in these hospital outcomes. Apart from the need for medical treatment there seemed to be three main reasons for applicants' eventual residence in hospital (irrespective of whether they had been admitted to Part III in the interim). First, many

157

hospital staff thought there was a "point of optimum recovery" during which a partially recovered patient quickly deteriorated if progress was not recognised and rewarded, especially by a move away from the hospital environment and regime.

Mrs D has been in ... [the geriatric hospital] for a year but has been personally independent for five months. In recent months her mood has changed from one of cheerful co-operation to general dissatisfaction and attention-seeking. This change is felt to stem from her long-stay in the ward as she feels she is fit in a hospital ward where everybody else is unfit. She goes out to church at weekends.

This applicant's attitude but not her physical state had changed but ward sisters, doctors and hospital social workers expressed strong feelings about the physical deterioration of some other hospital patients after their Part III application had been refused.

He was alert and highly motivated to move out of the hospital into Part III. When he was refused, he gave up hope, deteriorated and died within a few months.

A second reason for applicants continuing in hospital was that there was a group who were apparently "ineligible" for both Part III and hospital care. It seemed that it was often these applicants who experienced moves between different types of hospital as well as transfers between different wards within the same hospital (although transfers between wards were not monitored).

The generally accepted criterion for Part III care is that it should provide care similar to that which would be given by relatives in a private household. Unfortunately, some applicants were requesting residential care precisely because the care they needed was beyond the capacities of their relatives. Nevertheless, it was the authority's policy not to equip Part III Homes with power assisted hoists or pulleys as it was anticipated that this would render Part III more like a hospital or nursing Home and might endanger the informal and homely atmosphere. An applicant who was heavy, could not rise from a chair unaided or get in and out of bed, could be considered "too bad" for Part III care because they were beyond the care of residential care staff just as they may have been of their relatives. As we have seen, there was statistical evidence that such applicants were less likely to be admitted.

A third reason for long-term hospitalisation was that a small group of applicants preferred hospital care. A few chose hospital because it was free whereas fees for care in Part III might require them to sell their house. There were also some applicants who found it easier to live within the more impersonal environment of a large institution. Some isolated male applicants who previously had had a nomadic existence, and others who had had problems with heavy drinking, could exist within a larger group but were unable to conform to the expectations of smaller group living.

Other applicants preferred hospital care because they felt secure in their relationships with hospital staff. They felt more comfortable in accepting help with their physical needs if their helpers were socially distant. Yet other applicants chose hospitalisation because they felt safer in a place which contained medical expertise. One old lady had had a gastrectomy, was on a strict diet and had spent several periods in

Part III care between frequent re-admissions to the geriatric and general hospitals. Always the pattern was the same. Whenever she was in Part III, she deteriorated and seemed to be increasingly apprehensive and bewildered. Whenever she was re-admitted to the geriatric hospital, she soon regained her spirits and confidence and her general health improved.

This old lady was one of a small number of applicants whose application did not apparently result in a permanent placement in either a hospital or a Home since they subsequently moved between institutions. Taking the sample as a whole six months after application, most cases showed either "no movement" (25%) or "only one move" (54%). If applicants stayed where they were, it was usually in a hospital or other institution; a single move, in most cases, was into Part III care. However, 21% of applications resulted in two or more moves during this six-month period. This included 8% of applications which resulted in three to six moves of residence. These "heavy movers" had, in nearly all cases, first been admitted to Part III care. Half had then returned to a private household in the community, before being re-admitted to hospital or coming back into Part III care on a long-term basis. The other half of this small group had, in most cases, been transferred directly into hospital from Part III Homes.

Applicants who were only marginally eligible for Part III care could experience frequent transfer between residential care and hospital. For example, a lady of 80 who had lived and managed on her own for six years was occasionally doubly incontinent and had extensive arthritis, poor sight and difficulty in rising unaided from a chair.

She was admitted to hospital following a fall. At application, she viewed the prospect of residential care with relief as she had become frightened of falling when alone and expected that life in a Part III Home would provide her with companionship and security. This security was not forthcoming.

This applicant spent two months in the general hospital and was then transferred to the geriatric hospital where she stayed for a further month before being admitted to a Part III Home. However, she was only there for two months before she was transferred back to the general hospital for one week, re-admitted to the Home for a month and then transferred back to the geriatric hospital. There, she died within three weeks of her last admission.

This old lady's double incontinence and immobility meant she was only marginally eligible for Part III care. So, within the six months between her application and death she experienced six transfers between hospital wards and a Part III Home.

Transfers between Homes and hospitals were sometimes also precipitated by the increasing dementia or difficult behaviour of applicants. This especially applied to those who wandered out of the Home and became lost.

A further reason for "movement" was terminal illness. Amongst applicants who were interviewed in the small sample, there was an assumption that Part III care would provide the security they needed until their death. Most expected to die in the Home to which they were being admitted and heads of Homes expressed a willingness to retain residents until they died. Nevertheless, most (71%) of the deaths which occurred within six months of application happened in hospital. Only 16% occurred in Part III Homes, 8% in private households in the community and 6% either in private or voluntary Homes or in other institutions.

Death

One tenth (11%) of all applications received during the three years of the study had resulted in the death of the applicant during the six months after their application and one fifth (22%) resulted in death within a year - a figure similar to those reported in studies of populations in hospitals and Homes (Donaldson et al., 1980; Donaldson and Jagger, 1983; Goldfarb et al., 1966; Lieberman, 1961; Smith and Lowther, 1976).

In contrast to the other outcomes we have examined in this chapter, death was strongly related to the individual characteristics of the applicant. Death within six months was more likely to occur if applications related to people who were over the age of 80, male, had difficulty with climbing stairs or were unable to do so, and had difficulties with two or more self-care tasks. It was less likely to occur if the applicant was homeless, possibly because homeless applicants were not applying primarily for reasons to do with physical disability.

Within twelve months, death had followed 26% of applications from people with two or more self-care difficulties but only 14% of those from people who had one or no self-care problems. Over a quarter (27%) of applications from people who had problems with climbing stairs resulted in death within twelve months. Death occurred in only 13% of applications from those who had no difficulty with stairs.

Table 13.5

Quarterly Probability of Death within 1 Year

of Application

Quarter after application	Number of applications+	Within 1 Year	
		Number of deaths	Probability of death %
1st	743	42	5.7
2nd	701	40	5.7
3rd	661	34	5.1
4th	627	50	8.0

+ Based on 763 applications with twelve months follow up excluding five cases "not known if dead" and fifteen cases "dead - dates not known".

Similar relationships between sex, mobility and mortality after relocation have been found in other studies (Pablo, 1977) and between mortality and increasing difficulties in self care amongst people of all ages in private households (Warren and Knight, 1982). Some researchers

(Lieberman, 1961, 1974) have also suggested that death in old age is more likely after a relocation. For this reason, we expected that the probability of dying in our sample would be higher in the first and second quarter after an application, when moves were likely to take place, than in the third and fourth, and that it would also be higher immediately after applicants had moved to Part III than when they had settled in.

As can be seen from Table 13.5, these expectations were not fulfilled. The probability of death was also constant in each quarter of the first year after admission.

These results suggested either that relocation was not related to death in this sample or that other factors were influencing its effect. For example, some very ill people may not have moved because of their illness and died where they were. A further attempt was therefore made to relate death to number of moves.

Table 13.6

Number of "Moves" within Six Months of Application

and Death between Six and Twelve Months after Application

Between 6 and 12 months after application outcome was	Number of moves within 6 months of application				
	0	1	2	3-6	Total
	%	%	%	%	%
	(167)	(383)	(60)	(51)	(661)+
Death	15	10	17	20	13
Survival	85	90	83	80	87

+ Applications with at least twelve months follow up and excluding deaths within six months of application (eighty-two cases); death - dates not known (fifteen cases); not known if died (five cases).

χ^2 Trend (DF=1)= 0.66

χ^2 Overall (DF=3)= 6.0

As the number of moves during the first six months following application increased so too did the likelihood of death during the subsequent six months (Table 13.6). A higher proportion of applications resulting in only one move showed survival (ratio of survivors to deaths 9:1). Those who had two moves, more often had died (ratio of survivors to deaths 5:1). Deaths were most frequent amongst those who had had between three to six changes of residence during the six months following their application (ratio of survivors to deaths. 4:1). However, as many of these "heavy" movers had experienced one or more

161

hospital admissions, it is also possible that they were acutely ill and thus more likely to die.

Conclusion

The thrust of our earlier chapters has been the importance of applicants making a genuine choice over whether to enter Part III and the factors which made it difficult for them to do so. Encouragingly, in this chapter, we found that applicants' choices were related to outcome in that applicants who were reluctant to enter Part III were less likely to do so. Less encouraging is our evidence that contextual factors - i.e. where an applicant was, whether they were "homeless", and whether their relatives had "problems" - were also strongly related to outcome. Applicants exposed to these contextual factors were presumably less likely to be able to choose to discontinue their application, and further limitations on choice arose from the longer waiting times faced by those who wished to enter a particular Home. There were also indications that the applicants who had the greatest difficulty with self-care tasks were less likely than others to be admitted, especially if they were severely confused. Care of this very vulnerable group had implications for hospital provision and shortfalls in community services at the "heavy end".

Our findings on the repercussions of hospitalisation raise particularly serious issues. Applicants who were in hospital hardly ever returned to the community and they were much more likely to be in hospital at follow up than those who applied from private households. Medical personnel sometimes attributed deterioration in a hospital patient's health and morale to delays in admission to Part III. Case studies of the small number of applicants who moved frequently illustrated the difficulty they had in controlling their destiny. The ability of services to prevent admission to Part III or long-term institutional care will depend heavily on their capacity to respond appropriately to people who are being cared for in environments where they can no longer remain.

14 Outcome in alternative settings: condition of applicants on follow up

Introduction

Our analysis has led us to be critical of the way in which decisions to enter Part III were taken and to sympathise with applicants' common wish to avoid institutional care. We have not, however, shown that in the circumstances in which the applicants were, the decisions to enter Part III were wrong. Indeed, as we saw in the last chapter, staff in hospitals often felt that more patients should have entered Part III and would have done so if their "point of optimum recovery" had not been missed. In this chapter we examine the outcome of decisions for those who entered Part III, for those who remained in private households in the community or ended up in hospital.

The data and design on which we base this chapter were far from ideal for our purposes. We did not have the resources to carry out systematic interviews with a large sample of applicants at the point of application and again after a suitable standard interval. Nor were we able to reinterview the small sample. Instead, three months after the end of the three-year study period, a follow up date (31 August 1981) was set for reviewing the status of all applications received. Records had revealed that two-thirds (66%) of these applications related to applicants who were still alive on this date. In most cases, brief structured interviews were held with a principal professional caregiver (such as home help organiser or head of Home). Inevitably, these discussions took place over a period of several weeks but the caregivers were asked to recall and report the applicant's condition as it had been on 31 August and subsequent events were not included in the analysis. Information on all except six of the 615 surviving applicants was obtained (99% of those eligible) (Table 14.1). Of these, 64% were in Part III Homes, 17% in hospital and 12% in the community. A small number (7%) were in other locations such as private and voluntary Homes.

In assessing this material, it should be remembered that the data were collected from professionals in different settings who may well have applied different standards in giving their replies. Some respondents had "direct" knowledge of the applicants' situations, because they were in personal contact with them and providing a service directly. Others knew the applicants but their role was primarily to organise or administer services for the applicants' benefit (see Table 14.2).

Table 14.1

Applicant's Last Residence at Follow Up

At follow up applicants resident in	N	%
	(609)	
LA OPH		
Ordinary	357	59
HEMI	31	5
Hospital		
General	8	1
Geriatric	67	11
Psychiatric	33	5
Private/voluntary home	30	5
Other institution	11	2
Private household	72	12

The "other" group in Table 14.2 were 85 applicants who were "lost to the system". No professional who was in contact with them could be identified. Some of these applicants were still living in the borough but were not receiving any domiciliary or social services. Others had moved out of the borough either to live in a private or voluntary Home or to stay with relatives. Letters were sent to these applicants and their relatives and they were either visited by appointment or discussions were held on the telephone.

Professionals or relatives were asked questions about the applicant's mobility, mental state, activities and interests, how often and by whom they were visited and (for those in private households) the type and frequency of domiciliary services provided. At the end of these brief interviews each respondent was asked whether they thought the applicant was "suitably" placed (in their residence on 31 August 1981) and why.

We used the resulting data to compare "outcome" for applicants in the different settings in terms of:

* The degree to which they were assessed as suitably placed.

* Their physical and mental state.

* Visits from relatives.

164

* Involvement in activities.

We supplemented this data with more impressionistic case material gathered during the follow up.

Table 14.2

Source of Information about Applicant's Condition

at Follow Up and Nature of Respondent's Relationship

with Applicant

Source			Nature of relationship with applicant	
			Direct knowledge	**Indirect knowledge**
	(609)			
Social worker	(51)	%	18	82
Home help organiser	(25)	%	88	12
Head of OPH	(284)	%	100	(1)
Deputy/acting head of OPH	(124)	%	77	23
Other	(85)	%	92	8
Total "caregivers" interviewed	(569)	%	86	14
From records only	(40)	%	-	-

Overall: $\chi^2 = 248.34$ ***, DF = 4.

Suitability

Irrespective of their setting most of the former applicants were considered to be suitably placed. Nevertheless, as can be seen from Table 14.3 there were variations between settings in the degree to which this was thought to be so. Only 9% of those in Part III but 27% of those in hospital and 28% of those in the community were judged unsuitably placed. As we also see below, the reason for this unsuitability varied between settings.

Table 14.3

Suitability of Applicant's Last Residence at Follow Up

At follow up applicant resident in		% Considered not suitable
LA OPH	(388)	9
Hospital geriatric	(67)	23
psychiatric	(33)	41
Private household	(72)	28
Total	(609) +	15

Overall: $\chi^2 = 38.60^{***}$, DF = 3.

+ includes eight applicants in general hospital
   thirty applicants in private/voluntary homes
   eleven applicants in other institutions

Applicants in the community

Only seventy-two applicants were resident in private households at the date of follow up. Seventeen of these were regarded as unsuitably placed and these included sixteen who were living alone. If caregivers had noticed any mental disorientation or forgetfulness in the applicant the opinion was likely to be that it was not suitable for them to live alone.

In most cases, the ability of the seventy-two applicants in our sample to remain in the community was dependent upon a network of willing informal care and/or the provision of domiciliary health and social services. Their own determination was also important. For example, an alert and assertive man had had a leg amputated immediately prior to his application for Part III care. He was in severe pain and the prognosis for his other leg was poor. Despite this, he returned to his own home, admitting a district nurse to dress his leg, but insisting on doing all his own washing and cooking from his wheelchair. He relied on complicated arrangements with local shopkeepers, neighbours and a daughter who lived locally to get his shopping done, his pension collected and generally to provide daily contact with the local community.

Other applicants who remained in the community were more dependent on their families than the old man just described and yet others were maintained independently in their own homes solely by professional time and resources.

The follow up suggested that most people who refused long-stay care had little or no subsequent personal contact with social workers. However, three-fifths (60%) of the applicants living in private households at follow up had either a home help, meals on wheels, a district nurse or other service, but in over one third (38%) of cases there was no report of any services being provided (Table 14.4). About half the cases without a service may have had a low need for one in that they were not recorded as housebound or as showing any signs of confusion. More disturbing, perhaps, was the scarcity of intensive packages of services. Out of 35 former applicants who were recorded as housebound or confused, roughly two-thirds were receiving only one or two services.

Table 14.4

Applicants Resident in Private Household at Follow Up
(Services Received)

Services received	N	%
Any of:	(72)	
Home help	33	46
Meals on wheels	21	29
District nurse	23	32
Other	19	26
None	14	19
1 service	16	22
2 services	9	12
3 services or more	19	26
NR for all the above	14	19

Despite what might have been seen as a generally low level of service in a minority of cases, some social workers had put considerable time and effort into co-ordinating and modifying services to meet the needs of individual applicants. Comprehensive planning could be initially expensive of professional time. For example, two case conferences were necessary to plan and implement services for one disabled man confined to a wheelchair. These were attended by: a head hospital social worker, a hospital social worker, two rehabilitation officers, a physiotherapist, a home help organiser, a home help, a day centre worker for the disabled, a ward sister, a hospital doctor, a sheltered housing manager, a head occupational therapist and an occupational therapist. In addition a report was obtained from the general practitioner. To maintain him at home, this man was provided with meals on wheels seven days per week, a district nurse weekly and a male home help twice daily.

In the more encouraging case examples, there was evidence of the long-term beneficial effects of social work. One daughter said that the application for residential care for her mother had been made soon after the death of her own husband. At that time, she was exhausted by the physical demands of caring, the conflict between her adolescent daughter and her mother and the difficulties of adjusting to her own bereavement. Eventually, her mother had been admitted to hospital. Whilst submitting an application for Part III care, the hospital social worker had helped the daughter with the repercussions of her bereavement and assisted her to understand her own daughter's rebellious attitude. This enabled the caregiver and her daughter to perceive the applicant's needs with greater sympathy with the result that the application for Part III was withdrawn. At follow up, these three generations were living together relatively amicably. The caregiving daughter remembered the social worker's help with gratitude and said how relieved she was that her rejecting attitude towards her mother had been resolved.

Had similar social work time and skill been made available to other caregivers whose problems we examined in earlier chapters, it is possible that some of these applications also would have had a happier outcome.

The friendship and understanding of other professionals towards applicants could also be of crucial importance. The attitude of sheltered housing wardens, particularly to mental illness, could determine whether applicants were able to return from hospital to their sheltered housing.

A few mentally handicapped applicants were already known to social workers in the day and residential services and this enabled them to be considered for a wider range of services than Part III care. Although a Part III application was submitted for a mentally handicapped man of 65, a boarding out place was found for him. Two years later he was said to be settled happily, very fit, friendly and appreciative of his landlady's care. Facilities for the mentally handicapped enabled him to have holidays and to attend various social clubs. Other mentally handicapped applicants were, however, admitted to Part III residential care without first being considered for boarding out arrangements.

For a few applicants, rehousing or new friendships had apparently been all that was needed. One widow had been admitted to hospital suffering from malnutrition, the result of heavy drinking and depression. When rehoused in sheltered accommodation, she became friendly with another tenant, a divorced Irishman, with whom she was soon having meals, going to social clubs and apparently enjoying life.

Some applicants had found their own solutions through a housing transfer into non-sheltered accommodation. One applicant had neglected herself while living on the fifth floor. She herself obtained transfer to a ground-floor flat with windows overlooking the street and entrance to the flats. At follow up, she was no longer depressed over being housebound because she spent her time sitting at her window and chatting to passers-by.

However, for other applicants the cost of continued independence had been loneliness or physical deprivation. An old lady in a similar situation to our previous example had lacked similar initiative. When visited by the researcher in her bright, spotless seventh-floor flatlet, she was suffering from a serious heart condition which had made her housebound and ended her previous social contacts. Sometimes she sat on the balcony and tried to identify people in the streets below. She feared becoming ill in the night and dying on her own. The researcher wondered whether this situation could have been anticipated either when her illness was diagnosed or at the point of application when she might have been encouraged to apply for ground-floor accommodation in warden controlled sheltered housing or have been provided with a network of friendly visitors.

The most independent applicants had rejected not only Part III accommodation but also domiciliary services. One of them was described by a home help organiser:

> Apart from a weekly visit from her home help, she sees nobody. She is smelly, incontinent, can hardly get downstairs to her front door and has taken to locking herself in her upstairs flat. She refuses district nurse, meals on wheels or more frequent home help visits.

However, this applicant welcomed friendly visits and needed to be accepted on her own terms before she could willingly contemplate further help.

Other unhappy outcomes arose from circumstances which could not have been foreseen by the most skilled of social workers or in which they were powerless to intervene. One old lady had a grandson who visited uninvited and depended on her to supply money for his food and social activities. He painted her rooms and furniture "strange" colours, meddled with her electrical equipment rendering it dangerous and invited his friends in. The old lady had sustained inexplicable injuries and bruises but nevertheless was loyal to her grandson for he was her only living relative.

Others found themselves losing even those elements in their life which had led them to refuse residential care. One old man lived and slept in one room and refused a long-stay Part III placement because he did not wish to part with his cat. Because he allowed the cat to mess in his flat the home help organiser eventually decided that either the cat went or the home help would be withdrawn. This forced the old man to part with his cat, who was his only constant companion and the reason for his decision to struggle on in the community.

Although some applicants had returned to live with relatives, changes of role could make their lives also unsatisfactory. A nearly blind man, previously regarded as "the man of the house", returned home following a stroke to be dominated by his active, articulate wife and adult unemployed son. Hemiplegic and unable to speak clearly, he spent most of the time sitting silently in a chair with no interests apart from his talking book and weekly lunch club for the disabled.

The financial and emotional strains placed on caregivers by applicants living with them had seldom been eased as a result of the application. An unmarried journalist caring for his chairbound and incontinent mother revealed that he still knew nothing about attendance allowance, disposable sheets, incontinence laundry services, adapted clothing for the disabled, incontinence pads or the possibility of obtaining a review of his mother's drugs (about which he was worried) through a referral to a consultant geriatrician.

There was a small group of twenty-five applicants who, despite being regarded by their social workers as in "urgent" need of residential care remained in the community. At follow up it was found that half of them had died, but seven were still living alone in their own homes, which was where they chose to be. Although one had recovered her health and was now fit and mobile, the others were maintaining themselves with considerable difficulty, often refusing services and depending heavily on relatives and friends. The degree of independence enjoyed by such applicants who returned to live in private households appeared open to question. From the descriptions we received, their quality of life often appeared low and their personal freedom seriously restricted. Further investigation would be needed to determine whether and how their situations could be improved. Some at least appeared to us to have received too little attention from services and to have been failures of community care. Despite often refusing services this small number of applicants seemed to welcome continuing contact with a well-meaning person. Some social workers persevered in this situation; others seemed to accept an initial refusal as final.

Applicants in hospital

Over one quarter of applicants who were in hospital at follow up were regarded as unsuitably placed - usually because they were too mobile for care in a geriatric or acute hospital or too alert for care in a psychiatric ward. In the geriatric wards, there was said to be skilled nursing care for physical needs but lack of stimulus or interest for long-stay alert patients. In psychogeriatric wards, staff considered that they were not equipped to provide the quality of nursing care which ill or severely physically disabled patients required.

Some applicants in hospital required a kind of care which was not provided by hospitals or Part III. For example, one, regarded as unsuitable for Part III care, was in a long-stay geriatric ward at follow up. She was fixed into a sitting position by her arthritis and had to be lifted from bed to chair by a hoist. Her sight and hearing were unimpaired, she was alert and intelligent and an avid reader. Still in her early 70's, she was several years younger than other patients in the ward many of whom were confused and unable to hold a conversation with her. She had no relatives, few visitors and relied upon the friendship of the nurses for stimulation.

All too often it seemed that when some very old people realised that all the future probably held for them was life in a long-stay hospital ward which contained few other patients capable of making social contact, there followed a process of disengagement, withdrawal into a world of memory and acquiescence to dependency. Daily observation of the deteriorated condition of such patients also seemed to be a threat to the motivation and morale of the nursing staff and did little to reduce the underlying resentment which some had towards residential care services. Such strength of feeling amongst nursing staff might also have been a measure of the difficulties of maintaining therapeutic intentions while nursing deteriorated patients on a long-stay ward.

Applicants in Part III

Three-fifths of the applicants alive at the follow up date were in ordinary Part III Homes and a further 5% in Homes for the elderly mentally infirm. Nearly all (91%) of these applicants were thought to be suitably placed, the remainder being considered too confused for care in "ordinary" Part III Homes or (four applicants) too fit and active for care in a Home for the elderly mentally infirm.

Ten of the sixty applicants who were interviewed in the small study had already been admitted to Part III care prior to their interview and so they could be asked what they liked and disliked about their experience. These interviews provided admittedly sparse impressionistic material but they could be used along with material from the follow up to identify some initial reactions to life in Part III care.

All those interviewed said they appreciated the good food, warmth and attractive surroundings of the Homes. The standard of furnishings and comfort was something which several had not expected. One said it was "like the Hilton". The friendliness of the staff was also appreciated and one resident (who had previously been cared for by relatives) valued the "no fuss" attitude of staff towards helping her with personal care tasks. Other residents also (especially those who had been living with relatives) said that they felt more independent since their admission to Part III which was something they had not anticipated.

The characteristics of life in residential care disliked by residents who had recently been admitted stemmed from their feeling of insecurity and loss of independence. The most common dislike was removal of their pension book and lack of information about how much spending money they would have. Although these new residents said they did not need money for anything specific, they sought the security of having money to spend without having to ask relatives for it. There were some who were worried because they did not know how much they would have to pay for care in a Part III Home and (as their pension book had been removed) were unsure how they could manage the fees. An applicant admitted as an emergency to Part III worried because she no longer had her pension book:

> I don't know how I pay here - I'm in the dark - no one comes near. I do like it here very much - but what if they turn me out. I just hope I've enough [saved] not to be kicked out.

Another shock to new residents was the sudden awareness that they could lose their place in the Part III Home during hospitalisation. For example, one man said that he did not intend to tell the head of Home about a pain in his stomach in case she had him admitted to hospital.

Although before admission most applicants in the small study said that they would not mind sharing a bedroom, when interviewed after admission some described conflicts in shared bedrooms which had arisen over minor yet irritating habits. For example, one man was unhappy because another resident in his room was asthmatic and coughed continually during the night. Furthermore, since his bereavement he had become used to reading himself to sleep, but now the other residents in the room wanted the light turned off early. A general lack of privacy and control over their environment was a difficult situation for these new residents.

Our evidence, impressionistic though it was, suggested wide variations in the residents' overall response to Part III. Friendships between applicants could be an important influence on their quality of life and sometimes on their application. Two old ladies who were both mildly confused and frail became friends when they were patients in the same geriatric ward. Fortunately, the importance of this relationship was recognised and they were admitted together to the same Home to share a bedroom. This arrangement proved crucial, for individually they were disorientated and dependent but together they were able to compensate for each other. They went everywhere together, shared the same meal table, sat side by side in the lounge, were together on outings and even shared each other's visitors.

Although no residential care staff would admit to having a "favourite resident", nevertheless "special" residents did exist. Often these had made obvious progress since their admission to residential care. When one old lady was first admitted from hospital to a Home she could hardly walk and could not eat because of a sore mouth. A team effort from care assistants, the cook and domestic staff eventually resolved the problem through liquidising her food and tempting her to eat. At follow up, "a miraculous change" was described. She was eating solid food and was mobile and alert although still incontinent. Her incontinence mattered less to the care staff than her observable improvement which they knew resulted from their care. Where such natural affinity existed between a resident and the head of Home or care staff, there was a tendency for them to say:

> We would never part with her - unless we had to.

However, whereas incontinence could be regarded sympathetically in one resident, it could be considered a reason for another resident "not being suitable" for Part III care. Incontinence of faeces was difficult for residential care staff and other residents to tolerate, and if it was accompanied by depression and ambivalence about being in a Part III home, the reaction of staff towards the applicant could be somewhat less warm and spontaneous.

One man in his 70's had not wanted to come into Part III care. He had a large anal cyst which caused him to be incontinent of faeces but he was otherwise physically well, mobile and alert. He was so embarrassed about his incontinence that he stored his faeces in his socks in order to dispose of them later. This proved intolerable to residential care staff and after seven months he was admitted to hospital ostensibly for further assessment but it seemed that long-stay care in hospital might eventually be the likely outcome for him.

Informal relationships between residents and staff which supplied real roles to residents arose in unplanned ways. In some Homes, it had long been the custom for a group of volunteer residents to join a group of staff in the washing and drying of crockery after the evening meal. This shared activity was followed by a cosy cup of tea round a table in the empty dining room during which staff and residents chatted, gossiped and shared stories about their lives as equals. When the Homes were supplied with washing up machines, however, the reason for this important period of friendly interaction between residents and care staff no longer existed.

Some recently admitted residents expressed disappointment that the company for which they had hoped in Part III care was not forthcoming. One applicant, despite her loneliness, decided to return to her own flat after a period in Part III and said of other residents:

> They were all so ill and confused that it depressed me. The residents depressed each other because secretly they were all missing their own homes and felt that they had been "put away" by their families.

Mental and physical state

In addition to asking professionals for their opinions on suitability, we were interested in whether the mental or physical state of the applicants appeared to justify their longer-term placement in a particular setting.

As can be seen from Table 14.5 those in the geriatric hospitals typically appeared to have more severe physical and mental disabilities than those elsewhere. For example, in the geriatric hospital, 81% of applicants were described as having difficulty with their mobility. This is proportionately twice as many as applicants with mobility problems in other settings. Two thirds of those in the geriatric hospital were described as "confused" a slightly higher proportion than applicants in the psychiatric hospital who were confused (56%). One in three applicants in Part III (36%) were also described as confused - roughly twice as many as applicants in private households (16%). Interestingly, nearly one third (31%) of the small group who were

172

resident in the psychiatric hospital at follow up were apparently neither immobile or confused.

Table 14.5

Applicant's Mobility/Confusion and Last Residence at Follow Up

At follow up applicant resident in:

At follow up applicant has difficulty with	LA OPH	Hospital		Private household	Total
		Geriatric	Psychiatric		
	%	%	%	%	%
	(388)	(67)	(33)	(72)	(609) +
Mobility only	29	26	13	38	28
Confusion only	23	11	31	14	21
Both	13	55	25	2	18
Neither	35	8	31	47	33

+ Total includes eight applicants in general hospital
thirty applicants in private/voluntary Homes
eleven applicants in other institutions

More detailed information about difficulties with mobility and confusion confirmed these variations between settings. Half of the applicants who were in the geriatric hospital at follow up were described as bedfast or confined to a wheelchair. By contrast, one third of the applicants who were either in a Part III Home or in a private household were said to be able to walk outside, unaccompanied and without undue difficulty or risk. One third of all those in any type of hospital were said to be "totally disorientated" compared with only 14% of those in Part III and 6% of those in private households. The most common mental state in Part III and the community was said to be "alert in the environment" which meant that the old person managed in familiar surroundings but might be less certain outside them.

Visitors

Our third criteria for a "satisfactory outcome" was frequency of visiting. In fact, however, frequency of visitors varied little by setting, for informal caregivers apparently remained faithful irrespective of where the applicants were resident. Although rather more applicants in private households (87%) received regular visitors, so too did three-quarters of those in Part III Homes and two-thirds (67%) of hospital patients. However, 8% of Part III residents and 4% of hospital patients had nobody to visit them. They therefore lacked someone from outside the institution to "speak for them". We felt that such old people should be systematically identified and offered contact with volunteers who could act as advocates if necessary. Overall, three-quarters of all applicants (75%) were being visited regularly at follow up by their relatives or friends, a further 11% had less frequent visits (three visits per year or less), but 7% of applicants had no relative or friend alive or well enough to visit them.

This regular visiting did not necessarily mean that relatives found visiting easy and there were some indications that caregiving relatives of applicants in Part III or hospital had not been entirely relieved of their "burden" despite being freed of their daily care tasks. Just as applicants had experienced change, so too had their relatives been required to adjust to becoming visitors in a residential environment. For some, this experience had meant new types of stress. They no longer had control over the applicants' care and plans for their future residence, and some also felt nervous or powerless when faced with the regime and norms of hospital or residential Home (Gibson, 1983, 1984).

One niece said she had felt distressed and helpless when her aunt was transferred without warning or explanation from a general to a psychogeriatric hospital. For her, a loss of dignity and the beginning of institutionalisation was symbolised by the fact that her aunt's hair had been cut and her belongings taken away.

Other relatives described feeling nervous in their relationships with hospital or residential care staff. One daughter regularly visited her mother in a long-stay psychogeriatric ward. She said that the nursing staff were kind but their way of maintaining "a lively atmosphere" in the ward was to provide noisy music from the radio and loud activity in the ward. The daughter knew that her mother liked quietness and order and was not deaf. Her mother felt embattled and assaulted by the continual noise which surrounded her on the ward. This daughter was distressed because she felt the incompatible surroundings were increasing her mother's disorientation but she felt powerless and did not know what to do. Confident and decisive in other situations, this daughter was tense and nervous of being perceived by the hospital staff as a "complaining relative". For her mother's sake, she felt that she must appear appreciative of everything that the nurses did.

The quality of relationship between visitors and Part III residential care staff was also important. Residential care staff sometimes described residents in terms of their visitors, "She's got a nice daughter", or "They come and work her up." Visitors who complained about the care their relatives received in the Home or who caused an elderly resident to feel depressed or unwanted by a speedy and insensitive visit or by not visiting when expected, made residential care staff feel "low" for the sake of the resident. By contrast, however, one new resident in a Home was frequently visited by her son who always came in with a smile, called the care staff by their Christian names, and was generous in sharing his car with other residents when taking his mother on outings. He provided laughter and relief in an otherwise monotonous day and sometimes staff as well as residents were grateful to such visitors for outside stimulus.

Activities and interests

A rather different way of obtaining indications of the quality of lives of applicants was to ask professional caregivers to respond to a brief checklist of activities. They were asked whether the applicants could and did engage in each activity, could but did not choose to, or were unable to because of disability or mental confusion.

Table 14.6

Applicant's Activities and Last Residence at Follow Up

At follow up applicant resident in

Applicant's interest/activity	LA OPH %	Hospital Geriatric %	Psychiatric %	Private household %	Total %	χ^2 (DF = 6)
	(388)	(67)	(33)	(72)	(609) +	
Initiates conversation						80.14***
Can but does not	18	61	22	12	23	
Can't do	1	3	12	2	2	
Speaks when spoken to/watches/listens						67.60***
Can but does not	8	42	12	6	12	
Can't do	1	-	3	2	1	
Watches TV						75.69***
Can but does not	32	68	34	15	34	
Can't do	4	8	25	16	7	
Listens to radio						68.36***
Can but does not	56	82	34	34	56	
Can't do	3	3	28	8	5	
Reads newspapers/ magazines						60.41***
Can but does not	45	77	53	31	48	
Can't do	4	6	25	17	7	
Looks at pictures						49.25***
Can but does not	48	71	47	32	49	
Can't do	4	5	5	15	6	

+ Includes eight applicants in general hospital
    thirty applicants in private/voluntary homes
    eleven applicants in other institutions

All but two of the activities about which questions were asked showed the highest level of activity amongst applicants resident in private households and the lowest amongst those resident in geriatric hospitals. The two exceptions were knitting and sewing which few did. Six of the activities about which we asked are presented in Table 14.6.

Compared with applicants in Part III Homes at follow up those in private households were between two and four times more likely to be described as unable to take part in some specific activities. It is difficult to know whether this was because activity was stimulated in residential care or because those in private households lacked motivation. Perhaps the self-care activities of daily living in private households took precedence over watching TV or listening to the radio. It is also possible that aids to assist sight and hearing were more often provided to Part III residents.

The most striking finding of this part of the research was the consistently lower participation of applicants who were patients in the geriatric hospital in all the activities in the checklist. Even compared with those resident in the psychogeriatric hospital at follow up, geriatric hospital patients less often listened to the radio, watched TV, or looked at pictures in magazines, even though they were judged able to do so. More worrying was the apparent disinclination of three-fifths of applicants in geriatric wards to initiate conversation and of two-fifths to answer when spoken to.

The reasons for this picture of apparent inactivity and lack of communication with those around them can only be a matter for conjecture. Certainly, Part III Homes had more organised social activity and applicants in psychiatric hospital were known to be younger and more mobile and perhaps therefore able to make use of the extensive occupational therapy department provided in the psychiatric (but not the geriatric) hospital. However, further research on the quality of life in geriatric wards and its determinants seems essential.

Finally, we wished to know to what extent applicants who had been admitted to a Part III Home had regular activities outside, or whether they had become "housebound" in Part III, as many had been prior to their application.

A quarter (151) of all the 609 applicants followed up were said to have pursued an activity other than those discussed so far. These miscellaneous activities were analysed to determine how many involved going out on a regular basis. Only fifty-eight applicants (i.e. 15% of those in Part III at follow up) had at least one activity which involved "going out", a proportion similar to that reported by Willcocks et al. (1982) in their national study. As a result of hard work by residential care staff and the voluntary work organiser some Homes had regular outings, for example, to social afternoons run by the British Legion or church groups. Because comparable information on all applicants prior to admission was unavailable, it is not known whether applicants' social activities increased or declined after they became Part III residents. Interviews with the small sample of applicants, however, would indicate that their social activities tended to increase after admission to Part III compared with the isolated and housebound existence some had previously experienced either in their own or in their caregivers' households.

Conclusion

The findings reported in this chapter reflect those of Dodd and his colleagues (1980) in that in our sample Part III was found to contain fewer old people judged unsuitable for their setting by its staff than those in long-stay geriatric or psychogeriatric wards. Our findings also supported other evidence (Wade et al., 1983) that life in geriatric wards was unstimulating for long-stay patients. A number of implications arise from these findings.

First, the apparently depressing situation of many former applicants now in the community or in geriatric wards emphasised the degree to which these applicants - and no doubt others - faced a sort of Hobson's choice. Many had not been provided with an attractive alternative to Part III, or even, if they were in the community, intensive services. Some of these should in our opinion be regarded as failures of community care.

Second, the proportion of applicants both in Part III and in the community who were physically and mentally spry was influenced by the tendency of the less fit to die or go to hospital. A policy of excluding relatively fit applicants from Part III would therefore produce a disproportionate increase in the average level of disability of Part III residents. The issue of excluding fit people who may choose to enter Part III is therefore a serious one not only for ethical reasons but because of its practical implications for running the Homes.

Third, if such a policy is pursued it is important to learn two rather different lessons from the geriatric hospital. In the view of the staff, the hospitals were unsatisfactory environments for their patients. Many were not undertaking activities within their ability which they might have enjoyed. It is clearly vital that Part III is not similarly overwhelmed by a concentration of severely disabled residents.

Finally, the lessons of the data were not all negative. The successful resolutions of their problems which some applicants who remained in the community had found in changes of housing, the pleasurable surprise which Part III provided for some applicants, suggested that applicants can be provided with something better than Hobson's choice. In the next chapter we examine the effort made in the authority to provide a better set of options for potential applicants and the problems faced in doing so.

15 Developments

Introduction

Our analysis has been based on the assumption that clients considering Part III should as far as possible make a choice which is based on accurate information and an awareness of alternatives. This in turn implies the need for good assessment and the development of resources to reduce the constraints on choice which arise from hospitalisation, "homelessness" and the exhaustion of relatives.

In practice, developments do not flow easily from research findings. Over the period of the research, economic difficulties provided a depressing backcloth to efforts to develop services for applicants or potential applicants for Part III. Nationally, the falling rate of provision in local authority residential Homes (Grundy and Arie, 1982) was coupled with an increase in the private sector. The problems of elderly people in acute hospital beds, especially in surgical and orthopaedic wards remained unresolved and their effects are vividly described in the Lancet leader, August 1982. By 1981, publications about "crisis" in services were appearing (Snow, 1981). Such difficulties were experienced in the study authority as elsewhere but there were, nevertheless, opportunities for fostering relevant changes. Joint finance provided the seed corn for a number of experiments; vacant staff flats or even vacant wards could be put to new uses, valuable sites could be sold generating finance for new ventures; key staff left - being allowed in some cases to implement new ideas almost as a parting gift - while "new brooms" were appointed and allowed initial licence to introduce new practices. In the event, a number of exciting developments did take place. In this chapter we look briefly at the operations of the panel to which we fed back our findings, describe some of the developments which took place, and finally assess their impact and the lessons they provided for developing a policy of community care.

The panel

The multi-disciplinary panel was set up before the research began and its explicit purpose was to agree criteria for eligibility for care in psychogeriatric and geriatric wards, and in "ordinary" Part III Homes as compared with those for the elderly mentally infirm. The implicit purpose was to clarify and resolve the conflicts which had arisen between health and social services around the care of the elderly.

Panel members included the assistant director for residential services, two consultants (a consultant geriatrician and a consultant psychogeriatrician), a specialist in community medicine, a leading general practitioner, principal officers in fieldwork and residential services, the area nursing officer, an administrative/clerical officer and the social services research and development officer. Panel members invited the researcher to attend as an observer.

Although most panel members had considerable executive powers, they attended as individuals rather than as representatives and were not bound to represent sectional interests. It was generally agreed that the absence of an official remit or role enabled members to express their views freely and to resolve some of the inter-professional and organisational conflicts which had arisen.

Ideas for resolving these conflicts often involved blurring the distinction between Part III Homes and other institutions. There were suggestions for nursing wings in Part III Homes, for the "triple" use of residential care sites and for a new type of provision which was halfway between Part III and hospital care. Such solutions required joint planning between housing, area health and social services authorities, but while the panel often suggested that it would be desirable to have a representative from the housing department at their meetings, they were unable to obtain one. Nevertheless, there was close collaboration between the assistant director for residential services, the director of social services and the director of housing and the panel benefited from these relationships.

The work of the panel was conducted in four main phases. For the first three months the panel met weekly and, with the help of the referring social workers, considered all applications for Part III care.

In the second phase, also lasting three months, the panel met less frequently and considered only applications from old people described as "confused" or admitted as "emergencies" to Part III care, and applications which presented particular problems of eligibility.

The panel's consideration of individual cases increasingly stimulated discussion of broader issues of policy, practice and procedures. At the end of this second phase, the researcher submitted an analysis of 322 applications for Part III care received in the previous year. This provided the panel with facts where previously there had been only impressions. The third phase of the panel's work consisted of the production of a report which gave the panel's response in policy and planning terms to the findings which had been presented. (A summary of the researcher's report and the response of the panel is presented in Appendix 4.)

Phase four lasted nearly a year and during this time much previous work bore fruit. The panel evolved basic criteria for eligibility for Part III, and for geriatric and psychogeriatric hospital care. There were also several other developments during this period some of which are described in more detail later in this chapter.

Unfortunately, because of staff shortage there was at this time no assistant director responsible for research, development and training, these responsibilities being carried by the director of social services along with his other duties. Similarly, the social services research officer had many other responsibilities. There was therefore no person whose main remit was to translate potentially fruitful ideas into plans of action and obtain finance for them. If an assistant to the research and development officer had been in post, it seems probable that more progress could have taken place in integrating care from health and social services and in communicating the reasons behind suggested changes to all levels of staff.

This final period of the panel's existence was marked by cutbacks in services. Whereas moderate national economic constraint had produced an atmosphere of challenge and manageable crisis, the new constraints depressed morale and curtailed any activity which was not essential to maintaining day-to-day practice. The panel members increasingly felt that there was little purpose in discussing innovations or improvements as it seemed unlikely that even present standards could be maintained in future. This atmosphere of constraint and retraction, coupled with the retirements of key people, such as the specialist in community medicine and the assistant director for residential services, resulted in the panel winding up its activities and ceasing to meet.

Changes in procedures

The panel was as concerned as the researcher to improve the assessment of applicants. They interpreted assessments widely to include the provision of information and the chance to review the applicants' situations in Part III. A number of relevant developments took place aiming to:

* Improve assessment practices and quality of information obtained through changes in Part III assessment/application forms.

* Improve quality of medical information on applicants.

* Improve information on Part III to applicants to assist them to make a considered decision.

* Improve information to applicants on the Homes they might enter through head of Home visits and trial days.

* Review new residents in Homes.

As will be seen below these developments had varying degrees of success.

New application forms

The process of designing a new application form was lengthy and involved senior social workers from different settings. The eventual form was longer and more client centred than the previous one. For the first time, it explicitly sought information about the applicants' attitudes to residential care, what types of regime they considered would be most appropriate to them and whether they had a preference for particular Homes or localities. The social workers thought that there should be more explicit information about the physical and mental disabilities of applicants and their recent social history, so that the types of services required to help them in their own homes could be more accurately identified.

There were some complaints about the new application forms arising particularly from the fact that they were on "no carbon required" pads which were expensive to produce and bulky to carry around. However, these saved much clerical time as information could be included in the client's file, sent to the Home and also recorded for statistical purposes without the need to photocopy.

Another complaint arose from the length of the form. There were two schools of thought. Those workers who operated as "specialists" with the elderly or those who were particularly interested in this client group liked the extra detail and felt that it reflected the quality and length of the assessments required. Other social workers, however, considered that as decisions about eligibility and placement were eventually taken by residential services, only brief information about applicants should be sought from referring social workers. Overall, the impression was that information on applicants improved after these forms were introduced.

Medical assessment

The need for a comprehensive medical, functional and social assessment at the time of application was often discussed at panel meetings, but there were disagreements over who should conduct the medical assessment. General practitioners had often known the applicant and his family over years, but the consultant geriatrician had a medical team which specialised in assessment and treatment of elderly people. However, the expertise of hospital teams might lead them to suggest medical procedures which could overload diagnostic facilities (for example, through requests for the analysis of blood samples) or might be regarded by general practitioners as a "trespass" on their professional function.

A further problem was that consultants who made domiciliary visits to elderly applicants were paid a fee whereas a general practitioner was not. General practitioners nationally were therefore unwilling to do extra medical assessments on Part III applicants unless they were paid a fee for this service. Skilled negotiation by the community physician and the general practitioner on the panel found an "unofficial" way round this national problem. If a general practitioner submitted the report of a medical assessment to another doctor, no fee was required, whereas if this report was sent to a social services department, a fee was sought. Therefore, the local general practitioners agreed to submit a medical report on all Part III applicants providing this was sent to the specialist in community medicine and not to the social services department.

Throughout the years of the study, the local general practitioners sent medical reports to the specialist in community medicine, who then summarised the key factors in writing for residential services managers. The original report was then resealed and sent via the residential services section to the general practitioner who would be attending the new resident in the Home. Such a compromise partially met the need for a medical assessment on all Part III applicants, but unless the results of such an assessment were clearly described to either the applicant or the informal caregivers, it was of little use to a referring social worker when considering alternatives to Part III care.

One of the most important functions of these reports from general practitioners was that medical information on a new resident was available to the doctor who attended the Home. Medical notes on old people who were admitted to Part III care took at least three months to pass through the hands of the family practitioner committee. Unless the new general practitioner telephoned the previous one he had to treat a new resident without any medical records. If the original general practitioner had already sent the medical notes to the family practitioner committee, such information had to be given from memory.

Information "package"

The research suggested that applicants often had little knowledge of what Part III care entailed. To meet their needs, a working party, consisting of principal officers from residential and fieldwork sections and from the finance department produced an information package. It included a simple "do it yourself" assessment sheet which enabled applicants (or their caregivers) to assess how much they would probably be required to pay. Another document gave simple information about Part III Homes and the types of facilities they offered. This package was to be given to applicants and their caregivers during the social workers' initial visit. After a week the social workers would call to discuss the information and ensure that applicant and caregiver understood the implications of the decision.

Head of Home assessment

It was decided that heads of Homes should be more intimately involved in assessment and placement. When a place in a Home became available, the head visited the applicant and made arrangements for a trial day at the Home. It was expected that this would ensure that the applicant was still eligible for care and would be able to manage in the particular Home in which the vacancy was offered. At the same time, the applicant should gain information about the Home's regime and the reassurance of being received by someone who was already familiar.

Unfortunately, heads of Home were not always clear about the purpose of their visits and they lacked experience and skill at interviewing applicants in a non-residential environment. In most cases, friendly contacts were made between the heads of Home and the prospective residents but there were times when the familiar head of Home was not on duty during the "trial" day. Furthermore, the referring social workers and the heads of Home were not always aware of which information had been given to the applicants by the other. This sometimes resulted in applicants lacking information.

Heads of Homes attended group meetings organised by a new principal officer. These meetings increased the interaction of senior residential care staff and afforded opportunity for sharing problems such as uncertainty about the purpose of assessment visits prior to admission and the skills required to fulfil these.

Review of new residents in Homes

As a further step towards a more client centred approach, a review of new residents was piloted over several months by the research and development officer and the researcher. The review was conducted three months after admission and involved discussion with the head of Home, the applicant, an informal caregiver (invited by the applicant) and any care assistant or domestic staff who had had particularly close contact with individual applicants.

All the new residents were highly articulate about their feelings and welcomed the opportunity to review their position, discuss difficulties, suggest improvements and state their hopes for the future. The informal caregivers who attended these meetings were also happy to be asked their views. Not uncommonly, feelings and opinions which residents expressed through the medium of a review meeting were unknown previously either to the head of Home or to the care staff.

These meetings also revealed (to the surprise of some heads of Homes) that junior care assistants often had a great deal of information about the residents' problems and abilities. In fact, the junior staff (and sometimes the domestics) could know much more about individual residents than the heads of Home. The person who usually helped a resident to bath could be an important confidante for this was the only time a resident was alone in a room with an individual staff member.

The information which emerged during these meetings was simple but important. For example, a man who was a double amputee and in severe pain, had a blind wife who was also a resident in the Home. It was assumed that such a devoted couple would wish to spend most of their time in close proximity. However, at review they were seen separately and this enabled the husband to describe his exasperation at always being "the eyes" for his wife. Fond as he was of her, he longed for periods away from her and for masculine company over a game of cards. He also complained of severe pain which caused sleepless nights. As a result, more effective pain control was obtained for him and care staff involved him in card playing groups and other activities apart from his wife.

The conclusions of both the research and development officer and the researcher after these pilot review meetings was that systematic review would be a worthwhile job. However, considerable work would be required to dovetail information routinely collected on application forms with similar information collected on review and so produce an accurate assessment of improvement or deterioration. Such reviews could provide the basis for a systematic computerised census of residents which would give aggregated information on key factors such as their mobility or confusion. A rather different problem was that the reviews encouraged residents to say where they would like to be at a time when the economic need to maintain full bed occupancy did not facilitate extending transfers between Homes or indeed transfers between Part III care and sheltered housing.

Developments in resources

The access to data on the characteristics of applicants and the reasons for their application enabled service managers to identify gaps in provision and to present a case for change based on information as well as on professional opinions and idealism. The research had shown that a surprisingly high proportion of applicants could look after themselves given appropriate help apart from being unable to climb stairs or prepare a meal. To enable such applicants to retain their independence, other immediate crises had to be overcome. Some were occupying a hospital bed mainly for social reasons but were not fit enough to return home, some had homes which were unsatisfactory for them, others were unable to continue living with their relatives. Conversely, a number of applicants might have benefited from Part III but had deteriorated during their stay in hospital to the point where they were ineligible. Four developments during the project were designed to overcome these problems:

1. A "heavy" home care scheme providing intensive domiciliary support over a limited period.

2. Assessment flats in which applicants could live for limited periods to see if they were capable of independent living.

3. "Special" sheltered housing providing more intensive support than ordinary sheltered housing.

4. Part III maintenance groups designed to maintain the morale and functioning of Part III applicants in hospital.

The extent to which the repercussions of these developments could be monitored varied, for effects were likely to be cumulative and to continue after the end of the research. Research resources were also limited and so monitoring of the effects of developments had to be selective.

"Heavy" home care

The interim analysis of applications and the discussions of the inter-disciplinary panel revealed that some applicants were applying for residential care mainly as a result of a crisis in their own lives or the lives of their caregivers. The first chairman of the inter-disciplinary panel was subsequently appointed as home care organiser for the authority and she used the experience gained during panel discussions to establish a home care service aimed at assisting prospective applicants through these crises and facilitating their discharge from hospital.

It was anticipated that this service might delay or prevent the need for residential care, or at least would enable some applicants to make a more considered decision when they were not in a state of upheaval. The scheme was jointly financed by health and social services for an experimental period. As a result of its apparent success, the scheme was eventually put on to a permanent basis and was expanded.

Initially, a centrally based team of six specially trained home helps was set up. These were all car drivers and could visit old people as often during the day (or night) as required and vary their hours of work so that they could be available to give help at times of special need (such as early mornings and evenings). It was envisaged that during particular crises (such as a sudden bereavement), such home helps could be resident with the old person until the family was able to organise a more permanent arrangement.

Referrals for the scheme included all age groups, with four out of five being people over the age of 65 and 41% over 75. Most referrals for heavy home care were received from the casualty department of the acute general hospital. Very few came from psychiatric or geriatric hospitals whose patients the scheme had been intended to service. The heavy home care service was fulfilling a valuable function, but was not being delivered to the clientele for whom it had been planned.

Assessment flats

Interim analysis of Part III applications indicated that applicants resident in hospital at application would benefit from assessment in a

non-institutional environment.   Also, some Part III residents whose
condition had improved after their admission wished to return to a home
of their own but their ability to do so was in doubt.   There was a need
to establish a resource where such hospital patients and Part III
residents could have the opportunity of trying to care for themselves
and yet remain in touch with help should they need it.   To meet the need
a scheme for "assessment flats"   was set up.   This scheme was also

Table 15.1

Assessment/Rehabilitation Unit:

Characteristics of Residents +

	%
	(37)
Sex	
Female	65
Age	
Under 65 years	11
65-74 years	41
75-84 years	41
85 years or more	8
Admission from:	
LA OPH	54
Hospital	43
Private household	3
Discharge to:	
Sheltered housing	36
Private household	15
"Special" sheltered accommodation	12
Part III Home	9
Hospital	9
Boarding out/other	9
Still in unit	9
Length of stay	
0-12 weeks	65
13-25 weeks	23
26 weeks or more	13

+   For period September 1980 to February 1983.

jointly financed, initially on an experimental basis.   Subsequently, assessment flats became a permanent resource in the authority and their numbers were increased.

The scheme started by using four vacant staff flatlets attached to one of the Part III Homes. Although they had a separate entrance from the Part III Home, they were part of the same building and there could be telephone contact between the flats and the residential staff on night duty in the Home. The panel proposed that these flatlets should be turned into an assessment unit and staffed by a full-time occupational therapist. There was a special arrangement with the housing department which ensured that any resident in an assessment flat who was regarded as capable of independent life within ordinary sheltered housing would be provided with such accommodation on discharge. The objectives of the project were:

* To assess the client's ability to live independently.

* To continue rehabilitation of patients discharged from hospital.

* To evaluate housing needs and the most suitable placement on discharge.

* To continue intensive support immediately following discharge from the assessment flat.

The flatlets were to be entirely for elderly people who could be admitted from any source - a private household, hospital or a Part III Home.

Only fifty people passed through the unit during the first five years of its existence, too small a number to have an appreciable impact on the total number of applications. Initial results, however, were very promising (Table 15.1).

The flats seemed to open a route from Part III to the community. A follow up found that of twenty people admitted from Part III to the assessment flats only four returned to Part III, one went to a relative's household, five to special sheltered housing and ten (50% of this group) to an independent life in an ordinary sheltered housing environment.

In the same study, a similar number of assessment flat residents were admitted from hospital (including the geriatric and psychogeriatric hospitals). Here again, only two returned to a hospital. One quarter went into Part III care and half into ordinary sheltered housing.

"Special" sheltered housing

The interim analysis of research data showed that at least one third of Part III applicants were able to look after themselves - in the sense that they could eat, wash, dress and go to the toilet unaided. Partly in response to this finding, a special sheltered housing scheme was devised. It provided an alternative to Part III care for applicants who wished to look after themselves and were able to do so if given episodic help at particular times.

The scheme was developed collaboratively by senior managers in the social services and housing departments. It was decided that Part III Homes in the authority which did not contain lifts would be gradually closed and their valuable and extensive sites sold. In their stead, the housing department over an extended period would make available and maintain several complexes of special sheltered housing units.

These special sheltered housing schemes would be staffed by a full-time head of unit, a deputy and three full-time care assistants. A midday meal would be provided in a communal dining room and tenants in the special sheltered housing flatlets would be eligible for ordinary domiciliary services such as home helps, visiting chiropody and district nurses. Elderly people would retain their status as tenants and would be eligible for financial and other benefits which were not available to Part III residents. They could, for example, claim attendance allowances, social security supplementary benefits and additional needs allowances. For those with savings, the charges for accommodation and care would be lower than in Part III and, in contrast to the situation in Part III, the old people's rights of tenure would not be prejudiced by admission to hospital.

Every prospective special sheltered housing tenant would have to satisfy criteria for eligibility for Part III care. Owner occupiers would be eligible for these tenancies, unlike those of ordinary sheltered housing. Applications were to be submitted by both the housing department (from the housing list) and the social services.

Nearly half (45%) of the applicants for special sheltered housing had previously been local authority tenants. One fifth (22%) had previously owned their homes and a similar number had rented them privately. The rest had not had tenure or ownership of homes of their own because, for example, they had lived in the household of relatives. As Table 15.2 shows there were proportionately twice as many local authority tenants applying for special sheltered housing as there were for Part III care. As the previous accommodation of these applicants was likely to have been larger than the flatlet to which they were moving, the potential advantage to the housing stock of the local authority was clear.

The advantages to the social services department were perhaps less obvious. Applicants for special sheltered housing, by comparison with applicants for Part III care, were younger (the percentages over 85 years old were 12% and 39% respectively), were more often married (28% and 8% respectively) and were hardly ever severely confused (one special sheltered housing applicant only compared with 17% of applicants for Part III care). Careful monitoring of Part III applications showed no drop in the number of applicants who were alert and reasonably mobile, the group which the special sheltered housing scheme had been expected to divert from Part III, although, as discussed later, a higher proportion of more disabled applicants were admitted in the third year.

A pilot survey conducted by the social services department of ordinary sheltered housing tenants and of Part III residents suggested that, in terms of dependency, special sheltered housing tenants fell between tenants in ordinary sheltered housing and residents of Part III Homes. For example, the mean age of tenants in ordinary sheltered housing in 1983 was 74.9 years compared with the mean age of special sheltered housing tenants in 1981 of 77.8 years. The mean age of Part III residents in 1980 was 81.6 years.

The residents in the special sheltered housing unit who are described in Table 15.2 were in the first unit to be opened in the authority and so could be atypical. The first unit had been the result of much effort and negotiation. It was the prototype for more extensive development of special sheltered housing in the authority and much depended on its success. For this reason we obtained details of the residents admitted to the second special sheltered housing unit (although this was opened after our study ended). The residents admitted to the second unit

Table 15.2

Comparisons between Applicants for "Special" Sheltered

Housing and Applicants for "Ordinary" Part III

	Special sheltered+ % (78)	Ordinary Part III++ % (970)		DF
Sex			2.09	1
Male	32	24		
Marital status			38.69***	1
Married	28	8		
Age			28.68***	2
Up to 74 years	36	18		
75-84	53	43		
85+	12	39		
Residence at application			45.05***	2
Hospital	8	46		
Private household	82	45		
Usual household composition			20.54***	3
Alone	53	53		
With other elderly only	32	15		
And/or younger generations	2	15		
Tenure			31.74***	3
Owner occupier	22	19		
LA rented	45	21		
Privately rented	22	23		
Physical state			8.04**	1
Incontinent	-	11		
Mental state			35.14***	
Generally confused	1	17		
Occasionally confused	3	20		
Outcome			26.12***	3
Changed mind before admission	24	8		
Changed mind after admission	-	4		
Admitted to hospital within 3 months after admission	1	4		

+ Some questions contained a high percentage of no records. Re-allocation of these could reduce the size of the difference although they would be likely to remain statistically significant.

++ Includes applicants for HEMI.

Note:

The percentages do not add to 100 because some categories are not presented.

differed in that they were more likely to be living alone and less likely to be married. In this way, they were more similar than the first group to Part III applicants, and the long-term effect of this development may therefore be greater than the effect in the first year.

Hospital maintenance groups

The concern of panel members (and especially consultants) about the deterioration of hospital patients led to a suggestion of "maintenance groups" within the hospital environment. Reduction in the number of beds in the psychiatric hospital meant that there were vacant ward villas. It was anticipated that Part III applicants would live together in a ward villa where they would be able to enjoy greater independence. Furthermore, it would be possible to appraise their need for continued residential care and to assess whether some might be capable of looking after themselves in the community (for example, in sheltered housing).

As Part III applicants from the psychiatric hospital were on average younger and waited longer than others for a Part III vacancy, their need for a maintenance procedure seemed particularly important. Sadly, however, the projected maintenance group in the psychiatric hospital never started, for although the staff resources and accommodation were available, long-standing and unresolved conflicts between management and unions over staff deployment and cuts meant that the staff necessary to run the group could not be found.

Although a Part III maintenance group was established for a short while in the geriatric hospital, economic constraints again led to its being discontinued, although it was said to have been an effective way of maintaining physical abilities and morale.

Overall changes

The provisions we have been discussing were unlikely to affect the demand for Part III as measured in the number of applications. Typically they catered for a small number of people many of whom were not on our evidence likely to apply for Part III. This did not, however, mean that the number of applications were unaffected. During the course of the research the number of applications increased by a third between the first and second year of the study (June 1978 - May 1979/June 1979 - May 1980, not financial years as in the table below). As can be seen from Table 15.3 there was a drop following the study. Applicants decreased by 46% in two years, from 395 in the financial year 1981/82 to 212 in 1983/84.

The explanations for these changes are unclear but may well be different. At the start of the project, applications may have been discouraged by the institution of the panel which resulted, in the social workers' view, in decisions being taken by people who did not know the applicant, and who did not even necessarily work in the social services department. Also at this time there existed an informal filtering of applications whereby social workers contacted clerks in the residential services general office and gained information about where vacancies existed and the current size of the Part III waiting list.

Speculation about the drop in applications between 1982 and 1984 must be even more uncertain, since by that time we were no longer in close touch with the authority. The drop coincided, however, with a reduction of approximately 100 beds in the authority's old people's homes caused by the closure of Homes. This year also saw a period of industrial action when residential staff refused to accept any but "emergency admissions". Interestingly, there was a sharper drop in admissions from hospital than in those from the community. Social workers may have considered that old people in hospital were not in so much risk as those in private households.

Table 15.3:

Applications Registered in Consecutive Financial Years

Financial year	No of applications	% from hospital
1979-80	369	49
1980-81	384	45
1981-82	395	48
1982-83	317	44
1983-84	212	38
1984-85	230	43

The initial rise in demand followed by the sharp drop in demand as measured by number of applications could not be plausibly associated just with increases or decreases in alternative resources. These changes happened against a background of rapid expansion nationally in private Homes between 1979 and 1984 and we have no way of knowing how many prospective applicants for Part III care went into private residential care instead. We were not aware of any decreases in alternative resources large enough to explain the rise in applications between 1979 and 1980. Between 1982 and 1984 there was an increase of forty-two people supported by the local authority in private and voluntary Homes and also an increase of thirty-eight special sheltered housing units. Neither increase is sufficient to explain plausibly a drop of 183 applications.

There were also changes in practice and in the ways prospective applicants for Part III care were assessed which were partly influenced by this study. A system of multidisciplinary panels was set up in Area offices and these considered whether prospective applicants had been offered a full range of services and whether appropriate medical, functional and social assessments had been made available. These developments happened after the research ended, they were not monitored and so we have no way of knowing how many prospective applicants were "prevented" from needing Part III care.

Conclusion

This chapter has shown how the study authority used the research findings and confronted problems relating to assessment and resources which had been identified. We have also seen how difficult it was to introduce innovations which would divert potential applicants from Part III. In this way we have perhaps come close to the question with which we started. Why is it that successful polices of community care are so difficult to put into effect?

Some of the difficulties are shared with other promising innovations.

The reluctance of some social workers to carry out detailed assessments as required by the new form may have reflected a lack of interest in work with the elderly and the demands of other work which would make other changes in work with the elderly difficult to achieve. Difficulties in acquiring resources and the need for lengthy negotiations with staff and unions have no doubt delayed or prevented many more innovations than Part III maintenance groups. Other difficulties, however, arose from the situations of Part III applicants and are worth examining in more detail.

The basic problem is illustrated by our finding on special sheltered housing. Part III applicants share needs for adapted housing and extra care with a large number of elderly people who do not apply for residential care. Typically, these other elderly people are not in situations where they are cared for by people who are unable or unwilling to do so for much longer. Such degrees of dependency require speedy provision which may not be available in relation to special sheltered housing - only 10% of those applying for this resource applied from hospital. Therefore, such resources which are intended to divert potential applicants from Part III may be taken up by old people who wish to become special sheltered housing tenants but who would not have applied for Part III care in any event.

Efforts to overcome this situation may be influenced by the apparent success of the special assessment flats. Even our unsystematic evidence suggested that these flats not only diverted applicants from Part III but enabled some to leave Part III altogether. Their success might have been greater if there had been enough flats to ensure that vacancies in them were as easy to get as Part III beds, that they could be systematically offered to all Part III applicants and to all new residents three months after their admission.

Such a policy would require a determined targeting of resources at Part III applicants and new residents and a willingness to allow some resources including Part III to be under-used. It would also require attention to the assessment procedures for various resources and to establishing procedures for review. As it is difficult to predict who will apply for Part III, it would have to be accepted that resources designed to act as alternatives to Part III will be used by old people who would not otherwise become applicants. A policy of community care which relied on reducing need for Part III rather than simply reducing Part III places would, therefore, be expensive and difficult to implement.

Taken together, the developments emphasise the importance of joint finance and of the interchange between health and social services staff that took place in the panel. Panel members showed that even against a background of conflict and economic constraint innovations in care could be implemented. Although these may not always have reached the populations for whom they were primarily intended, they undoubtedly extended the range of choice and service available to other very old people.

191

16 Conclusions

Introduction

Twenty years before this study, Professor Peter Townsend (1962) reported on a survey of residents in Homes for the elderly suggesting that for many their admission to residential care was unwelcome and unnecessary.

> The majority of residents are not so handicapped by infirmity that they could not, given a small amount of support from domiciliary social services, live in homes of their own in an ordinary community. A large number enter Homes for reasons of poverty, lack of housing, social isolation and absence of secondary sources of help among relatives and friends, and they do so unwillingly. Few of them take the initiative themselves and rarely are they offered practical alternatives - such as housing, emergency grants and services or permanent help from the domiciliary services. Nearly all, once admitted, are expected to stay permanently, although the great majority, or so it seems, would prefer not to do so.

Sadly, Townsend's findings have been repeated in later research. There is now increasing evidence that most applicants:

* Do not want to enter long-stay Part III care (Shaw and Walton, 1979; Stapleton, 1976; Willcocks et al., 1982).

* Are generally not heavily dependent on others for help with self-care tasks (Bebbington and Tong, 1986; Bowling and Bleathman, 1982; Booth et al., 1983b; Wade et al., 1983).

* Are often not receiving intensive packages of services (Avon, 1980).

And that

*   In the opinion of social workers, around a third of applicants could be kept out of residential care given adequate resources (Avon, 1980).

*   Experimental, and in some circumstances, traditional services can keep some of them out (Challis and Davies, 1985; Levin et al., 1983).

In these respects, it is striking how far our findings confirm other research. We, like others, have found that applicants:

*   Often applied for Part III reluctantly and at the instigation of others.

*   Were not severely dependent.

*   Often had not had an adequate medical and functional assessment.

*   Often had poor housing or lacked a home of their own.

*   Were usually visited regularly by relatives whose problems often contributed to the reasons for application.

In addition:

*   Half of the applicants admitted from the community had not been receiving home help.

*   Social workers considered that up to a half of the applicants could remain in the community given adequate resources.

We know of no evidence that contradicts these conclusions. The question is not whether this situation exists but what should be done about it.

Implications

The implications of our findings are in two main groups. First, some have relevance to broad preventive measures which might, for example, ensure that becoming housebound does not lead to social isolation, that homelessness does not remove the power of choice, and that those overwhelmed by bereavement are identified and helped. If services were offered when relationships between applicants and relatives were being re-aligned in response to an old person's disability, subsequent conflict and crisis might be avoided. The second and main focus of our research, however, has been on situations and the context in which applications were made and it is about these that we have most to say. Here our approach differs in emphasis from that of other researchers in the field.

Traditionally, applications have been examined in terms of criteria and need which have often been based on measures of disability. Obviously, the State cannot afford to subsidise fit old people in an old people's home simply because they want to become residents. Nor can Homes take old people irrespective of how disturbed or disabled they may be or how they will fit into the current group of residents. For these reasons criteria of eligibility are required, and although they are applied flexibly in individual cases, they do affect the average levels of disability in old people's homes. For their part, researchers have been concerned with whether residents meet these criteria of eligibility - in short whether they need to be in Homes at all.

While we acknowledge the importance of criteria, our own emphasis has been on the even greater importance of choice. In our view, the aim of policy should be that no old person should enter an old people's home permanently unless they have made a considered and informed choice for admission or are too confused to weigh up alternatives. Our criticisms are not that many residents do not need to be in Part III - indeed, our evidence suggests that some patients in long-stay wards would be better off in Part III care - it is rather that they have been given too little real choice over their admission. Similarly, serious attention should be given to the wishes of those old people who, although not seriously disabled, nevertheless define themselves as needing Part III care.

The problem of providing choice does not arise primarily from the disabilities of the old people or the strains on their carers. These difficulties were generally not so severe that they could not have been managed or alleviated while the old people remained in the community. Choice was difficult to provide because of the context within which the application was made - often a hospital or the home of a relative who was unwilling to continue to provide care. It was the context of applications that appeared to have the greatest influence on the likelihood of an applicant progressing to long-term institutional care in a Home or a hospital ward.

The first problem in providing greater choice in such situations is that of resources. Our data support a determined policy of community care; they do not suggest that such a policy will be cheaper (as against more effective) than one which relies more heavily on institutions. On the evidence of this as of other studies (Levin et al., 1983; Plank, 1977), the average level of community services available to individuals as an alternative to Part III is low and would need to be increased. These services will almost inevitably be rationed on the basis of disability (a weak predictor of institutional admission) and will, therefore, serve many old people who would not be expected to enter Part III. In order to cope with "crises", it will be necessary to keep spare capacity in expensive resources such as heavy home care.

A determined policy of community care may also, in the long term, increase the average level of disability in Part III - hence requiring additional expenditure on staffing and facilities in the Homes without reducing the number of Part III places needed. Like Townsend (1962) we have argued that many potential residents could be cared for in the community, but like Bond and Carstairs (1982) we would also argue that there are others in the community or in hospital in need of Part III care. Indeed, applicants who on follow up were not in Part III were more likely than those who were in to be considered by professionals as misplaced.

For these reasons we would argue that determined efforts should be made to ensure that no one enters Part III unless they want to or the step is unavoidable and that those eligible for Part III and who wish to enter are not kept out. Experiments may be needed to adapt and equip Homes (for example, through the provision of hoists) to accommodate some old people who are currently excluded because of their disability. This might also ensure that the more disabled do not wait longer for admission than the less disabled. Such a policy should diminish some sources of demand for Part III by diverting potential applicants. It might increase other sources of demand by accepting for Part III some who are in unsatisfactory situations in the community or in hospital and who would usually be excluded. Whether the net effect would be to increase or decrease demand could only be determined by experience.

A second difficulty in implementing a determined policy of community care is that it requires a degree of collaboration between departments and professions which is hard to achieve. Interests conflict - for example, it is not in the interests of the housing department to keep sheltered housing units vacant to accommodate old people in crisis, nor do general practitioners necessarily wish to bear the consequences of maintaining very frail old people in the community at a high cost to relatives. All service providers could put to good use the resources that would be released if certain difficult or very disabled old people were not in their care.

Thirdly, a policy of community care requires a high degree of internal coherence. Applications may be discouraged by industrial action, the reduction of places in old people's homes or by arranging that decisions are reviewed at more than one level. However, there is little virtue in discouraging applications if the needs of those who might have applied are not addressed, and relevant resources provided. Unless alternative resources are provided when they are needed to the people who might otherwise apply for Part III, they will meet additional needs without reducing demand for Part III. Thus, the procedures for dealing with applications need to go hand in hand with the provision of appropriate resources and policies over their use and allocation and with improvements in practice. In more detail attention needs to be paid to:

Assessment

Our evidence suggested that many applicants were being admitted to Part III on the grounds that they lacked basic care or were at risk when the specific self-care difficulties or risks they faced had not been identified. A determined policy of community care would require that applicants should not be admitted to Part III unless the particular problems which made it difficult for them to look after themselves, or which caused anxiety to them or their caregivers had been identified. In particular:

* There would be an integrated medical, social and functional assessment prior to admission which would result in an integrated care plan.

* Applicants and their relatives would be told the results of this assessment if they wished to know.

* Assessment would include detailed appraisal of specific difficulty at particular times.

* Practical solutions would be offered and reviewed if tried.

* Social workers making the assessments would have appropriate training and an interest in the elderly.

Measures to support carers

Despite evidence that services can relieve the burdens of those caring for old people (Levin et al., 1983), the problems of carers are still given low priority by social services departments. In relation to applicants and potential applicants, these priorities would need to be changed so that:

* All those providing care to applicants (including neighbours) were identified and contacted by those assessing for Part III.

* The problems of carers and their conflicts with applicants were identified by professionals and discussed.

* Services were offered where appropriate and acceptable and, if possible, before the carer had reached a point where only the admission of the old person would do.

Measures to counteract the effects of hospitalisation

Ways would have to be found of overcoming the dilemmas which arise when an old person is blocking a hospital bed but cannot for the moment cope at home. In particular:

* Applicants would not usually be assessed in hospital on their ability to remain in the community.

* Rehabilitation and convalescent facilities would be developed and these would be offered before a decision was taken on permanent residential care.

* If other research confirmed that "a point of optimum recovery" existed, methods should be tried to prevent the deterioration of Part III applicants in hospital wards (for example, through Part III maintenance groups) and to ensure that as far as possible they were discharged before deterioration.

Measures to counteract housing problems

A key element in the demand for Part III was that an applicant was in a place (hospital, a relative's home, private old people's home, very unsatisfactory housing) where they could not remain. In this sense they suffered from a particular kind of housing problem, although one which was exacerbated and complicated by other factors. On the policies we are discussing applicants would not enter Part III simply as a solution to a housing problem. For example:

* Inter-disciplinary assessment and liaison between social services departments, housing departments and other professionals would in some cases enable one room to be made warm, safe and free from smell.

* For those applicants willing to accept it, the provision of sheltered housing would be expedited, especially if they were living in detrimental conditions, or with families who were unwilling to continue caring for them.

* Widows and widowers who had given up their homes to live with children would be eligible to apply for sheltered housing and given appropriate support when they first moved in.

* Younger more mobile applicants from psychiatric hospitals would

always be considered for other types of provision such as boarding out, sheltered housing or small group Homes which might be more suitable for some than a residential Home.

Measures to improve the quality of decisions

In our view, applicants and caregivers should make decisions about Part III on the basis of information which is accurate, as comprehensive as possible, and made available to them in a way they can understand. In particular:

* Applicants should be informed about alternatives to Part III that might be available to them and about conditions in Part III.

* Applicants should know that they do not have security of tenure in Part III, but that they may be transferred to hospital if their condition deteriorates.

* It should be possible for decisions to enter Part III to be reversed at least three months after admission.

* It should also be possible for residents whose condition improved after a more extended stay in Part III to be rehabilitated into sheltered housing or accommodation of their own.

Finally, we have shown that the evaluation of alternatives to Part III cannot rely simply on demonstrating that they cater for very disabled old people in a satisfactory way. In evaluating alternatives, what is at issue is the operation of a complex system of care which may go wrong not because the component parts are faulty but because they do not fit together satisfactorily. For these reasons the operation of community care policies must be monitored through, for example, occupancy rates, the waiting times for Part III, the number of applicants receiving low levels of services, the number of emergency admissions, the number of applicants admitted with low levels of disability and the rate of applicants from different hospitals and area offices. It is also important to monitor the number of admissions to private Homes or long-stay hospital wards. Pressures on old people to enter private Homes may be as great as in the case of Part III and the safeguards against unnecessary admission less. Such monitoring would need to be complemented by less structured methods of collecting data such as conversations with residents, social workers, nurses and consultants. Action would be taken on the basis of the experience gained. For example, Homes could be closed or their use changed if they were shown to be consistently under-occupied. Further attention might be focussed on area offices which produced an unusually high or low number of referrals.

Conclusion

It would be a pity if this book came to be seen as yet another attack on old people's homes. The constraints on choice and conflicts which residents experience before admission must have further complicated the tasks of residential care staff. The main problem lies not in the Homes but in the way in which or circumstances in which decisions to enter them are taken.

197

From the evidence of the follow up study some very disabled old people can maintain themselves in the community on their own, and some very confused old people can continue to live with their carers. Too often, however, the choice of old people seems to lie between life in an old people's home or geriatric ward, which is feared and unwanted, or a lonely and undignified life, dependent on exhausted relatives or spent next to a unemptied commode. Inevitably, the choices will continue to be limited and the needs of old people and their caregivers will to an extent still conflict. Nevertheless, the service developments and, in our view, increasingly good practice observed over the course of the project suggest that these dilemmas can be reduced. The challenge for professionals, as for researchers, is to show more clearly how this can be done and how the "need for care" can be recognised and met.

Appendix 1
Social and service characteristics of the study area

Introduction

In Chapter 1, we said the choice of the study area was primarily based on two factors. First, senior managers in both health and social services intended to review and develop their practice regarding residential care for the elderly and so improve collaboration. Second, the social services department had coterminous boundaries with the area health authority which would simplify the research and facilitate understanding of the organisational and procedural influences on applications for Part III.

This appendix compares the population and service characteristics of the study area to other areas. The study took place during the Rayner Review of DHSS Statistics. Statistics on service provision were not consistently available. We have had to make do with those that could be obtained.

The Small Area Statistics from the 1981 Census of Population have been used to provide comparative statistics on the social characteristics of the elderly population. As the the elderly population are in many respects different from those of the whole population, for example, in marital status and tenure, only those statistics available for the elderly population or for persons of pensionable age have been used.

Social characteristics

On most indicators of social characteristics of the elderly population there were few differences of any likely importance between the study area, outer London and England.

Some indicators, however, were of general interest to planning and evaluating services for the elderly. In the study area, approximately:

* One in four of all persons were of pensionable age or lived with persons of pensionable age.

* Six in ten elderly persons were women.

* Over seven in ten men aged 65 years and over were married. Elderly women were only about half as likely to be married.

* Four in ten persons of pensionable age lived alone and about half of those living alone were aged 75 years and over. Six in ten persons of pensionable age lived with others.

* A small percentage of persons of pensionable age lived in accommodation which lacked the basic amenities of exclusive use of a bath and inside toilet. This rose to one in eleven of persons aged 75 years and over.

The effects of age, gender, marital status and household composition on the rate of applications for Part III were discussed in Chapter 2 and that of the suitability of accommodation in Chapter 9. On these indicators, (the frequency of) elderly persons (with these social characteristics) in the study area were similar, on average, to those in outer London and England. However, in comparison with other authorities, the study area had higher proportions of persons of pensionable age living in owner occupied and private rented accommodation. The frequency of housing association accommodation among the elderly (2.5%) was, although not presented separately, similar to that found elsewhere.

Social service provision

The rate of permanent residents in local authority homes for the study area was slightly higher than the averages for outer London and England (Table A1.1). The rate of permanent admissions appeared to be much higher than that found elsewhere. At the time of the study, however, the authority appears to have counted transfers between Homes and re-admissions after short-term discharges (for example, admissions to hospital) as "permanent admissions", while more stringent criteria were followed elsewhere. We calculate that the rate of permanent admissions following a new application (a definition more in keeping with that used in other authorities) was 5.8 per 1000 aged 65 years and over.

Nationally and in outer London the rate of elderly residents in local authority homes declined slightly over the study period. A downward trend was also apparent in the study area.

The pattern of domiciliary social service and related provisions for the elderly in the study area differed in some respects from that found in other authorities though missing information makes firm conclusions difficult. Provision of sheltered housing, day care, home help (Table A1.2), meals and aids, but not adaptations, were all lower in the study area than national averages. With the exception of sheltered housing and regular day care places in local authority homes, the study area also had lower levels of domiciliary social service provision than the averages for outer London during these years.

Table A1.1

Levels of Social Services Residential Provision

	Average annual rate over study period		
	Study area+	Outer London	England

Residents

Number of LA supported elderly
permanent and short-stay
residents per 1000 population
65 years and over in:

LA homes	16.9	12.9	14.9
Voluntary/private homes	2.8	4.1	2.2

Admissions to LA homes

Number of elderly permanent
admissions per 1000
population aged 65 years and over ... 9.0++ ... 4.9 ... 5.2

% elderly permanent admissions
aged 85 years and over ... 32.0 ... 39.0 ... 36.0

Number of elderly short-stay
admissions per 1000 population
aged 65 years and over + ... 4.1++ ... 5.6 ... 7.5

+   Average based on two years as the figures were not available
for 1981.

+ + These rates may be unreliable, see text.

<u>Sources:</u>

     DHSS Personal Social Services LA Statistics:
The Statistics of Residential Accommodation for Elderly and for
Younger Physically Handicapped People.
       LA supported residents years ending 31 March 1979 to 1981,
RA/79/1 to RA/81/1.
       All residents in local authority, voluntary and private
homes years ending 31 March 1979 to 31 March 1981, RA/79/2
to RA/81/2.
OPCS Final Revised Mid-year Population Estimates 1978-1980
(unpublished).

Levels of Sheltered Housing and Social Services

Domiciliary Provision

	Average annual rate over study period+		
	Study area	Outer London	England

Sheltered housing++

Number of specially
designed dwelling units per
1000 aged 65 years and over:

	Study area	Outer London	England
With warden service	15	15	27
With no warden service	18	9	31

Day care for elderly

Rate per 1000 population
aged 65 years and over:

	Study area	Outer London	England
Day centre places	1.4	4.4	2.9
Regular day care places in Local authority homes	0.6	0.5	1.1

Home help

	Study area	Outer London	England
Number of elderly cases per 1000 population aged 65 years and over	71.8	91.6	95.0
% elderly cases aged 75 years and over	74.6	72.7	67.6

Meals

	Study area	Outer London	England
Number of main meals provided to elderly at home per 1000 population aged 65 years and over	295	509	387

Aids and adaptations

Number of cases of assistance to
elderly per 1000 population
aged 65 years and over:

	Study area	Outer London	England
Communication	8.7	19.4	12.7
TV/radio (supply/licence)	0.6	4.5	2.7
Other personal aids	21.9	38.3	28.2
Adaptation to private dwellings	6.9	6.6	3.3
Adaptation to LA dwellings	3.0	3.2	2.2

+ Averages have been based on one or two years only in some cases when, for example, the study area failed to return information in time or the format of published information was altered.

+ + Sheltered housing provision relates to 30 September 1977, and is taken from Bacon, V. Local Authority Housing for Elderly People, Social Services Buildings Research Team, Oxford Polytechnic. Extra units were developed by the Authority during the study period.

Sources:

DHSS Personal Social Services LA Statistics:-
Adult training centres for the mentally handicapped and day centres for the mentally ill, the elderly and the younger physically handicapped: years ending 31 March 1979, 1980, 1981, England. A/F79/8, A/F80/8, A/F81/8.

Home help service: years ending 31 March 1979, 1980, England. A/F79/1, A/F80/2.

Meals services: years ending 31 March 1979, 1980, England. A/F79/2, A/F80/2.

Domiciliary services, meals, aids and adaptations: year ending 31 March 1981, England. A/F81/18.

Aids to households: year ending 31 March 1980, England. A/F80/4.

OPCS Final Revised Mid-year Population Estimates (unpublished) 1978 - 1980

Health service provision

The rate of available beds in geriatric units was slightly higher, the average length of stay longer and the discharge rate lower than the national average (Table A1.3). It was not possible to obtain consistent information on psychogeriatric bed provision.

Rates of elderly persons treated by the home nursing service (district nurses) were slightly higher than the national average. The rate of provision of health visitors in the study area was similar to the national average (excluding school health visitors and assuming the concentration of domiciliary health visitors' work on the elderly was similar in the study area to the national average).

Table A1.3

Levels of Health Service Provision

	Average annual rate over study period		
	Study area	Outer London	England
Geriatric units			
Average daily available beds per 1000 population aged 65 years	9.1	4.6	7.7
Average duration of stay (days)	112.5	72.3	71.2
Discharges and deaths per 1000 population aged 65 years	26.5	21.4	37.2
Domiciliary			
Elderly persons treated by the home nursing service per 1000 population aged 65 years and over	221.9	+	202.1
Health visitors per 1000 population aged 65 and over + +	1.3	1.0	1.2

+ Data not readily available for outer London.

+ + Based on whole time equivalents, figures rounded to nearest 10 as at 30 September of each year excluding school health visitors.

Source:

DHSS 1985: NHS hospitals in England based on SH3 hospital return (unpublished).

NHS health visitors based on SR7 annual census of non-medical manpower (unpublished).

204

Conclusion

The authority was, in many relevant respects, similar to the general run of authorities in England. However, it differed in having more elderly persons living in owner occupied and private rented accommodation, slightly higher rates of both social and health service residential provision and rather lower levels of social service domiciliary provision. In none of these respects was it extreme. Other work in the Unit, Gorbach and Sinclair (1981), suggests that authorities which make relatively low domiciliary provision tend to concentrate this provision on the more elderly and hence more disabled section of the population. It is from this sector that Part III applicants are most likely to be drawn. This may explain the similarity in the levels of domiciliary services found among Part III applicants in this study to that found in others.

Appendix 2
Methodological issues

Methodological issues in the large-scale application study

Content of forms

When the researcher first had contact with the authority, it had no aggregated information on the numbers of old people applying for residential care or their characteristics. At the beginning of the research, the authority reviewed its Part III waiting list, determined the criteria for what constituted an application and began numbering applications.

The application forms were used to provide coded information on:

* Demographic characteristics (for example, age, sex, marital status).

* Setting at application (for example, hospital or private household).

* Accommodation (for example, suitability and tenure).

* Physical and mental state of applicant.

* Applicants' care network (for example, services received, next of kin, contact with friends and relatives).

* Applicants' mood and attitude to residential care.

* Reason for application.

* Status of application (for example, planned, emergency).

* Degree of urgency accorded to the application by the referring social worker.

In order to achieve consistency over time, all the coding was carried out by one of us (JW). The coding was done on the basis of all the relevant data on the form. Comparisons were made between forms completed in different years to see whether the information recorded was changing over time in a way which suggested that different coding conventions were being developed, or whether there were real changes in the applicants coming forward.

Three further checks were made. First, the quality of the data we coded was sometimes apparent from the number of "no record" codes which were common for some codes but not others. We did not use some information because of this. On other occasions we have commented on the implications of lack of information. Second, we made made comparisons between hospital and community applicants to see if the information on them varied by setting. Finally, and importantly, the small intensive study in which interviews were held with a sample of sixty applicants, caregivers and social workers indicated whether information given verbally differed from that contained in the relevant application form.

Uses and limitations of data

Application forms represented the social workers' views of what constituted a good "official" case for admission and were the documents used during the decision-making process. Their use enabled us to see how the applications and the resultant decisions were being justified.

Although information on forms included some reliable standard data (for example, on age, sex and setting at application), it almost certainly reflected the social workers' knowledge of the case, their enthusiasm for work with the elderly, their views on what factors constituted "eligibility" and their interpretation of imprecise terms such as "confusion". Inevitably, the forms were in many ways "political" documents and far removed from structured questionnaires which form the basis for much social research.

Despite its limitations, we believe that information from the application forms can be used to provide:

* <u>Basic information on the applicants</u> (for example, age, sex and marital status) which is of interest in its own right and can be compared with information gathered from other sources (for example, in the census).

* <u>Data on the "official" reasons put forward for application.</u> Irrespective of whether these were the "true" reasons as perceived by the applicant, caregiver or social worker, the application forms provide the best source of data on the "official" reason.

* <u>Information on the basis on which these arguments for care are presented</u>. The accuracy, nature and comprehensiveness of this data are themselves matters for investigation and reflect on the validity of the official reason.

Used with care, the data can also be employed in two other ways - to examine associations and to provide a minimum estimate of the prevalence of problems in the sample. For example, the finding that in this study privately rented housing provided a worse standard of accommodation than local authority housing was, on the basis of other evidence (1981 Census), not likely to reflect social worker bias. The number of applicants recorded as living in houses with an outside WC will almost certainly be an underestimate of the true number.

Changes in the characteristics of applicants over the study period

As will be seen from Table A2.1 there were fewer applications received during the first year of the study than in the two subsequent years. Although applications increased by one third between the first and second year of the study, it seemed probable that the lower number in the first year of the study reflected the degree of informal filtering of applications where there was doubt about eligibility or speed of admission. In the initial year these informal discussions had sometimes resulted in a formal application not being made.

Our data suggested that emergency admissions were more frequent during the first year than in the two subsequent years of the study.

Table A2.1

Planned/Emergency Admissions and Year of Study

| | Year of study | | | |
	1 June 1978 - 31 May 1979	1 June 1979 - 31 May 1980	1 June 1980 - 31 May 1981	Total
Initial admission	%	%	%	%
	(289)	(383)	(381)	(1053)
Planned	83	91	92	89
Emergency	17	9	8	11

Overall: $\chi^2 = 13.97^{***}$, DF = 2.

The accuracy with which emergency admissions were registered by clerks in the general office may have varied during this time especially if an applicant who was initially admitted as an emergency subsequently completed an application for long-term care. Conversely, it may also have been that the increase in the number of applications occurred entirely among what was termed "planned" admissions.

Treatment of re-applications

During the study period, 887 of the 1053 applications referred to persons who made only one application for Part III, and 166 cases involved re-application.

The sample of 970 applicants used in the main analysis of characteristics is based upon the 887 applicants who did not subsequently re-apply and the first application of those who did. Re-applicants differed from the rest in that at "earliest" application they were more likely to be women, to live alone in a private household, to have a walking problem and to change their mind regarding applying for Part III at that stage. Few, one in four, were admitted as a result of their initial application. On second application two in three were applying from an institution and many of these now had no other home.

Table A2.2

Long-Stay Re-applications and Year of Study

| | Year of study | | | |
| Long-stay applications | 1 June 1978 - 31 May 1979 | 1 June 1979 - 31 May 1980 | 1 June 1980 - 31 May 1981 | Total |
	%	%	%	%
	(289)	(383)	(381)	(1053)
One application only	88	85	81	84
Applicant re-applied				
Initial application	11	8	5	8
Second application	1	8	13	8
Third application	-	-	1	-

One v. more than one application: $\chi^2 = 5.76$, DF = 2.

On most characteristics, for example, confusion, re-applicants were similar to those with only one application. On two characteristics of applicants, however, there was a significant trend over the three years. Their age increased from 60% of applicants aged 80 years and over in the first year to 64% and 68% in the later years of the study. This appeared to be accounted for by a similar increase in the percentage of applications arising from a re-application. The age of initial applicants did not increase over the study period.

Levels of response in the outcome studies I and II

Outcome study I involved a follow up of all 1053 applications for ordinary Part III registered with the social services department between June 1978 and 31 May 1981 in terms of the location of the applicant as at 31 August 1981 (Table A2.3).

Follow up was achieved on 99% of the 1053 applications; only six applicants could not be traced. For 5% of deaths the date of death could not be found.

Outcome study II of the large-scale study, involved interviewing key people who knew about applicants' physical and mental condition, activities, etc. The appropriate sub-group was obtained by excluding 89 "previous" applications from the 1053 registered. Of the remaining 964 "latest" applications, 349 related to applicants known to have died by the follow up date of 31 August 1981 and a further six to applicants for whom no contact was made. This left a sample of 609 applicants eligible for follow up and in confirmed locations. The apparent anomaly between 964 "latest" applications and 970 "earliest" applications was accounted for by six applicants whose latest application was for special sheltered and hence excluded from these analyses.

Location at Follow Up: 31 August 1981

Location	N	%
Total	1053	100
Survivals		
Part III	388	37
Hospital - general	16	2
- geriatric	95	9
- psychiatric	39	4
Private/voluntary home	32	3
Other institution	17	2
Private household	117	11
Deaths		
Date known	331	31
Date not known	18	2

Information was obtained by interviewing professionals and other workers directly or indirectly involved with the care of the applicant.
The types of respondents reflected the location of applicants at the follow up date. Interviews were successfully conducted for all but forty applicants (7%) about whom only incomplete or indirect information was available. About half of these were applicants resident in private or voluntary homes; while it was not possible to obtain a personal interview some information was obtained by telephone.

Methodological issues in the small-scale study

Sample selection and level of response

From early August 1981, at the same time each week, the weekly inflow of applications for permanent admission to Part III was listed. The following types of case were then excluded:

* Applications for special sheltered accommodation.

* Applications from long-term hospital patients (i.e. in hospital more than six months prior to application).

* Re-applications from ex-residents of local authority homes who had been admitted to hospital.

* Applications from out county, private/voluntary homes, group homes, "boarding out", etc.

* Applications from the general hospital. This criterion was relaxed during the study.

The remaining applications, i.e. from private households, geriatric hospital and psychiatric hospital, constituted the sampling frame. This was stratified according to the following four categories as interim analysis of the large-scale study had shown fairly similar proportions of applications from each of these sources:

* Applicants from hospital usually living alone.

* Applicants from hospital usually living with others.

* Applicants from private households usually living alone.

* Applicants from private households usually living with others.

Applications were then randomly selected (by rolling a dice) from each of these categories to select four applications each week until fifteen in each category were successfully included.

By the eighth week, however, it was apparent that to compensate for failures all eligible cases were being selected. A decision was made to continue selecting all eligible cases each week until the quotas were reached.

Sampling and interviewing took about 28 weeks to complete. On average there were about nine applications registered per week. Overall about half of those were eligible by the above criteria. Almost all, 94%, of these eligible were selected and a half of those selected were successfully interviewed. These are averages and during the early interviewing period the proportion of successful interviews was higher.

Various problems occurred during the interviewing period which led to delays and a slight alteration in the sample. In the eighth week, during September, the flow of applications from the geriatric hospital was interrupted for a month owing to an infection on the wards. During November, social workers from the geriatric hospital were consistently under pressure of work arising from shortage of staff.

Negotiations with the principal social worker at the general hospital resulted in agreement for her social workers to participate in the study. Eventually five out of the sixty cases in the sample were from the general hospital. All eligible cases which failed because of "pressure of work" are included in the response rates quoted below even though in some cases the social worker was not approached (Table A2.4).

Letters explaining the purpose and confidentiality of the interviews were sent to applicants and to their informal caregivers, appointments were offered and an opportunity given for these to be confirmed or refused.

Applicants in the small-and large-scale studies were compared on characteristics recorded on the application form and their outcomes. Differences between the applicants in the large-and small-scale study were small, and with one exception, not statistically significant. In the small-scale study inadequate basic care or risk was more frequently asserted with recorded evidence than without though there was very little difference in the frequency of the assertion itself. This difference could reflect improved recording practices, the new application form or changes in coding. This and the other non-significant differences would not alter the conclusions drawn from the small-scale study as these were not based on the prevalence of applicants' problems.

The reasons for refusal in Table A2.4 reflect difficulties and delays in the decision-making process. The small sample is likely to underestimate these difficulties. In other ways it is believed to be representative.

Table A2.4

Reasons for Non-Response

	Reasons+	Cases
	N	%
	(69)	(61)
Social worker refused because:		**52**
Pressure of work	18	
Possible distress to applicant/difficult case	12	
Applicant confused/ill	10	
Social worker left/delayed/case lapsed	**12**	**20**
Case closed because:		**26**
Emergency admission only	4	
Applicant changed mind	4	
Applicant unsuitable	2	
Applicant ill (withdrew)	2	
Applicant died	4	
Applicant refused	**1**	**2**

+ More than one reason was given for eight cases.

Social workers in small sample

Thirty-five social workers were interviewed in the small-scale study. Between them they also covered an estimated 62% of the 197 applications made in the last six months of the large-scale study (excluding applications for special sheltered accommodation, from applicants resident "permanently" in institutions, and from out county sources). It should be remembered that data collection on the large sample finished before the full sample had been drawn for the small-scale study. As almost all the social workers from the geriatric and psychiatric hospitals were interviewed, there was a lower representation of social workers who supported applications from the community. This arose in part from staff movements and the higher number of social workers in area offices presenting only one application over a long period of time.

Content of interviews

As far as possible, similar questions were asked of applicants and their informal caregivers except that caregivers were asked more detailed questions about the nature and repercussions of their caregiving duties. Interviews with applicants and informal caregivers were lengthy, usually lasting around one hour or more. Interviews with referring social workers were briefer.

To assist interviewers to conduct briefer interviews with applicants who were particularly frail or tired some questions were designated as less important than others. Seven essential areas of questioning were identified.

1. The <u>context of the application</u> including <u>quality of applicants' present lives.</u> Applicants were asked about their personal "roots", previous occupations and interests, and events which they thought had started their present difficulty, their current social contacts and the gains and losses they had experienced during the process leading to their need for residential care.

   The nature of their social isolation was explored, and the number and nature of their social contacts (or lack of them) identified.

2. <u>Lack of self-care ability and mobility problems.</u> Applicants and caregivers were asked how applicants managed tasks at each period of the day - starting with the time they usually got up - and also about sensory abilities, dexterity, balance, incontinence, memory and pain.

3. <u>Risk.</u> Applicants and caregivers were asked about risk, and attempts made to discover who was worried about what and whether this anxiety had arisen from the experience of a dangerous event or was a worry about anticipated danger.

4. <u>Stress on informal caregivers.</u> The "closest" informal caregivers were asked about the types of caregiving task which were stressful and the repercussions of this stress on their family and social lives, on their physical health and on the quality of their relationship with the applicant. Parallel, but less detailed questions were asked of applicants about their perceptions of their caregivers' burdens.

5. <u>Lack of, or unsuitable, accommodation.</u> Interviewers explored the specific environmental problems which existed in relation to stairs, warmth, security and nearness to shops and friends. Information was also sought about how, why and when tenure or ownership of homes had been relinquished.

6. <u>Attitude to Part III and decisions to apply.</u> Applicants and their caregivers were asked whether the applicant had reached a definite decision about entering residential care, whether they had visited a Part III Home, what they expected to gain and miss on admission and whether there had been adequate time to make the decision. Their knowledge of alternatives to residential care was assessed by use of a brief checklist of services such as home help, sheltered housing and day care. Applicants in hospital were asked special questions

about whether, and how, they felt being in hospital had affected their decision.

7. <u>Services</u>. Applicants and their caregivers were asked about the advantages and shortfalls of the services they had received, and about their contact with the social worker who had submitted the application. Social workers were asked more detailed questions about the professional problems and issues which were raised by the application in question.

Limits and uses of data

The data provided by these interviews were used in a variety of ways:

* Some questions were closed and the replies counted and reported as for an ordinary questionnaire.

* Some questions invited lengthy replies, for example, the applicant's perceptions of the origins of their troubles, and these were classified or rated by the principal researcher.

* Case histories have been used to illustrate particular points and draw on all the material available from the three interview schedules, the interviewer's opinions and the application form.

* Applicants have been divided into groups, again on the basis of material from all five sources.

The number of applicants included in the study was small enough for the principal researcher to get to know the material on each of them intimately. This provided a depth to our understanding of the processes leading to applications and an opportunity to compare the perceptions of different actors in the same situation.

Conclusion

A number of different issues have been discussed in this appendix for both the large-and small-scale studies. The link between them is that each issue potentially could have introduced biases which would have altered the description of findings, their analysis and conclusions.
   We have concluded that in the large-scale study:

* The levels of response in outcome studies I and II were high and we succeeded in gaining relevant information from almost all of the appropriate samples of applicants on their states at follow up.

* The exclusion of the second or later application for those who re-applied for admission to Part III from the description and analysis of the characteristics of applicants would not affect conclusions from that analysis.

* The combined analysis of applicants and outcome over the three-year period of the study was not affected by underlying real trends in applicants' characteristics and the changes which did occur would be unlikely to lead to alterations in the conclusions.

and in the small scale study:

* The social workers interviewed reflected the variety of those who would be submitting applications for Part III in the study area at that time although community social workers were somewhat under-represented.

* The applicants' characteristics and outcomes in this study were similar to those in the large-scale study.

Overall, we conclude that both studies are adequate for the purposes for which they were intended and used.

Appendix 3
Information on outcome

Introduction

As you will recall from Chapter 13, the residence of the applicant at the time of application was key in suggesting where, if not Part III, the applicant was likely to reside at follow up. About two-thirds of persons resident at application in a private household were admitted to Part III and a similar proportion were admitted from those resident in hospital at application. Those not admitted to Part III, however, tended to remain within the same sector, i.e. private household or hospital, from which they applied.

The three tables in this appendix provide a tabular summary presenting the number of applicants with selected characteristics who were resident in private household or hospital at application and the percent that at follow-up had been admitted to Part III (Table A3.1), were resident in a hospital (Table A3.2) or were resident in a private household (Table A3.3). This sample of 967 applications includes those with a follow-up of at least six months. The first row of Table A3.1, for example, indicates that on 114 applications the applicant was male and resided in a private household at application. By the time of follow up, 61% of the applications had resulted in admission to Part III. The small percentage of other outcomes, eg. to private or voluntary home, boarding out, death, etc., are not presented so looking across tables, the percentages will add to less than 100%.

We hope that these tables will help others studying applications for admissions to Part III to make comparisons to the data in this study.

Table A3.1

Applications with Part III Outcome by Selected Characteristics and Residence at Application

Residence at application

Selected characteristics at application	Private household (N)	%	Hospital (N)	%	Total+ (N)	%
All applications	(432)	65	(444)	69	(967)	68
Sex						
Male	(114)	61	(90)	67	(224)	66
Female	(318)	67	(354)	70	(743)	69
Age						
Under 80	(160)	61	(161)	76	(353)	69
80 and over	(271)	69	(281)	65	(611)	68
Difficulty climbing stairs						
None	(119)	69	(99)	75	(248)	73
Some	(199)	65	(116)	67	(345)	67
Can't do	(101)	62	(195)	66	(320)	66
Number of self-care difficulties						
0-1	(99)	66	(120)	75	(248)	71
2-3	(175)	64	(234)	70	(443)	68
4-8	(151)	66	(76)	55	(252)	64
Confusion						
Not mentioned	(268)	63	(264)	73	(584)	69
Occasional	(93)	75	(103)	71	(218)	74
Severe	(71)	61	(77)	51	(165)	57
Problems with						
Confusion only	(78)	72	(93)	68	(185)	69
Mobility only	(213)	63	(201)	72	(446)	68
Both	(86)	66	(85)	57	(196)	64
Neither	(54)	63	(63)	78	(135)	73
Homelessness						
Not homeless	(312)	62	(253)	69	(287)	62
Homeless	(108)	75	(165)	70	(194)	75
Applicant's attitude to Part III was						
Positive/accepting	(231)	68	(255)	74	(526)	72
Reluctant/negative	(86)	59	(83)	69	(186)	63
Doesn't understand/ other	(26)	58	(46)	43	(79)	49
Social worker's presentation of urgency						
Urgent/before event	(175)	74	(61)	66	(274)	73
As soon as possible	(151)	62	(101)	73	(266)	67
Not urgent	(38)	50	(2)	50	(43)	49
In hospital bed/other	(22)	55	(240)	70	(278)	68

+ Includes fifty cases "in Part III" and forty-one "in other institutions" at application. Numbers in subtotals may not add to the total for the residence group as "no records" are not presented.

Table A3.2

Applications with Hospital Outcome
by Selected Characteristics and Residence at Application

Residence at application

Selected characteristics at application	Private household (N)	%	Hospital (N)	%	Total+ (N)	%
All applications	(432)	5	(444)	17	(967)	10
Sex						
Male	(114)	8	(90)	12	(224)	13
Female	(318)	4	(354)	18	(743)	14
Age						
Under 80	(160)	6	(161)	13	(353)	12
80 and over	(271)	5	(281)	19	(611)	15
Difficulty climbing stairs						
None	(119)	3	(99)	12	(248)	12
Some	(199)	6	(116)	13	(345)	12
Can't do	(101)	6	(195)	22	(320)	18
Number of self-care difficulties						
0-1	(99)	4	(120)	14	(248)	13
2-3	(175)	3	(234)	16	(443)	14
4-8	(151)	8	(76)	24	(252)	16
Confusion						
Not mentioned	(268)	4	(264)	14	(584)	12
Occasional	(93)	4	(103)	14	(218)	12
Severe	(71)	10	(77)	32	(165)	26
Problems with						
Confusion only	(78)	5	(93)	17	(185)	11
Mobility only	(213)	4	(201)	15	(446)	9
Both	(86)	8	(85)	26	(196)	15
Neither	(54)	4	(63)	10	(135)	6
Homelessness						
Not homeless	(312)	5	(253)	13	(287)	7
Homeless	(108)	6	(165)	3	(194)	15
Applicants attitude to Part III was						
Positive/accepting	(231)	5	(255)	11	(526)	8
Reluctant/negative	(86)	3	(83)	19	(186)	10
Doesn't understand/other	(26)	4	(46)	33	(79)	20
Social worker's presentation of urgency						
Urgent/before event	(175)	3	(61)	16	(274)	6
As soon as possible	(151)	7	(101)	16	(266)	10
Not urgent	(38)	-	(2)	-	(43)	-
In hospital bed/other	(22)	-	(240)	17	(278)	14

+ Includes fifty cases "in Part III" and forty-one "in other institutions" at application. Numbers in subtotals may not add to the total for the residence group as "no records" are not presented.

**Applications with Private Household Outcome
by Selected Characteristics and Residence at Application**

Selected characteristics at application	Residence at application					
	Private household		Hospital		Total[+]	
	(N)	%	(N)	%	(N)	%
All applications	(432)	23	(444)	3	(967)	12
Sex						
Male	(114)	18	(90)	3	(224)	11
Female	(318)	24	(354)	3	(743)	12
Age						
Under 80	(160)	28	(161)	4	(353)	14
80 and over	(271)	19	(281)	2	(611)	10
Difficulty climbing stairs						
None	(119)	21	(99)	3	(248)	11
Some	(199)	23	(116)	4	(345)	15
Can't do	(101)	23	(195)	2	(320)	9
Number of self-care difficulties						
0-1	(99)	27	(120)	3	(248)	13
2-3	(175)	24	(234)	3	(443)	11
4-8	(151)	18	(76)	3	(252)	12
Confusion						
Not mentioned	(268)	26	(264)	4	(584)	14
Occasional	(93)	16	(103)	2	(218)	8
Severe	(71)	18	(77)	1	(165)	9
Problems with						
Confusion only	(78)	19	(93)	1	(185)	9
Mobility only	(213)	25	(201)	4	(446)	14
Both	(86)	15	(85)	2	(196)	8
Neither	(54)	30	(63)	5	(135)	15
Homelessness						
Not homeless	(312)	25	(253)	4	(287)	25
Homeless	(108)	15	(165)	1	(194)	4
Applicants attitude to Part III was						
Positive/accepting	(231)	19	(255)	2	(526)	10
Reluctant/negative	(86)	33	(83)	2	(186)	17
Doesn't understand/ other	(26)	23	(46)	7	(79)	11
Social worker's presentation of urgency						
Urgent/before event	(175)	14	(61)	3	(274)	10
As soon as possible	(151)	27	(101)	4	(266)	13
In hospital bed/other	(22)	32	(240)	2	(278)	5

+ Includes 50 cases "in Part 3" and 41 "in other institutions" at application.
  Numbers in subtotals may not add to the total for the residence group as
  "no records" are not presented.

Appendix 4
The panel: response to central government guidelines, interim research report and eligibility criteria agreed

Introduction

Panel members wished to produce agreed guidelines for eligibility for care in an ordinary Part III Home, a Part III home for the elderly mentally infirm, geriatric and psychogeriatric hospitals.

These are examples of the types of agreements reached. First, panel members agreed their response to central government guidelines.

Second, they responded to a research analysis and report of the first 322 Part III applications received during the study period. Panel members selected paragraphs from this interim report. These paragraphs are presented in italics. They are followed by the panel's response to the findings in each paragraph and its recommendations for action.

Finally, panel members agreed a broad spectrum of disability which indicated which people were more appropriate for care in an ordinary Part III Home or in a home for the elderly mentally infirm. Applicants requiring further assessment or regarded as inappropriate for any type of Part III care would be considered eligible for long-term care in a geriatric or psychogeriatric hospital bed.

Central government guidelines - ordinary Part III

The panel concurs with the views of the DHSS (A Memorandum of Guidance, July 1977), which says:

> Residential Homes are primarily a means of providing a greater degree of support for those elderly people no longer able to cope with the practicalities of living in their own homes, even with the help of domiciliary services. The care provided is limited to that appropriate to a residential setting, and is broadly equivalent to what might be provided by a competent and caring relative able to respond to emotional as well as physical needs. It includes, for instance, help with washing, bathing, dressing, assistance with

220

toilet needs, the administration of medicines when a resident falls sick, the kind of attention someone would receive in his own home from a caring relative under guidance of the general practitioner or nurse member of the primary health care team. However, the staff of the Home are not expected to provide the professional kind of health care that is properly the function of the primary health care services; nor should residential Homes be used as nursing Homes or an extension of hospitals.

In considering "criteria" for Part III Homes, the admission and retention of residents must also take into account the well-being of the elderly already in residence. The panel also recognises that to disregard the needs of staff in residential homes, is to invite patterns of care which might be less than satisfactory.

Government guidelines - Homes for elderly, mentally infirm

For the purpose of this paper, the panel wishes to refer to H.M.72/71, "Better services for the elderly, mentally infirm", which relates to the category of mild dementia, which it states should be nursed in Homes for the elderly, mentally infirm.

> This is by far the largest of the three categories of elderly persons with dementia. Those in this category are mildly confused, and may have a tendency to wander, but, though occasionally restless, over-active, noisy, or aggressive, do not need continuous nursing care. Their condition may be associated with certain physical disorders, such as some degree of incontinence. Given appropriate care and support, particularly at night, they can be looked after satisfactorily at home or in a residential Home. The local authority, health and social services thus have a large and vital part to play.

In addition, Homes for the elderly, mentally infirm should take people with mild degrees of psychiatric or behavioural upset, such as do not require mental hospital treatment but are so odd as to be intolerable to the ordinary population of the Part III Home.

The report of the panel

(A report based on the analysis of 322 applications by the National Institute for Social Work, May 1980)

The panel felt that some of the observations made by the study would support local rather than borough-wide initiatives, for example, the use of a Health Centre where multi-disciplinary assessment and other linked developments might be attempted. It was felt that multi-disciplinary assessments should be intensified and that full support should be available by the combined geriatric services to provide follow-up treatment.*

The social services department is considering an experimental "prevention" service, serving a selected district of the borough where support services would operate in an integrated and flexible way, in order to minimise the demands on health and social services residential resources. The panel felt that such a project had great potential as an eventual model for a borough-wide preventative approach, and was

221

consistent with its own thoughts on the role of field services for the very elderly.

Essential to any such effort would be ease of access to services. The panel favoured a central point providing information and advice for inquiries, both night and day, which could also mobilise required help.

1. *Assessment*

a. *The environment in which applicants are living when assessed appears to influence how their capacities are perceived, and described, and might also affect an applicant's motivation and performance with regard to self-care tasks.*

   Further work would be needed to clarify whether applicants assessed in hospital are likely to be seen as "worse" than similar applicants in the community and hence rejected for Part III when suitable for it, or discouraged from returning to the community when they could manage there with appropriate support.

   The importance of assessment was endorsed by the panel for both pre-and post-admission stages. The panel was particularly concerned that the motivation of "hospital" Part III applicants should be sustained if not strengthened.

Recommendations

i. Consideration should be given to ways of maintaining and improving motivation amongst hospital applicants for Part III. Essential to such an objective was assessment.

ii. In view of the "disabling" effect which hospitalisation has on many elderly people, ways must be sought to relocate them satisfactorily and speedily, once their medical needs are resolved.

iii. "Assessment should be recorded in a form which is as standardised as possible.

b. *There are ambiguities over the meaning of words like "incontinence", "confusion" and "depression" which are used in assessment. Some of the conditions described under these terms might respond to medical treatment, as might some of the sensory defects which were also common in the sample. Consideration might be given to ensuring appropriate medical assessment.*

   The Sub-Group recognised the treatment possibilities which an adequate medical assessment might enable, thereby broadening disposal options.

---

* The Consultant Geriatrician's view was that an intensive geriatric medical assessment was desirable for all applicants for long-stay Part III accommodation. The panel recognised the immense potential of volunteer workers to encourage motivation, and felt full advantage should be taken of this possibility. (The attention of the panel was drawn to the Geriatric Hospital "Part III Maintenance Group".

Recommendations

i. Elderly persons who display incontinence, confusion, depression, or sensory defects, should be more thoroughly investigated as a precondition to entering Part III. One implication of this would be the need for medical data of greater depth.

c. *"Assessment" is usually conducted in terms of difficulties of applicants' rather than in terms of their interests, ambitions and potentials. Planning for communal life in a residential home and appropriate placement implies a need for such information, particularly if applicants are to be helped to maintain contact with their previous networks.*

The positive aspects of an applicant's life, for example, existing social contact, and hobbies, were important to a sensitive and planned care programme.

Recommendations

i. This dimension should be incorporated in the Part III application form, currently being revised.

2. *Applicants Living Alone (50% of Sample)*

Most of these applicants were said either to lack basic care or to be "at risk". Most were visited frequently by relatives and provided with many domiciliary health and social services. Further understanding of the nature of "risk" in this group might elucidate what it involved, who was most worried by it, and the precise measures needed to combat it.

The panel shared the report's view that the term "at risk" required elucidation.

Recommendations

i. The term "at risk" be studied by classifying situations which are thought to place the elderly "at risk" (The NISW Researcher has been invited to consider this as a further project for her work in Croydon).

ii. On the application form the term "at risk" should not be used without specifying reasons.

3. *Applicants Living With Other Elderly People (14% of Sample)*

These applicants received neither as many services as those alone, nor as few as those with families including younger people. Yet a higher proportion of this group than others had been admitted to hospital by the time their application was made. The types of domiciliary service which enable one elderly person to care for another may differ from those appropriate for applicants living alone, and eligibility for services is also affected by applicants living alone, and by the presence of other, apparently active, although elderly people in the household. There seems to be considerable scope for preventive work with this group.

The panel endorsed the recognition by the report of "considerable" scope for preventative work with this group, particularly as the higher incidence of hospital admissions tended to indicate a greater prevalence of pre-admission crisis. It seems to be the case that elderly carers "soldier on" longer than younger carers. It was very important to identify early signs of the need for support services, though at the same time recognising the reciprocal dependency which often arose between elderly carers and the cared-for.

Recommendations

i. In order to provide a support input of sufficient sensitivity, contact should be made with the elderly household as early as possible as a prelude to any major decisions needing to be made with the clients. (It was felt that Good Neighbour Schemes, working in partnership with the Fieldwork Service Group, might provide such a level of familiarity with the needs of these households, perhaps more appropriately in the early stages, than the statutory services).

4. *Applicants Living With Families Containing Younger Generations (19% of Sample)*

There was evidence of stress, conflict, and depression amongst these applicants and their caregivers. Despite this, very few families in this group were receiving statutory domiciliary services. It may be wondered whether such services might be a more effective measure for preventing the need for residential care with this group than they may be with applicants alone, and at risk. Preventative work would imply the identification, prior to application of those "at risk" of entering Part III care.

The researcher's impressions were that the problems of many caregivers appeared to be long-standing, and largely unrecognised until a Part III application was made.

Most applicants living with younger families had given up their own homes. It would be worth exploring how these decisions came to be made, and what types of provision might have been appropriate to the old person at that time, and to the families after they received them.

As with the group in 3, above, there seemed a problem of access to support at a sufficiently early stage (though not necessarily with the dimension mentioned above, of mutual dependence). The panel felt that publicity on service availability might be of particular relevance to such households. Part III applications in some cases need not proceed to completion if a pre-emptive supportive approach is adopted, for example, shared care between community and Part III.

Recommendations

i. Earlier contact should be made by the statutory services with these

224

households, though in the earlier stages it might be more appropriate and acceptable to families if Good Neighbour Schemes fulfilled this role, working in partnership with the statutory services.

ii. Greater effort should be made to reach such families with information about services, and this particular finding should be communicated to the voluntary sector.

iii. Maximum support should be given by the statutory services to the NISW suggestion to carry out a study of "support needs for caring (younger) relatives", which should embrace the nature of "risk" and "burden".

N.B. The panel acknowledged that an early intervention scheme would inevitably lead to a different pattern of demand on services.

5. *Applicants Living In Private/Voluntary Homes Or Housing Associations (9% of Sample)*
   The lack of clear contracts of eligibility for residence in some Homes or Housing Associations means that some old people can be told to leave or refused re-entry when admitted to hospital. An impression is that some applicants entered this private or voluntary accommodation when they were relatively mobile, but that they could not be retained when they became more frail or confused. Unlike private tenants, they had no legal right of tenancy or redress.

   The relatively large population of such premised in Croydon aroused the concern of the panel in view of its future implication to the Part III service, as well as for the distress caused to such applicants through enforced "transfer".

Recommendations

i. Efforts should (somehow) be made to ensure that the terms and rights of elderly people entering such establishments in Croydon should be as explicit as possible.

ii. A further examination should take place of these applications with a special reference to the increasing numbers, and reasons for applications amongst this category.

6. *Applicants In Hospital At Application*

   47% of the applicants were in hospital at application - a classification which cuts across the living groups previously discussed.
   Little information was available on applicants' recent histories of hospital admissions and transfers between hospitals. Enquiry into a few individual cases indicated that a hospital admission could set in train a whole series of disruptive events which culminated in long-stay institutionalisation. The nature of this process requires further study as does its effect on particular small groups, such as the blind.
   Further enquiry might also be made into applicants, who were "resident in hospital only", and into how this situation came about.

It would also be interesting to know whether the provision of suitable accommodation might enable some homeless applicants to continue a degree of independent living for a little longer.

The panel recognised that adequate assessment and rehabilitation opportunities in hospital were as crucial to a patient's well-being as appropriate "placement" opportunities, post-treatment.

Recommendations

i. In view of the occurrence of elderly patients releasing their home whilst having long periods of treatment in hospital, fieldworkers and hospital staff should be offered guidance on advice to be given to clients and families regarding disposal of accommodation, to encourage maintaining existing accommodation for as long as possible.

ii. The danger of institutionalisation might be relieved if within the treatment programme, formal social/medical prognoses were made, and that once the patient's potential had been recognised, every encouragement should be given to their motivation within a rehabilitation programme.
    In addition, the panel identified further important issues on which it made the following recommendations:

R.i. The housing department should be made aware of the report, and possible implications for its service, and invited to join the panel's discussion.

R.ii. In particular, the views of the housing department should be invited on the potential of further flexible use of sheltered accommodation, and the possibility for group living in Council property.

R.iii. Greater provision for the elderly mentally infirm, either residential or community, should be sought.

The panel had become aware that waiting time for a place in a Home for the elderly mentally infirm is substantially longer than that for a non-specialist Home.
The Chairman was requested by the panel to circulate the report as widely as possible, particularly to those organisations and working parties with a planning responsibility for services for the elderly.

Table A4.1

Panel Criteria for Part III Application - EMI

The table below identifies the range of "behaviour" associated with acceptance and non-acceptance (in principle) of applicants/residents for the Part III service (EMI) assuming that the criteria overleaf are satisfied in all respects other than "behaviour".

	Incontinence	Socially un-acceptable behaviour	Aggression	Over-activity	Noisy	Wandering
Features normally associated with acceptance or appropriateness	Occasional accidents. Incontinence due to change of surroundings or illness. * Needs toiletting after meals. Irregular incontinence due to dementia.	Oddities or eccentricities in manner of apparel.	Occasional swipe and/or bad word.	Needs to wander round the home indoors.	Occasional explosion or rebellion against authority.	Walks ++ but finds own way back to EMI Home.
Features requiring further assessment	Incontinence for medical/physical reasons - to be referred to geriatrician.	Alcoholism.	Persistent intimidatory displays which frighten other residents.	Persistent restlessness accompanied by raised heart rate i.e. 90/min.		
Features normally associated with inappropriateness	Smearing or incontinence for physical reasons. persistent incontinence of urine due to dementia.	Sexual displays Persistent stealing. Fire-risk behaviour Dirty and disgusting habits with faeces etc.	Violence persistent or sporadic towards other residents.	Restlessness leading to risk of injury.	Persistent screams and bangs and repetitive noises.	Defeats double handle doors and cannot find own way back to Home.

* A month's settling period is normal.

Table A4.2

Panel Criteria for Part III Application - Ordinary

The table below identifies the range of ability and behaviour associated with acceptance and non-acceptance (in principle) of applicants/residents for the Part III (ordinary) service.

	Mobility	Dressing	Feeding	Continence	Sleep	Social relations	Co-operation	Bathing	Medication	Communication	Orientation
Features normally associated with acceptance appropriateness	Mobile including stairs.	Dresses correctly unaided.	Feeds correctly unaided at appropriate times.	Fully continent.	Regular pattern.	Normal relations.	Actively co-operation.	Can bathe without assistance.	No medication.	Normal contact.	Mentally alert.
	Mobile not stairs.	Dresses imperfectly but adequate.	Feeds adequately with maximum supervision.	Occasional accidents of urine.	Needs hypnotics.	Selective relations.	Passively co-operative.	Needs occasional supervision.	Occasional medication.	Slight difficulty due to physical disability. Can indicate needs.	Short-term memory retention.
	Mobile with aid.	Dressing with minimum supervision.				Family relations.	Requires frequent encouragement and/ or persuasion.	Needs constant supervision/ help.			
	Mobile in chair, little supervision.					Accepts others but loner.					
Features requiring further assessment	Mobile in chair, high level of supervision.	Dresses inadequately unless continually supervised.	Needs continual supervision, e.g. physical handicap or medical problem.	Incontinent of urine.	Wanders.	Mood swings, refuses to accept others.	Rejects assistance and shows some independence/ poorly directed actively.	Total rejection of washing.	Requires DDAs i.e. morphine.	Language problem. Lack of understanding.	Disorientated.
Features normally associated with in-appropriateness	Needs one-to-one support.	Unable to dress or retain clothing due to mental/ physical impairment.	Unable to feed because of mental impairment.	Double incontinence.	Sleep reversal.	Socially unacceptable, i.e. aggressive.	Completely resistive or withdrawn.			No effective contact.	

Bibliography

Audit Commission (1983), *Social Services: Provision of Care to the Elderly* (London: HMSO).

Audit Commission (1985), *Managing Social Services for the Elderly More Effectively* (London: HMSO).

Avon (1980), *Admissions to Homes for the Elderly: A Survey of Alternatives* (Avon County Council, Social Services Department, unpublished).

Bacon, V. (1980), "How much housing for the elderly?", *Housing Review*, May-June, pp. 93-95

Barnes, C.D. (1980), *The Restless Tide: A Study of Admission into Homes for the Elderly* (Surrey Social Services Department, Training and Development Division).

Bebbington, A. and Tong, M. (1986), "Trends and changes in old people's homes: Provision Over Twenty Years" in K. Judge and I. Sinclair (eds.) *Residential Care for Elderly People*. (London: HMSO).

Bird, B. and Kirkman, D. (1974), "Needs of the elderly and handicapped: a summary of the progress report on the pilot survey", *Clearing House for Local Authority Social Services Research*, Birmingham, no.2.

Bond, J. and Carstairs, V. (1982), *Services for the Elderly* (Scottish Home and Health Department).

Booth, T.A., Barritt, S., Berry, S., Martin, D.N. and Melotte, C. (1983a), "Dependency in residential homes for the elderly", *Social Policy and Administration*, vol. 17, no. 1, pp. 46-62

Booth, T.A., Phillips, D., Barrett, A., Berry, S., Martin, D.N. and Melotte, C. (1983b), *A Follow-up Study of Trends in Dependency in Local Authority Homes for the Elderly 1980-1982* (University of Sheffield: Joint Unit for Social Service Research).

Bowling, A.C. and Bleathman, C. (1982), "The need for nursing and other skilled care in local authority residential homes for the elderly: research report no. 5., overall findings and recommendations", *Clearing House for Local Authority Social Services Research*, Birmingham, 17 December, no. 9. pp. 1-65.

229

Bowling, A.C., and Salvage, A. (1984), *Prevention of Admission to Residential and Long-stay Hospital Care in City and Hackney* (unpublished).

Brearley, C.P. (1982), *Risk and Social Work* (London: Routledge & Kegan Paul).

Butler, A., Oldman, C. and Greve, J. (1983), *Sheltered   Housing for the Elderly: Policy, Practice and the Consumer* (London: Allen & Unwin).

Cartwright, A. (1982), "The role of the general practitioner in helping the elderly widowed", *Journal of Royal College of General Practitioners*, no. 32, pp. 215-27 (Gale Memorial Lecture, 1981).

Cason, J.S. (1972), "Burns in the elderly" in A. Nelson   (ed.), *Medical Aspects of Home Hazards* (London: Medical Commission on Accident Prevention).

Central Statistical Office (1982), *Social Trends*, no. 12 (London: HMSO).

Challis, D. and Davies, B. (1985), "Long term care for the elderly: the community care scheme", *British Journal of Social Work*, vol. 15, no. 6., pp. 563-79.

Chartered Institute of Public Finance and Accountancy (1983), Personal Social Services Statistics, 1982-83 Actuals. London: CIPFA

Clarke, M., Hughes, A.D. and Dodd, K.J. (1979), "The elderly in residential care: patterns of disability', *Health Trends*, vol. 11, pp. 17-20.

Department of Health and Social Security (1978), *Social Service Teams: The Practitioners' View* (London: HMSO).

Department of Health and Social Security (1981), *Growing Older* (London: HMSO).

Department of Health and Social Security Welsh Office (1978), *A Happier Old Age* (London: HMSO).

Department of Trade and Industry (1983), *Home Accident   Surveillance System: 1982. Presentation of Twelve Months Data*   London: (Department of Trade and Industry Consumer Safety Unit).

Dodd, K., Clarke, M. and Palmer, L. (1980), "Misplacement of the elderly in hospitals and residential homes: a survey   and follow-up', *Health Trends*, vol. 12, pp. 74-76

Donaldson, L.J. and   Jagger, G.   (1983), "Survival and   functional capacity: three year follow-up of an elderly population in hospitals and homes" *Journal of Epidemiology and Community Health*, vol. 37, pp. 176-9.

Donaldson, L.J., Clayton, D.G. and Clarke, M. (1980), "The   elderly in residential   care: mortality   in   relation   to   functional   capacity", *Journal of Epidemiology and Community Health*, vol. 34, no. 2, pp. 96-101.

Eastman, M. (1982), "Granny battering: a hidden problem",   *Community Care*, 27 May, no. 413, pp. 12-13.

Equal Opportunities Commission (1981), *Behind Closed Doors* (Manchester, Equal Opportunities Commission).

Equal Opportunities Commission (1982), *Caring for the   Elderly and Handicapped: Community Care Policies and   Women's Lives* (Manchester: Equal Opportunities Commission).

Exton-Smith, A.N. (1977), "Functional consequences of ageing: clinical manifestations" in A.N. Exton-Smith and J. Grimley Evans (eds.), *Care of the Elderly: Meeting the Challenge of Dependency* (London: Academic Press).

Gibson, F. (1983), "Visiting relatives in residential care". *New Age*, Summer, pp. 36-37.

Gibson, F. (1984), "An enriching experience", *Social Work Today*, 24

January, pp. 20-22.

Glennerster, H., Korman, N. and Marslen-Wilson, F. (1983), *Planning for Priority Groups* (London: Martin Robertson).

Goldberg, E.M. (1970), *Helping the Aged* (London: Allen & Unwin).

Goldberg, E.M. and Connelly N. (1982), *The Effectiveness of Social Care for the Elderly: An Overview of Recent and Current Evaluation Research* (London: Heinemann Educational).

Goldberg, E.M. and Neill, J.E. (1972), *Social Work in General Practice* (London: Allen & Unwin).

Goldberg, E.M. and Warburton, R.W. (1979), *Ends and Means in Social Work* (London: National Institute Social Services Library no. 35).

Goldfarb, A.I., Fisch, M. and Gerber, I.E. (1966), "Predictors of mortality in the institutional aged', *Disorders of the Nervous System*, vol. 27, pp. 21-29.

Golding, K. and Cooper, M. (1981), *Alternatives to Residential Provision for the Elderly: Final Report* (Essex County Council, Social Services Department).

Gorbach, P. and Sinclair, I.A.C. (1981), *Pressure on Health and Social Services for the Elderly*, Working Paper (London: National Institute for Social Work).

Grundy, E. and Arie, T. (1982), "Falling rate of provision of residential care for the elderly", *British Medical Journal*, vol. 284, no. 6318, pp. 799-802.

Hunt, A. (1978), *The Elderly at Home* (London: HMSO).

Hunt, L.B. (1983), "Community services for community care", *Health Trends*, vol. 15, no. 2, pp. 77-81.

Huntingdon, J. (1981), *Social Work and General Medical Practice. Collaboration or Conflict?* (London: George Allen & Unwin).

Isaacs, B. (1976), *The Giants of Geriatrics* (University of Birmingham), Inaugural Lecture.

Isaacs, B. and Evers, H. (1984), *Innovations in the Care of the Elderly* (London: Croom Helm).

Isaacs, B. and Neville, Y. (1976), "The needs of old people", *British Journal of Preventive Social Medicine*, no. 30, pp. 79-85.

Isaacs, B., Livingstone, M. and Neville, Y. (1972), *Survival of the Unfittest* (London: Routledge & Kegan Paul).

Jones, D.A., Victor, C.R. and Vetter, N.J. (1985), "The problem of loneliness in the elderly in the community: characteristics of those who are lonely and the factors related to loneliness", *Journal of the Royal College of General Practitioners*, vol. 35, no. 272, pp. 136-39.

Kay, D.W.K., Beamish, P. and Roth. M. (1962), "Some medical and social characteristics of elderly people under state and welfare homes", *Social Research Monograph*, vol. 5, pp. 173-95.

Keeble, U. (1979), *Aids and Adaptations*, Occasional papers on Social Administration No. 62 (London: Bedford Square Press).

Kirkman, D.R. (1984), "The non-use of community social services by the frail elderly: a case study in an outer London borough", M. Phil thesis, Goldsmith's College.

The Lancet (1982), "The old woman with a broken hip" (editorial), ii, pp. 419-20.

Latto, S. (1984), *Coventry Home Help Project*, 2 vols. (Coventry Social Services Department).

Levin, E., Sinclair, I.A.C. and Gorbach, P. (1983), *The Supporters of Confused Elderly People at Home*, Report to the DHSS (London: National Institute for Social Work).

Levin, E., Sinclair, I. and Gorbach, P. (1985), "The effectiveness of the home help service with confused old people and their families",

Research, Policy and Planning, vol. 3, no. 2, pp. 1-7.

Lieberman, M.A. (1961), "Relationship of mortality rates to entrance to a home for the aged", *Geriatrics,* vol. 16, pp. 515-19.

Lieberman, M.A. (1974), "Relocation, research and social policy", in J.F. Subrium (ed.), *Late Life: Communities and Environment Policy* (Springfield, Illinois: C.C. Thomas).

Lowther, C.P. and McCleod, H.M. (1974), "Admissions to a welfare home", *Scotland Health Bulletin,* vol. 32, no. 1.

MacLennan, W.J., Isles, F.E., McDougall, S. and Keddie, E. (1984), "Medical and social factors influencing admission to residential care", *British Medical Journal,* vol. 288, no. 6418, pp. 701-03.

Millard, P. (1983), "Depression in old age", *British Medical Journal,* vol. 287, no. 6389, pp. 375-76.

Mitchell, S.J.F. and Earwicker, J. (1982), *Getting People Placed* (London Borough of Hammersmith and Fulham).

Morley, K. (1982), "New venture for the elderly", *Health and Social Services Journal,* 13 May.

Murphy, E. (1982), "Social origins of depression in old age", *British Journal of Psychiatry,* vol. 141, pp. 135-42.

National Assistance Act (1948), (London: HMSO)

Neill, J.E., Fruin, D., Goldberg, E.M. and Warburton, R.W. (1973), "Reactions to Integration", *Social Work Today* vol. 4, no. 15, pp. 458-65.

Neill, J.E., Warburton, R.W. and McGuiness B. (1976), "Post Seebohm social services: the social worker's viewpoint", *Social Work Today,* vol. 8, no. 5.

Neill, J.E. (1982), "Some variations in policy and procedure relating to part III applications in the GLC area", *British Journal of Social Work,* vol. 12, no. 3, pp. 229-45.

Nissel, M. and Bonnerjea, L. (1982), *Family Care of the Handicapped Elderly: Who Pays?* (London: Policy Studies Institute).

Norman, A.J. (1980), *Right and Risk: A Discussion Document on Civil Liberty in Old Age* (London: National Corporation for the Care of Old People).

Office of Population Censuses and Surveys (1971), *Census* (London: HMSO).

Office of Population Censuses and Surveys (1981), *Census* (London: HMSO).

Ovenstone, I.M.K. and Bean, P. (1981), "A medical social assessment of admissions to old people's homes in Nottingham", *British Journal of Psychiatry* vol. 139, pp. 226-29.

Pablo, R.Y. (1977), "Intra-institutional relocation: it's impact on long-term care patients", *The Gerontologist,* vol. 17, no. 5, pp. 426-35.

Parkes, C.M. (1969), "Broken heart: a statistical study of increased mortality among widowers", *British Medical Journal,* pp. 740-3.

Parkes, C.M. (1972), *Bereavement* (London: Tavistock).

Plank, D. (1977), *Caring for the Elderly: Report of a Study of Caring for Dependent Elderly People in Eight London Boroughs* (Greater London Council).

Post, F. (1972), "The aetiology of mental breakdown in old people", in Cape (ed.) *Symposia on Geriatric Medicine* vol. 1. (Birmingham: West Midland Institute of Geriatric Medicine and Gerontology).

Royal College of General Practitioners (1972), *The Future General Practitioner. Learning and Teaching* (London: The Royal College of General Practitioners).

Shaw, I. and Walton, R. (1979), "Transition to residence in homes for the elderly", in D. Harris and J. Hyland (eds.), *Rights in Residence* (London: Residential Care Association).

232

Sinclair, I.A.C., Crosbie, D., O'Connor, P., Stanforth, L. and Vickery, A. (1984), *Networks Project: A Study of Informal Care, Services and Social Work for Elderly Clients Living Alone*, Report to the DHSS (London: National Institute for Social Work).

Smith, R.S. and Lowther, C.P. (1976), "Follow up study of two hundred admissions to a residential home", *Age and Ageing*, vol. 5, no. 176, pp. 176-80.

Snow, T. (1981), *Services for Old Age: A Growing Crisis in London* (London: Age Concern).

Social Services Committee (1984), *Further Report from the Social Services Committee. Session 1983-84, Public Expenditure on the Social Services* (London: HMSO).

Stapleton, B. (1976), *A Survey of the Waiting List for Places in Newham's Hostels for the Elderly* (London: Borough of Newham, Applied Research Section).

Thomas, S. (1985), "Prevention better than cure", *Action Baseline*, no. 30.

Tinker, A. (1977), "What sort of housing do the elderly want?", *Housing Review*, May-June, pp. 54-55.

Tinker, A. (1984), *Staying at Home: Helping Elderly People* (London: HMSO).

Townsend, P. (1962), *The Last Refuge* (London: Routledge & Kegan Paul).

Wade, B., Sawyer, L. and Bell, S. (1983), *Dependency with Dignity* (London: Bedford Square Press).

Wager, R. (1972), *Care of the Elderly: An Exercise in Cost Benefit Analysis Commissioned by Essex County Council* (London: Institute of Municipal Treasurers and Accountants).

Warren, M.D. and Knight, R. (1982), "Mortality in relation to the functional capacities of people with disabilities living at home", *Journal of Epidemiology and Community Health*, vol. 36, pp. 220-23.

Wenger, G.C. (1984). *The Supportive Network: Coping With Old Age* (London: Allen & Unwin, National Institute Social Services Library, no. 46).

Wheeler, R. (1985), *Don't Move, We've Got You Covered* (Institute of Housing).

Wicks, M. (1978), *Old and Cold: Hypothermia and Social Policy* (London: Heinemann).

Wilkin, D., Mashiar, T., and Jolley, D.J. (1978), "Changes in behavioural characteristics of elderly populations of local authority homes and long stay hospital wards, 1976-1977", *British Medical Journal*, vol. 2, pp. 1274-76.

Willcocks, D., Peace, S., Kellaher, L. and Ring, J. (1982), *The Residential Life of Old People: A study in 100 Local Authority Homes*. 2 vols. Research Reports nos. 12, 13 (Survey Research Unit, School of Applied Social Studies & Sociology, Polytechnic of North London).

Wright, K.G., Cairns, J.A., and Snell, M.C. (1981), *Costing Care: The Costs of Alternative Patterns of Care for the Elderly* (Sheffield University).

Index

assessment:
    flats for, 184-6
    functional, 141
    GPs and, 181
    heads of homes and, 182
    improving, 180
    inadequacy, 139
    informing applicants of, 12
    medical, 181-2
    necessity of, 147, 178
    needs of, 100
    NISW report, 222-3
    panel and, 222-3
    psychiatric, 140
    research findings and, 195-6
    risk and, 73
assistant social workers, 11
attendance allowance, 126, 128, 187
Audit Commission, 2
Avon study, 133

balance, 52, 65, 74
basic self care: difficulties with, 24-7, 39, 51-60, 105, 150, 152, 162
Bebbington and Tong, 32
bed, going to, 59-60 see also getting up
bereavement, 20, 36, 38-9, 45, 78, 117, 140
blindness, 46-7 see also visual handicap
boarding out schemes, 131, 168
Bond and Carstairs, 194
Booth et al., 3
Bowling and Salvage, 147
braille, 61
burglary, 67

care, institutional: paradox of, 3, 4, 5
caregivers:
    age, 85
    anxiety, expression of, 68
    applicants, conflicts with, 12, 38, 41
    applicants, relations with, 91-3, 100
    applicants living with them, 85, 89, 91, 93, 96, 97, 98-9, 105
    basic self care and, 60
    changes in situation, 80-3
    contextural features, 85-101
    daughters and sons, differences between, 78
    depression, 98
    employment, 90-1
    family relationships, 93-5
    family situation, 89
    health, 85-7, 99
    homes, visiting, 137
    housing, 103
    identity of, 76-7
    networks, 27-30
    origins of care, 75
    other responsibilities, 76
    problems, 27-30, 32, 75, 81-2, 86, 90, 96-9

rehabilitation from, 185-6
review of new residents, 182-3
sharing rooms, 139
short stay in, 127, 128, 137, 146, 152
"special" residents, 171-2
spending money in, 139, 171
transfers, 159, 183
trial days, 12, 182
unsuitability of for some residents, 3, 194
visitors, 174
see also following entry and applicants for Part III homes;
applications for Part III homes
Part III homes for the elderly mentally infirm, 25, 140, 150, 154, 170,
220, 221, 226, 227
physiotherapy, 144
Plank, D., 133
pop-in centres, 38, 40, 107, 123, 126
private Homes, 20, 23, 119, 154, 178, 190, 197, 225-6
private households:
    applicants in at follow up, 167, 172, 173, 176
    applications from, 31, 113, 156, 157, 216
privately rented accommodation, 21, 106
psychiatric day centres, 126
psychiatric hospitals, 20, 28, 154, 157, 172, 173, 176, 189, 197
psychogeriatric hospitals, 176, 179, 204:
    condition of, 8-10

Rayner Review, 199
rehabilitation, 117, 129, 147:
    lack of, 144
relatives:
    absent, 69
    care from, 83
    conflict with, 45
    visiting, 42
researchers' report, 179, 221-6
research findings: implications of, 193-5
resources:
    development of, 178, 183-9
    targeting of, 191
risk, 24-7, 33, 62-75:
    attitude to, 62, 64, 66, 67-70, 72-3
    background to, 70-2
    freedom to live at, 62, 73
    types of, 64, 65-7

self care see basic self care
services:
    attitudes to, 127-8
    caregivers and, 195-6
    collaboration between, 2, 4, 10-11, 144, 179, 180, 191, 195
    communication, 116
    crisis in, 178
    cutbacks in, 180
    knowledge of, 127-8, 133
    lack of comprehensive provision, 128-33
    non-substitutable, 4